Bion in the Consulting Room

Bion in the Consulting Room addresses the long-unanswered question of Bion's clinical and supervisorial technique and examines the way Bion's conceptual model and clinical practices informed his theoretical work.

As Bion wrote about technique so rarely, the authors set about looking at many of his clinical and supervisorial examples to infer what might be learned from them. This book factors in the four distinctive periods of Bion's clinical and supervisorial work in chronological order: the group period of the 1940s; the period of the psychosis papers in the 1950s; the epistemological period of the early 1960s; and, finally, the period of his international group seminars in the late 1960s and 1970s. In all four periods, the authors examine and analyze his method of clinical inquiry, or how he went about knowing and experiencing his analysands and supervisees. The authors offer a uniquely overarching view of his method of clinical inquiry, uncovering an amazing consistency in how Bion went about his work both as a psychoanalyst and supervisor.

This illuminating book is essential reading for psychoanalysts, psychotherapists, and psychologists interested in the work of Wilfred Bion and the importance of his legacy in contemporary practice.

Joseph Aguayo, PhD, is a training and supervising analyst at the Psychoanalytic Center of California and a guest member of the British Psychoanalytical Society. He holds PhDs in both Clinical Psychology and European History from UCLA. He contributes to leading psychoanalytic journals and has co-edited *Wilfred Bion: Los Angeles Seminars and Supervision* (2013) and authored *Introducing the Clinical Work of Wilfred Bion* (2023).

R.D. Hinshelwood is a fellow of the British Psychoanalytic Society and fellow of the Royal College of Psychiatrists; he has previously served as the clinical director at the Cassel Hospital, UK. Hinshelwood is the author of numerous publications, including *Melanie Klein: The Basics* (2017) and, recently, *W.R. Bion as Clinician* (2022).

Sira Dermen was a training and supervising analyst of the British Psychoanalytical Society. She was Honorary Senior Consultant at the Portman Clinic and was in full-time private practice. She has written on violence and perversion. She passed away in 2023.

Nicola Abel-Hirsch is a training and supervising analyst of the British Psychoanalytical Society and works in private practice in London. She is the author of numerous publications, including *Bion: 365 Quotes* (2019), and she is the editor of Hanna Segal's last book, *Yesterday, Today and Tomorrow* (2007).

The Routledge Wilfred Bion Studies Book Series
Series Editor
Howard B. Levine, MD

Editorial Advisory Board
Nicola Abel-Hirsch, Joseph Aguayo, Avner Bergstein, Lawrence J. Brown, Judith Eekhoff, Claudio Laks Eizerik, Robert D. Hinshelwood, Chris Mawson, James Ogilvie, Elias M. da Rocha Barros, Jani Santamaria, Rudi Vermote

The contributions of Wilfred Bion are among the most cited in the analytic literature. Their appeal lies not only in their content and explanatory value, but in their generative potential. Although Bion's training and many of his clinical instincts were deeply rooted in the classical tradition of Melanie Klein, his ideas have a potentially universal appeal. Rather than emphasizing a particular psychic content (e.g., Oedipal conflicts in need of resolution; splits that needed to be healed; preconceived transferences that must be allowed to form and flourish, etc.), he tried to help open and prepare the mind of the analyst (without memory, desire or theoretical preconception) for the encounter with the patient.

Bion's formulations of group mentality and the psychotic and non-psychotic portions of the mind, his theory of thinking and emphasis on facing and articulating the truth of one's existence so that one might truly learn first hand from one's own experience, his description of psychic development (alpha function and container/contained) and his exploration of **O** are "non-denominational" concepts that defy relegation to a particular school or orientation of psychoanalysis. Consequently, his ideas have taken root in many places.... and those ideas continue to inform many different branches of psychoanalytic inquiry and interest.[1]

It is with this heritage and its promise for the future developments of psychoanalysis in mind that we present *The Routledge Wilfred Bion Studies Book Series*. This series gathers together under newly emerging and continually evolving contributions to psychoanalytic thinking that rest upon Bion's foundational texts and explore and extend the implications of his thought. For a full list of titles in the series, please visit the Routledge website at: https://www.routledge.com/The-Routledge-Wilfred-Bion-Studies-Book-Series/book-series/RWBSBS

Howard B. Levine, MD
Series Editor

---

[1] Levine, H.B. and Civitarese, G. (2016). Editors' Preface, *The W.R. Bion Tradition*, Levine and Civitarese, eds., London: Karnac 2016, p. xxi.

Bion in the Consulting Room

An Implicit Method of Clinical Inquiry

Joseph Aguayo, R.D. Hinshelwood,
Sira Dermen, and Nicola Abel-Hirsch

Routledge
Taylor & Francis Group
LONDON AND NEW YORK

Designed cover image: "Orange" by Cheryl Yaney 1995, oil on paper, 25" x 26".

First published 2025
by Routledge
4 Park Square, Milton Park, Abingdon, Oxon OX14 4RN

and by Routledge
605 Third Avenue, New York, NY 10158

Routledge is an imprint of the Taylor & Francis Group, an informa business

© 2025 Joseph Aguayo, R.D. Hinshelwood, Sira Dermen, and Nicola Abel-Hirsch

The right of Joseph Aguayo, R.D. Hinshelwood, Sira Dermen, and Nicola Abel-Hirsch to be identified as authors of this work has been asserted in accordance with sections 77 and 78 of the Copyright, Designs and Patents Act 1988.

All rights reserved. No part of this book may be reprinted or reproduced or utilised in any form or by any electronic, mechanical, or other means, now known or hereafter invented, including photocopying and recording, or in any information storage or retrieval system, without permission in writing from the publishers.

Trademark notice: Product or corporate names may be trademarks or registered trademarks, and are used only for identification and explanation without intent to infringe.

British Library Cataloguing-in-Publication Data
A catalogue record for this book is available from the British Library

Library of Congress Cataloging-in-Publication Data
Names: Aguayo, Joseph Richard, 1946- author. | Hinshelwood, R. D., author. | Dermen, Sira, author. | Abel-Hirsch, Nicola, author.
Title: Bion in the consulting room : an implicit method of clinical inquiry / Joseph Aguayo, R.D. Hinshelwood, Sira Dermen, and Nicola Abel-Hirsch.
Description: Abingdon, Oxon; New York, NY : Routledge, 2024. | Includes bibliographical references and index.
Identifiers: LCCN 2023030752 (print) | LCCN 2023030753 (ebook) | ISBN 9781032506333 (paperback) | ISBN 9781032513768 (hardback) | ISBN 9781003401926 (ebook)
Subjects: LCSH: Bion, Wilfred R. (Wilfred Ruprecht), 1897–1979. | Psychoanalysis. | Psychotherapy. | Psychoanalysts—Supervision of.
Classification: LCC RC438.6.B54 A48 2024 (print) | LCC RC438.6.B54 (ebook) | DDC 616.89/17—dc23/eng/20231016
LC record available at https://lccn.loc.gov/2023030752
LC ebook record available at https://lccn.loc.gov/2023030753

ISBN: 978-1-032-51376-8 (hbk)
ISBN: 978-1-032-50633-3 (pbk)
ISBN: 978-1-003-40192-6 (ebk)

DOI: 10.4324/9781003401926

Typeset in Times New Roman
by codeMantra

Contents

Introduction   1
JOSEPH AGUAYO

1 **Working Clinically with Groups**   11
R.D. HINSHELWOOD

2 **Tracing the Clinical Trajectory and Technical Relevance of Bion's Cases and Theorizing from the 'Psychosis' Period (1950–1957)**   33
JOSEPH AGUAYO

3 **The Psychosis Papers (1958–1959)**   57
SIRA DERMEN

4 **Clinical Restlessness: The 1960s**   76
NICOLA ABEL-HIRSCH

5 **Wilfred Bion's Clinical Seminars in North and South America and Europe, 1967–1978: A Clinical Method of Inquiry as an Implicit Theory of Psychoanalytic Technique**   95
JOSEPH AGUAYO AND SIRA DERMEN

6 **The Brazilian Clinical Seminars**   121
NICOLA ABEL-HIRSCH

7 **Conclusions on Bion's Method of Clinical Inquiry: Similarities and Differences**   131
JOSEPH AGUAYO, R.D. HINSHELWOOD, SIRA DERMEN AND NICOLA ABEL-HIRSCH

Index   *153*

Introduction

Joseph Aguayo

Prelude

Just after the publication of Wilfred Bion's *Los Angeles Seminars and Supervision* (Bion, 2013), a distillation of his clinical work undertaken in the United States in 1967, the thought occurred to one of the co-authors (Joseph Aguayo) that it might be important to see how Bion's actual clinical practices informed his theory-building. Blending clinical with historical research trajectories, he approached British colleagues (Sira Dermen and Bob Hinshelwood) about melding an experientially near yet close chronological reading of Bion's clinical work from his group period in the 1940s through to the *Clinical Seminars* period of the 1970s. Having consulted with both Hinshelwood and Dermen for years on matters of historical research along with analytic case discussions, he sought to bring these important realms of discourse together. He also invited Los Angeles colleague Barnet Malin (whose father, Arthur Malin, also an analyst, had originally recorded Bion's *Los Angeles Seminars* back in 1967) to form what then became an Anglo-American research group.

After 2015, when more of Bion's clinical and supervisory examples came to light—for example, his *Buenos Aires Seminars and Supervisions* of 1968 (Bion, 2017a), there were fresh examples, such as his own case presentations and some rather extensive supervisions with colleagues such as Horacio Etchegoyen. These publications were of interest insofar as they could illuminate Bion's clinical approach during the time of his extensive theoretical work enshrined in his four epistemology monographs of the 1960s (Bion, 1962, 1963, 1965, 1970). These books almost exclusively focused on theory-building, such as container–contained, the Grid, and transformations in knowledge and O. Along with the new epistemology, post-Bionian writers have generally paid little attention to his clinical work in the 1960s and 1970s, although there are notable exceptions (Ogden, 2007).

Rather than take the path of an *extensive secondary literature review of Bion's theoretical evolution*, a new question arose: could Bion's extant clinical work be studied and understood as its own separate domain, an implicit theory of practice—implicit because, aside from the famous but lamentably brief "Notes on Memory and Desire" (1967; republished, 2014b), Bion wrote very little about psychoanalytic

DOI: 10.4324/9781003401926-1

technique (Aguayo, 2014). Could a concentrated study of Bion's analytic examples throw fresh light on his well-known theories, which have been the subject of scores of papers and books for decades?

In the 1950s, when there seemed to be little conscious awareness of having a distinctive technique, Bion, as a member of the London Klein group, seemed disinclined to define his, or was perhaps disinterested. Like other London Kleinians, he did not realize that the "novelty of content" represented by the analytic treatment of psychotic patients in fact represented a "novelty of method" (Spillius, 1988, p. 5). With the appearance of new clinical seminar publications, however, these questions of implicit theories of technique received fresh impetus: more examples of his clinical and supervisorial work appeared with the publication of *Bion in Brazil: Supervisions and Commentaries* (from 1973; 2017b) and *The Clinical Thinking of W.R. Bion in Brazil: Supervisions and Commentaries* (2024). These newly published seminars now represent a more complete collection of Bion's clinical work in seminars from the 1970s than had already appeared—Brasília, São Paulo, New York, Rome, London (Tavistock), and Paris (1967–1979). Much of the content of these earlier published seminars contained fewer actual clinical examples of Bion's work for scholars and analysts interested in Bion's work to take note of. In effect, discussion of Bion's own clinical work has had to wait until recent years when so much of his actual clinical material has come to light.

Prior to 2013, the *Clinical Seminars* had essentially been treated as ephemera, a sort of late journalistic entry consisting of Bion's older ideas (Bion, 1980, 1990, 2000, 2005a, 2005b). In *Wilfred Bion: His Life and Works 1897–1979*, Gerard Bléandonu (1994, p. 247) understandably marginalized the significance of these *Clinical Seminars*, maintaining that they were essentially recitations of Kleinian ideas long familiar to him, but essentially strange and new to the audiences that listened to them:

> The public's desire was expressed in two opposite directions simultaneously. On the one hand, the questions asked aimed to elicit repetitions of statements he had already written and published, and avoided areas which were not part of his success. Rather than being party to work in progress, the audience came to see and admire the throned and crowned king.

Our research group has concluded that this older view needs to be reassessed and revised. Bion's more complete clinical work includes evidence of his practices during both the group and psychosis papers periods of the 1940 and 1950s. We have opened up inquiry into its existence as a separate domain worthy of intense study. Our group has met primarily online, and only periodically in person as a group, mainly at the pre-pandemic IPA Congresses. With each colleague choosing a particular period of Bion's clinical work—group (Hinshelwood), early psychosis (Aguayo), late psychosis (Dermen), epistemology during the 1960s (Abel-Hirsch), early clinical seminars (Aguayo and Dermen), and late clinical seminars (Abel-Hirsch)—we have met up over a 6-year period to share our current findings. There have been panel presentations on clinical Bion at the IPA Boston (2015), IPA Buenos Aires (2017), IPA London (2019), and IPA Vancouver (2021) Congresses. Specific topics have included: Bion's clinical approach in general, his group work, the three phases of his clinical approach, supervision work in Buenos Aires, and the continuities and discontinuities of his clinical practices. When other research obligations led Barnet Malin to take leave of our working group, we were fortunate to then enlist Nicola Abel-Hirsch as another seasoned analyst versed in Bion studies to join our group in 2019.

An Organizing Idea in Approaching Bion's Clinical Work—The Implicit Method of Clinical Inquiry

With the newly published clinical and supervisorial material, we have had to tackle the question of how we would approach Bion's practices in an experientially near yet contextual manner. Since Bion's clinical practices had received little formal study, we formulated our own method. Early on, Sira Dermen formulated the question that struck a responsive chord with other members of our team. In her IPA Boston paper of 2015, Dermen described what our group has termed "Bion's implicit method of clinical inquiry":

> These are some of the features of Bion's mind. But why do I find his method of enquiry clinically so useful? He shows in practice how to avoid foreclosure. His fundamental presumption is: "I am missing something". He does not treat *any* insight, however hard gained and temporarily illuminating, as a resting place. What matters is what happens next. His capacity to live with the uncomfortable premise that every gain in analysis will come at a cost—to patient and analyst alike—is remarkable. Insight is a way station on the stormy journey of therapy.
>
> I add that clinical Bion has also stood the test of time. I have focused on what there is to be learned from his method of clinical enquiry. I could have stressed that I find his clinical insights applicable to a wide range of patients, especially those we regard as recalcitrant, hard to reach, difficult to make emotional contact with. Personally, I gain a great deal of *practical* help from re-reading his clinical papers: how to keep on questioning my own understanding of the intransigent clinical situation, how to find a new direction which could open up a fruitful line of enquiry, and how to listen for a bit of collaboration from the patient when all I can hear is obstruction.

These initial ideas were further elaborated in Dermen's IPA panel contribution for the Buenos Aires Congress in 2017 when she returned to Bion's seemingly restless method of clinical inquiry, but now in the supervisory situation, a process that led him to ask questions of the supervisee as well as of the clinical material itself:

> Bion's clinical style is personal and reserved. It is personal in that when he speaks to a supervisee or patient, his voice is uniquely his own. Yet this has

nothing to do with his personality—in the sense of his own desires or group affiliations. His sole aim is to understand the patient. The truth can be reached only through its manifestation in a particular moment in the analysis, provided there is genuine contact between patient and analyst. Recourse to theory is dangerous because it freezes time, and it deadens the contact necessary for the emergence of the patient's personal truth. *Evasion* of contact is lethal for the same reason. Bion shows an acute awareness of the variety of specific ways in which the patient evades what he supposedly is coming to the analyst for. He is immensely acute in spotting psychic escape routes. If not spotted, such evasions result in a clinical situation I think most of us are familiar with: where many things appear to be changing, yet we feel fundamentally nothing is changing.

Our group found that we could further refine the approach in the various periods of Bion's professional evolution. Next to thinking about his cast of mind in any particular clinical situation, a concern with temporal factors arose. Was Bion's cast of clinical mind the same throughout the periods of his publications? Or did it evolve and change over time? Examining the question of continuity and discontinuity in his clinical practices then had to take up the specific ways in which Bion went about the process of inquiry at different points in time. For his part, Bob Hinshelwood (2018a) took up Bion's clinical practices during his group period, which began with his collaboration with his former analyst, John Rickman, in 1939 when war broke out. Our group has agreed with Hinshelwood that, from the beginning, Bion's clinical practices as a group psychiatrist needed to be considered as part of his method of clinical inquiry. It is well known that group therapists that favor the Tavistock method tend to exist in a camp separate from Kleinian psychoanalysts, who tend to become interested in Bion's work only after he became a graduated psychoanalyst in 1950. Grosskurth (1986, pp. 427–428) has detailed how Klein attempted to dissuade Bion from continuing his group work, hoping that he would turn his attention exclusively to psychoanalytic matters.

As distilled in his IPA London Congress paper of 2019 (Barahona, 2019, p. 1009), Hinshelwood reached the following conclusions that shed some orienting light on Bion's method of clinical inquiry:

John Rickman's encouragement here and during the Northfield Experiment in 1943 was crucial in the sense of how he understood the interview process and the psychoanalytic situation in field theory terms. For Rickman the first requirement of the analyst was to learn to accept any role the patient puts upon him. Hinshelwood explained that from Rickman's approach, a set of principles could be derived, which may be thought of as having influenced Bion, though the latter rarely spoke directly about field theory:

1. Subjective introspection by the analyst;
2. Reflection by the analyst on that experience;

3. The formulation of his/her experience in terms of the role in which the analyst feels he is cast;
4. The roles forming a narrative content of an implicit drama in the group that both are playing out.

Hinshelwood reiterated the main purpose of his paper, to make clear how Bion's early thinking remained present in his writing after 1948. The quality of the introspective function of the analyst was already present in his work and would be expanded in his later work on reverie, which demanded an authentic response in the analyst.

Hinshelwood stated that Bion was trying to introduce at this point the need for the analyst to pay attention to his own functioning—a double stance—we observe our patients and we observe ourselves observing our patient. "Bion's approach," he said, "remained consistent between very different early and late periods of his work" (Barahona, 2019, p. 1009).

Both Dermen's and Hinshelwood's (2018b) complementary ways of approaching Bion's clinical examples helped us to refine our working assumptions in how we approached the question of his overarching method of clinical inquiry. Fundamentally based on an introspective method in his group, individual psychoanalytic, and supervisorial work, Bion would pose a series of questions to himself, an organizing set of experiences about what he did and did not understand in the current situation. He made self-observations in the clinical setting, attempted to abstract from his findings, and retested them in the clinical situation, insatiably questioning and re-questioning his understanding. Taking his entire work as a psychiatrist and psychoanalyst as a whole—and this included both his group work as well as the *Clinical Seminars* of his late California period—a working formulation was framed and is herein tested out in a series of chapters that focus heavily on Bion's own clinical work as its own separate domain, one that needs to be articulated and ultimately integrated alongside his much better-known theoretical formulations.

Rounding out what Dermen and Hinshelwood had set forth in the method of clinical inquiry and early group and later psychosis periods, Nicola Abel-Hirsch has examined Bion's clinical illustrations in the four 'epistemological' books of the 1960s. This period presented its own unique challenges as Bion's few clinical examples have not elicited much attention from post-Bionian scholars. In attempting to redress some of these imbalances, Abel-Hirsch had arrived at her own conclusions by the time of the IPA Vancouver Congress in 2021: "Some light can be thrown on Bion's view of this by the following quote—written in his 1970's novel *A Memoir of the Future—The Dawn of Oblivion*":

P.A. [psychoanalyst]: ... Many analysts repudiate Klein's extension of psychoanalysis as elaborated by Freud. I found it difficult to understand Klein's theory and practice though—perhaps because—I was being analysed by Melanie Klein herself. But after great difficulty I began to feel there was truth in the interpretations she gave and that they brought illumination to many experiences, mine and others, which had previously been incomprehensible, discrete and unrelated. Metaphorically, light began to dawn and then, with increasing momentum, all was clear.

(Bion, 2014a, p. 121)

Abel-Hirsch (2021) continued:

In the quote we hear Bion say that he employed interpretations, based on his experience with Klein, without good results. He is asked why he didn't lose faith in psychoanalysis and responds that it became an issue of "discrimination"—I imagine between what should stay and what should go. Bion doesn't mention that he has been engaged in developing a new framework for analysis: alpha function, alpha and beta elements, container/contained, discipline of memory and desire, faith as a scientific tool, being rather than knowing! Instead, he first goes to what had struck the young Freud in the work of Charcot—the observation of unexplained facts until a pattern becomes recognisable, then to the significance of the "impressive caesuras" and the emergence within him of light thrown by Klein's interpretations (some 25 years earlier).

In the clinical accounts I have presented from the four books of the 1960's we have seen him documenting a lack of good results. We also see considerable "discrimination" taking place in the 60's, not only between what is to stay and what is to go, but also discrimination in the sense of differentiation. It is possible that making differentiations was unusually important to Bion—perhaps particularly in the 60's.

Review of Relevant Secondary Literature on Bion's Work

Before turning to the structure of this book, it is important to set out some of the relevant secondary literature in Bion studies in order to examine our claim of the somewhat different trajectory of our clinical research project. With over 12,000 titles in Bion studies that can be found in the Psychoanalytic Electronic Publishing (PEP) archive, the vastness of the secondary literature cannot be covered in any comprehensive way (Vermote, 2019). Instead we restrict ourselves to those well-known secondary sources that buttress our contention that Bion's actual clinical work has been the subject of less research focus, certainly far less than his formidable conceptual explorations.

The modern era of sophisticated studies of Bion's work was ushered in by Gerard Bléandonu's (1994) *Wilfred Bion: His Life and Works 1897–1979*. This full-length study typifies the kind of secondary Bion literature that emphasizes conceptual considerations and, less so, actual clinical examples of his work—and so, we examine it in some detail.[1]

Bléandonu was all-inclusive in covering all seasons of Bion's work: the group period, the psychosis period, the epistemology monographs of the 1960s, and the autobiographical/literary works. Bléandonu's overall trajectory was conceptual in nature, and we actually hear very little of Bion's clinical encounters with his patients or his supervisees. In looking at the balance of biographical, conceptual, and epistemological ground covered so well by Bléandonu, very little of his entire text of 287 pages covers any of Bion's actual clinical group or individual psychoanalytic cases. We do, however, learn a great deal about how Bion theorized in all seasons of his professional work, but precious little about how he actually functioned as a practicing clinician and psychoanalyst.

Other recent contributions also tend to overlook Bion's actual clinical work but do so for different reasons. Take an example from Italian field theory: in a number of post-Bionian books and papers, Giuseppe Civitarese and Antonino Ferro have vigorously engaged many of Bion's epistemological propositions, mainly in the service of extrapolating what is to be learned by contemporary psychoanalysts (Civitarese and Ferro, 2013; Civitarese, 2008, 2014, 2015, 2019). One representative work is Civitarese's *The Necessary Dream: New Theories and Techniques of Interpretation in Psychoanalysis* (2014). While Civitarese admirably extracts essential aspects of a theory of dreaming from Freud, Klein, and Bion, along with other more recent Bionian-inspired analysts such as Thomas Ogden (2007) and Antonino Ferro, these extracts are amalgamated in the service of dream theory in the new millennium; as a result, we read about how contemporary analysts work in the consulting room. Fair enough. While it is important for such work to continue to explore what is inspiring about Bion's theoretical work, this position is again derived from Bion's theoretical propositions, in effect rendering his epistemology a sort of 'memoir for the future,' much of which tends to minimize learning from his actual clinical work and supervision.

Still another very conceptually informed book—Rudi Vermote's *Reading Bion* (2019)—gives a nuanced view of how Bion effected a major shift when he transited from transformations in knowledge to transformations in infinity (or O). Since Vermote makes a special effort to present Bion's epistemological books—indeed, it is the central part of his book—I present some of its highlights, again to make the point that it too emphasizes the presentation and distillation of Bion's theoretical work while spending very little time discussing his actual clinical practices and case work. In his chapter on "Learning from Experience," for example, Vermote (2019, pp. 80–94) highlights how Bion was inspired by British empiricists such as David Hume, mathematical theories of functions, Freud's theories of dreaming, and his own experience in treating psychotic patients, all of which culminated in a new theory of how thinking emerges in the infant—and how it can go awry. It presents the theory of container–contained, complete with a new set of terms, such as: alpha-function, beta-elements, and contact barrier. But, like Bion's own books, there is little by way of clinical examples of these ideas.

Likewise, in Vermote's (2019, pp. 95–112) distillation of Bion's *Elements of Psychoanalysis* (1963). Again, the mode of presentation is primarily conceptual. So, the reader hears a great deal about how Bion devised the Grid for use by clinicians, so they might develop their own ways of thinking and intuition. Vermote (p. 95) emphasizes Bion's own accentuation of the analyst's valuing of not-knowing and openness; the absence of moral judgment; the focus on psychic functioning; a binocular view; the development of reverie and imagination; and also, looking for concurrencies he termed "constant conjunctions," a phenomenological approach of looking at 'what goes with what' in an ongoing fashion (p. 95). But again, like Bion's text itself, which in fact contained very few clinical examples, we see very little of Bion's actual clinical practices here. For the interested analyst, he or she would have to experiment with the Grid itself to see if there is any important clinical use that can be made of it. The same point recurs in Vermote's chapters (2019, pp. 114–139, 140–168) on Bion's other epistemological works, *Transformations* (1965) and *Attention and Interpretation* (1970). In his chapter on *Transformations*, for instance, we hear more of Bion's theoretical evolution—that, by that point, Bion had established three necessary theoretical structures: his distillation of Klein's ideas about the paranoid/schizoid positions; the model of container–contained; and the "selected fact." Again, the text leads the reader in the direction of more and more theoretical considerations—for example, Vermote's point that, by the end of *Transformations*, Bion posits the unknowability of how thought originates, let alone how it becomes transformed phenomenologically in the form of the ordinary manifest content of the night dream. He terms this unknowable realm 'O,' or infinity or ultimate truth, the noumenon, the Kantian 'thing-in-itself' which, in and of itself, cannot be known. But again, significant as these conceptual developments are, they come with next to no actual clinical examples of what these ideas looked like in Bion's consulting room.

It is at this point in Vermote's book that his central thesis becomes clear— that Bion's major innovation and lasting contribution to psychoanalysis was theory-building, which, as Vermote states, was the move from representations in thinking to experience that has not yet been represented, or what he terms the "not-yet-psychic." Also of interest is the fact that, within the current cache of Bion's actual clinical and supervisorial work, there is not one clinical example of what a transformation from the 'not-yet-represented' to the representational looked like in Bion's consulting room. Perhaps it is as Giuseppe Civitarese has said: Bion's epistemology was a clinical 'memoir for the future,' and it would be left to succeeding generations of analysts to extrapolate the clinical meaning of an epistemology that seemed to exist in its own disjunctive universe of discourse, separate from Bion's actual clinical practices.

Organization of the Chapters

We begin with Hinshelwood's chapter on Bion's group period, with its focus on clinical examples of his group work. It is followed by Aguayo's chapter on the first part of Bion's psychosis paper period (1950–1957)—with a particular and detailed analysis of "The Imaginary Twin" case of 1950 (Bion, 1967). The third chapter is Dermen's work on the last trio of Bion's psychosis papers (1958/1959) which emphasizes a very microscopic clinical view of how Bion worked with extremely disturbed patients as well as how he presented his clinical results. The fourth chapter, by Abel-Hirsch, on the clinical examples from Bion's epistemology period looks at the very few clinical examples from the period of 1962–1970 in the four epistemological monographs. Then, Chapter 5, by Aguayo and Dermen, on Bion's late *Clinical Seminars*, contains representative examples of both clinical and supervisorial work (e.g., Bion's clinical and supervisorial work in Los Angeles and Buenos Aires in 1967–1968 as well as in other cities). And finally, in Chapter 6, Abel-Hirsch takes up Bion's supervision work in a number of visits he made to Brazil during the 1970s.

In the Conclusions section, our research group distills the final results of what it has learned about Bion's method of clinical inquiry across the various periods of his professional existence as a psychiatrist and psychoanalyst. These conclusions attempt to meld together both a clinically close reading of Bion's individual and group clinical cases and his numerous supervisions. Our conclusions are meant as questions that we hope others will take up and explore further, especially in the direction of what light his clinical practices shed on his theoretical evolution, which continues to excite interest in our contemporary psychoanalytic universe.

Joseph Aguayo, Los Angeles

Note

1 A separate view that essentially maintains that Bion was *sui generis*, a sort of genius plant who could have taken firm root anywhere, has it that he existed quite apart from Melanie Klein's influence and that of the members of her London group (Symington and Symington, 1996). From the first chapter of their work, entitled, "The Theoretical Disjunction between Bion and Freud/Klein," Bion and Klein are pitted against one another as opposites—one emphasized a "positive," more searching mode of clinical inquiry while the other was overly consumed with pathological mechanisms. This view notwithstanding, the Symingtons' book also emphasizes theoretical considerations and discusses very few actual clinical examples from Bion's analytic work or supervisions.

References

Abel-Hirsch, N. (2021). 'Bion 1960–1975.' Panel contribution (unpublished). International Psychoanalytic Congress, Vancouver, July, 2021.

Aguayo, J. (2014). 'Bion's "Notes on Memory and Desire": Its Initial Clinical Reception in the United States—A Note on Archival Material.' *International Journal of Psychoanalysis*, 95: 889–910.

Barahona, R. (2019). 'Report on the Panel: "Did Bion Change His Mind? Three Phases of His Clinical Approach."' *International Journal of Psychoanalysis*, 100: 1009–1011.

Bion, W. (1967). 'The Imaginary Twin,' in W. Bion, *Second Thoughts: Selected Papers on Psychoanalysis*. New York: Basic Books.

———. (1962). *Learning from Experience* (London: Heinemann; reprinted in paperback, London: Karnac, 1984).

———. (1963). *Elements of Psychoanalysis* (London: William Heinemann Medical Books).

———. (1965). *Transformations* (London: William Heinemann Medical Books).

———. (1967). 'Notes on Memory and Desire.' *The Psychoanalytic Forum*, 2: 272–273, 279–290.

———. (1970). *Attention and Interpretation* (London: Karnac).

———. (1980). *Bion in New York and São Paulo* (Perthshire: Clunie Press).

———. (1990). *Brazilian Lectures* (London: Karnac).

———. (2000). 'Four Discussions with W.R. Bion,' reprinted in *Clinical Seminars and Other Works* (London: Karnac).

———. (2005a). *The Italian Seminars* (ed. by F. Bion) (London: Karnac).

———. (2005b). *The Tavistock Seminars* (ed. by F. Bion) (London: Karnac).

———. (2013). *The Los Angeles Seminars and Supervision* (ed. by J. Aguayo and B. Malin) (London: Karnac).

———. (2014a). *A Memoir of the Future, Book Three: The Dawn of Oblivion*. In The Complete Works of W.R. Bion, Vol. 14 (London: Routledge), p. 121.

———. (2014b). 'Memory and Desire.' A talk given at the British Psychoanalytical Society, 16 June 1965. In The Complete Works of W.R. Bion, Vol. 6 (London: Routledge), pp. 7–17.

———. (2017a). *Bion in Buenos Aires: Seminars, Case Presentation and Supervision* (ed. by J. Aguayo, L. Pistener de Cortinas, and A. Regeczkey) (London: Karnac).

———. (2017b). *Bion in Brazil: Supervisions and Commentaries* (ed. by J.A. Juanquiera de Mattos, G. de Mattos Brito, and H. Levine) (London: Routledge).

———. (2024). *The Clinical Thinking of W.R. Bion: Supervisions and Commentaries* (ed. by H. Levine, G. de Mattos Brito, and J.A. Juanquiera de Mattos) (London: Routledge).

———. (1994). *Wilfred Bion: His Life and Works 1897–1979* (London: Free Association Books).

Civitarese, G. (2008). 'Immersion versus Interactivity and the Analytic Field.' *International Journal of Psychoanalysis*, 89: 279–298.

———. (2014). *The Necessary Dream: New Theories and Techniques of Interpretation in Psychoanalysis* (London: Karnac).

———. (2015). 'Transformations in Hallucinosis and the Receptivity of the Analyst.' *International Journal of Psychoanalysis*, 96: 1091–1116.

———. (2019). 'The Concept of Time in Bion's "A Theory of Thinking."' *International Journal of Psychoanalysis*, 100: 182–205.

Civitarese G. and Ferro, A. (2013). 'The Meaning and Use of Metaphor in Analytic Field Theory,' *Psychoanalytic Inquiry*, 33: 190–209.

Dermen, S. (2015). 'Bion the Clinician.' Bion panel contribution (unpublished). International Psychoanalytic Congress, Boston, July 2015.

Dermen, S. (2017). 'Horacio Etchegoyen's Analytic Case Presentation to W.R. Bion—Buenos Aires, Argentina (July/August 1968).' Bion panel contribution (unpublished). International Psychoanalytic Congress, Buenos Aires, July 2017.

Grosskurth, P. (1986). *Melanie Klein: Her World and Her Work* (New York: Knopf).

Hinshelwood R.D. (2018a). 'John Rickman behind the Scenes: The Influence of Lewin's Field Theory on Practice, Countertransference and W.R. Bion.' *International Journal of Psychoanalysis*, 99: 1409–1423.

———. (2018b). 'Intuition from Beginning to End? Bion's Clinical Approaches.' *British Journal of Psychotherapy*, 34: 198–213.

Ogden, T. (2007). 'Elements of Analytic Style: Bion's Clinical Seminars.' *International Journal of Psychoanalysis*, 88: 1185–1200.

Ogden. T. (2012). 'Elements of Analytic Style: Bion's Clinical Seminars,' in *Creative Readings* (London: Routledge), pp. 117–137.

Spillius, E. (1988). *Melanie Klein Today, Vol. 2: Mainly Practice* (London: Routledge).

Symington, J. and Symington, N. (1996). *The Clinical Thinking of Wilfred Bion* (London: Routledge).

Vermote, R. (2019). *Reading Bion* (London: Routledge).

1

Working Clinically with Groups

R.D. Hinshelwood

Bion's first experiences of groups were like all of ours—family, school, and career. However, he was quickly confronted, at the age of 19 years, with the deadly experience of the First World War, when he became commander of a tank unit. When invited by Anthony Banet to talk about his war experience as late as 1976, Bion was quite open about it. But when asked if it contributed to his theoretical formulations, he replied "No, not really, but I suppose they had some influence" (Bion and Banet, 1976/1976, p. 149). However, despite this denial, a moment later in the interview he said: "The curious thing was the great relief I felt when it was over, and then the discovery that, in fact, it had left very deep marks indeed" (p. 150). He continued to reflect on how, at Oxford, he felt a generation apart from those a little younger who had not seen military service. One imagines that, as Gooch said: "[H]is life's work was to try and turn that [his desperate wartime experience] to good account so as not to stay completely stuck in a PTSD state. I think Bion never got over the [First World] War" (Gooch, 2011, p. 88).

He was left with a deep suspicion of authority and its potential for incompetence and for a crushing suffocation of the individual. The experience did in fact contribute significantly to the work with groups, not least in the Second World War, and his highly original 'experiments' with patients-as-soldiers at Northfield (see later). In the 1970s, he was still writing about groups and even took part in experiential group relations conferences at the A.K. Rice Institute in the US when he lived in Los Angeles. In fact, his late novels, the Memoir trilogy, read almost as a group session of part objects.

So, as Gooch said, he turned his war experience to good account in various ways until the end of his life. It was a productive background he drew on during the Second World War. And, subsequently, perhaps it helped him to orient himself to the tribal warfare of the British Society in the decades after the Controversial Discussions. Such controversies led, in my view, to a very useful (and humane) theory of transformations deriving from differing viewpoints around a group or organization.

But, for two decades, after 1918, Bion struggled to find his direction, only to find, in 1938, that he was embroiled in another war. But by then he was not so alone; he developed a mentoring relationship with John Rickman with whom he had had a brief first analysis. In 1942, Bion was appointed senior psychiatrist in a team charged with reconceptualizing the method of officer selection; Eric Trist was the psychologist in the team. He chose a group method to inquire about the suitability of applicants for commissions: "[This] method was so simple and so obvious, when it has been propounded, that its revolutionary nature can easily be lost sight of" (Bion, 1946/2014, p. 36). No specific observational material was given by Bion, but he described in rather general terms his method of approaching the task:

> In concrete terms, a group of eight or nine candidates, an 'eye-full' from the testing officer's point of view, was told to build, say, a bridge. No lead was given about organization or leadership; these were left to emerge, and it was the duty of the observing officers to watch how any given man was reconciling his personal ambitions, hopes and fears with the requirements exacted by the group for its success.
>
> (Bion, 1946/2014, p. 36)

So, they set up a situation of tension for the applicants for an officer commission and then observed, for each man, "their capacity for maintaining personal relationships in a situation of strain that tempted him to disregard the interests of his fellows for the sake of his own" (Bion, 1946/2014, p. 35). Bion's method was to create a social tension and see who managed it best. Implicitly, he is defining the role of leadership in this specific way—managing a personal tension within a group.

The Northfield Rehabilitation Experiment

In 1943, Bion was moved to Northfield Hospital in Birmingham to take over medical responsibility for the rehabilitation wing (also known as the training wing) for men who had broken down psychologically on active service (Bion and Rickman, 1943/2014). Again, he constructed a radical reconceptualization. We can consider the three detailed vignettes from Bion's account. In the ward, lack of discipline, untidiness, and, frankly, dirt indicated the low morale and neurotic despondency of the men and thus the problem the ward had to tackle.

Northfield Vignette 1

The rehabilitation unit was not one for verbal therapy. The men were instructed to form activity groups—car maintenance, carpentry, and the like. Once a day, at 12.10, the officers and men went on parade, a moment when instructions were given, problems displayed, and complaints discussed. It took several days for the men to realise that Bion meant business about requiring their co-operation:

> It had been my habit, on going the rounds of the groups, to detach one or two men from their immediate work and take them with me 'just to see how the rest of the world lives.' I was therefore able to communicate to this meeting

an interesting fact observed by myself and by others who had gone round with me. Namely, that, although there were many groups and almost entire freedom to each man to follow the bent of his own inclinations, provided he could make a practical proposal, yet very little was happening. The carpenter's shop might have one or two men at most; car maintenance the same; in short, I suggested, it almost looked as if the training wing was a façade with nothing behind it. This, I said, seemed odd because I remembered how bitterly the patients in the training wing had previously complained to me that one of their objections to the Army was the 'eyewash.' Its presence in the training wing, therefore, really did seem to be a point worth study and discussion. ... I turned the discussion over at that point as a matter of communal responsibility and not something that concerned myself, as an officer, alone.

(Bion and Rickman, 1943/2014, pp. 109–110)

Bion picked, as the significant feature, this inconsistency in the attitudes of the men in the ward. The group had complained about hypocritical eyewash in the army. But now, with the opportunity for a more genuine commitment to an activity, it was not being taken. He was clear that the individuals in the unit were to be collectively responsible for what happened in the ward. Bion placed himself in the role of the one who defined the problem, and the men were charged to address this as a communal responsibility they should take up.

It seemed that this was a challenge from the commander, and it set going a new tension among the soldiers. Although they were vulnerable patients in a hospital, Bion was attempting to establish roles much more like soldiers who were required to face up to a challenge and defeat it. It was as if he was defining a new role for the men—no longer as patients. So, it was a challenge to the men expecting some medical authority to treat them. His own role as a leader was limited, and the men's role was an active one.

In fact, to his surprise the wing became self-critical, and within a few days real contributions and real work began. He writes: "The Commanding Officer of the hospital remarked on the big change in cleanliness that had taken place" (Bion and Rickman, 1943/2014, p. 110). Bion had displayed the problem to the social group and he assigned them the responsibility that was theirs. This created new roles and a motivating tension.

Northfield Vignette 2

The second vignette is similar—the problem of engaging a group responsibility that infected everyone. He was told: "Only 20 per cent of the men are taking part and really working hard; the other 80 per cent are just a lot of shirkers" (Bion and Rickman, 1943/2014, p. 111). He continued:

I was already aware of this, but refused, at least outwardly, to have its cure made my responsibility. Instead, I pointed out that, at an Army Bureau of Current

Affairs meeting some weeks before, the discussion had at one point centred on just that question—namely, the existence in communities (and the community then under discussion was Soviet Russia) of just such uncooperative individuals as these and the problem presented to society by their existence. Why, then, did they sound so surprised and affronted at discovering that just the same problem afflicted the training wing?

The group were not satisfied with that. They wanted such men punished:

> To this I replied that no doubt the complainants themselves had neurotic symptoms, or they would not be in hospital; why should their disabilities be treated in one way and the disabilities of the 80 per cent be treated in another? After all, the problem of the '80 per cent' was not new; in civil life magistrates, probation officers, social workers, the Church, and statesmen had all attempted to deal with it, some of them by discipline and punishment. The '80 per cent,' however, were still with us; was it not possible that the nature of the problem had not yet been fully elucidated and that they (the complainants) were attempting to rush in with a cure before the disease had been diagnosed? The problem, I said, appeared to be one that not only concerned the training wing, or even the Army alone, but had the widest possible implications for society at large. I suggested that they should study it and come forward with fresh proposals when they felt they were beginning to see daylight.
>
> (Bion and Rickman, 1943/2014, pp. 111)

Bion is continuing to display the 'problem' as one for the whole group and not that of any particular individual. He has used his role, not to take responsibility, but to define the problem, which the group must then take responsibility for. There was a result from this re-presentation of their 'neurosis' and a realignment:

> It is worth remarking at this point that my determination not to attempt solution of any problem until its borders had become clearly defined helped to produce, after a vivid and healthy impatience, a real belief that the unit was meant to tackle its job with scientific seriousness.
>
> (Bion and Rickman, 1943/2014, pp. 111)

In this vignette, Bion was bringing out a tension again—those who complained about others had some responsibility for all. It was like the officer selection tests: the individual with his own needs had to pay attention to everyone else's.

These tensions placed individuals in different roles and with different responsibilities to carry out. By refusing "at least outwardly, to have its cure made my responsibility" (p. 111), Bion's 'therapy' entailed reconstructing the social reality of the unit. He was not 'treating' individuals but supporting them taking their own responsibility.

Northfield Vignette 3

The next example again continued to use responsibility for problems of the group. In this case, the tension was about a soldier's experience of feeling manly in the hospital:

> By far the largest group of men proposed the formation of a dancing class. Despite the veneer of a desire to test my sincerity in promising facilities for group activity, the pathetic sense of inferiority towards women that underlay this proposal, by men taking no part in fighting, was only too obvious.

In fact, Bion's response was not to dismiss the frivolous proposal but to tell the men to make proposals. So, he responded by taking them seriously, but on condition they continued with the responsibility for their suggestion:

> [I]n the end the class was held during hours usually taken up by an evening entertainment … In short, a proposal, which had started as a quite impractical idea, quite contrary to any apparently serious military aim, or sense of social responsibility to the nation at war, ended by being an inoffensive and serious study carried out at the end of a day's work.
> (Bion and Rickman, 1943/2014, p. 112)

Individuals moved into effective roles again under the ability of the leader to direct and support their efforts.

The General Method of Approach

These are vivid vignettes and they expose certain principles of Bion's approach. Bion did not simply start work on officer selection, or on rehabilitation of soldiers who broke down. He worked out very clear ideas derived from a social psychology orientation (Hinshelwood, 2018) which he had discussed for years with John Rickman (Vonofakos and Hinshelwood, 2012). We can examine some of these principles through the work on the two projects.

First of all, the War Office Selection Boards: from the account given, the selection of army officers meant observing an applicant's interest in his fellows while managing the strain of pursuing his own interests. Underlying that test were several important points:

1. First of all, the men were given a responsibility
2. This was a joint task to be achieved together
3. The setting was designed to create a specific stress (or he called it a tension) to pursue self-advancement while dependent on others
4. A specific role would emerge—a leader.

The selecting team set up the conditions based on the tension they believed underlies leadership and watched for who emerged in this test in the specific role of leader. The role of leader was implicit, though nevertheless very clear. A leader appeared to be defined as a person able to manage the conflicting stresses of his own needs plus the needs of others.

The second main innovation/experiment at Northfield Hospital was similarly about playing a role in a group task (such as the war or the rehabilitation ward's disorder). The notion of working within a set of social tensions is quite explicit here, though in a slightly different form from the officer selection test. In this instance, the leader was clearly identified: it was Bion. He had to identify the particular field of action. As Bion said, it was not formal parade-ground discipline that was needed to drive the men:

> I became convinced that what was required was the sort of discipline achieved in a theatre of war by an experienced officer in command of a rather scallywag battalion. But what sort of discipline is that? In face of the urgent need for action I sought, and found, a working hypothesis. It was, that the discipline required depends on two main factors: (i) the presence of the enemy, who provided a common danger and a common aim; and (ii) the presence of an officer who, being experienced, knows some of his own failings, respects the integrity of his men, and is not afraid of either their good-will or their hostility.
>
> (Bion and Rickman, 1943/2014, p. 106)

His thinking proceeded by analogy with the fighting front:

> The common purpose to be substituted for the fighting soldier's aim to defeat the enemy had to be found.
>
> (Bion, 1943/2014, p. 27)

But:

> What common danger is shared by the men in the rehabilitation wing? What aim could unite them?
>
> There was no difficulty about detecting a common danger; neurotic extravagances of one sort and another perpetually endanger the work of the psychiatrist or of any institution set up to further treatment of neurotic disorders. The common danger in the training wing was the existence of neurosis as a disability of the community. I was now back at my starting-point—the need, in the treatment of a group, for displaying neurosis as a problem of the group. But, thanks to my excursion into the problem of discipline, I had come back with two additions. Neurosis needs to be displayed as a danger to the group; and its display must somehow be made the common aim of the group.
>
> (Bion and Rickman, 1943/2014, p. 107)

Bion was using the terms of group dynamics: the need for a leader and the common purpose/task of the group (to fight the problem of the group). Again, there is an attempt to construct the tensions, and, in this case, roles were assigned (while in officer selection, the test was to see who would emerge as a leader).

It is well known that the experiment with the rehabilitation wing lasted only briefly and was closed by the authorities for reasons which have been subsequently debated (Main, 1975; Trist, 1985). Where it was successful, it appears that the vignettes point to the deliberate observance of certain principles:

- A clear leadership of a military kind
- The identification of a communal problem
- Assigning a responsibility role to the group
- The tension in that role (identifying the passive role of the patients with those they complained of, for instance)
- The mobilization of energy to meet the responsibilities of the new roles.

These principles, though somewhat different in the two settings, were nevertheless both designed around the ideas of tension, roles, and leadership. And, as he summarized: "The therapeutic occupation had to be hard thinking and not the abreaction of moral indignation" (Bion, 1948a/2014, p. 39). This must have rung a bell later when he was reading Freud's (1911) paper on the reality principle (Bion, 1957/2014), where Freud talks of the change in action from satisfaction in discharging impulses towards modifying reality. Bion's descriptions using the key terms of role, tension, and so on betray the influence of social field theory he had acquired from Rickman.

Group Work at the Tavistock Clinic

These elements of Bion's general principles cast a light forwards to his group work after the war and during the time he was training as a psychoanalyst, from 1945 until 1950 (when he became a member of the British Psychoanalytical Society) and, ultimately, to the end of his analysis in 1953.

Bion's first study group was held, it seems, on 1 January 1946. Bion immediately wrote to Rickman about what happened in the group (Letter from Wilfred Bion to John Rickman 2 January 1946; see Vonofakos and Hinshelwood, 2012, p. 89). I shall quote most of that report:

> We had our first Staff group meeting yesterday and I must say I thought the Tavvy came out of it very well. I think about 30 people showed up; this included psychiatrists, technical lay staff (P.S.W.s [personal support workers] and such like) and lay staff (clerks)—also Maberly[1] and Leonard Browne[2] who do not quite fit into any of the other categories.
>
> I opened the discussion by saying I wanted to know how many people would like to form a guinea pig group and what hours we could appoint for meetings and what fee we should pay the Clinic. I then stopped.

> Everyone seemed a bit sheepish and then a few people started talking to ease the tension. Leonard Browne said, could you give any indications about how groups behave? To which I replied, Just like this. Another awkward pause followed.

Here Bion is inviting the members as a group to observe for themselves. He is putting his finger on an immediate tension, as in the Northfield work, and asserting the group members' responsibility:

> And then further questions to all of which I responded with non-committal grunts. The group hunted round a bit and then Dr. Stein[3] took the floor to explain, since I wouldn't, what he thought Dr. Bion wanted. The group fell on this with gratitude and Dr. Stein took over the group.

Bion observed the hunt for a leader to explain and thus to reduce the tension. The group space needed a leader as the key role at this stage:

> Then they petered out again. Then the topic of Dr. Bion cropped up, but without much assistance from Dr. Bion. A certain amount of heat began to be generated at this point and I then intervened to point out that they were angry with me because it was becoming clear that when I had said "group therapy" I meant "group" therapy and not therapy by Dr. Bion. I said that when I hadn't taken the lead they had first fallen back on themselves and had then squeezed Dr. Stein into the job since I wouldn't.

Bion does help the group to observe what they have displayed: the need for Dr Bion, his disinclination to accept their dependence, the anger at his non-compliance, and their resort to an alternative leader. Bion continued:

> After this things followed pretty conventional lines with Maberly's hostility and anxiety becoming more and more marked every minute. I may be wrong but I am pretty sure Maberly was present as a spy from the enemy's camp. That is to say he spoke with the assurance of one who felt he had allies both in and outside the group.

Bion observed something like an alternative group, an anti-group forged in hostilities:

> Dicks[4] took what I thought a very good and illuminating point, I believe he had great private relief when I gave my interpretation that gp. th. meant therapy by the group and not by Dr. Bion. Nor was he the only one. At the end I pointed out there were two opposite anxieties—that they were all going to be treated as patients and another anxiety that they were not being treated as patients.

Here is a tension, a seriously felt conflict, affecting the members generally, presumably. Right or wrong, Bion was trying to display the tension of the group to the group, including the tension around the role the group had assigned to Dr Bion. His implication is that the group members will take his observations and do something with them.

There are a number of specific strategies Bion used here in his understanding:

1. First and foremost was Bion's recognition (by introspection) of the role he was put in by the group
2. The role was to be responsible for therapy of the group
3. Not only did he reflect on this, but he insisted that the members do so as well
4. When he declined the role required of him, he observed the tension in the field
5. Roles evolved from the conflict and tensions impacting on other members.

The evolving process of the group was permeated by strong emotions—not just anxiety but also a build-up of hostility. In relation to these principles, Bion established that: the psychoanalyst (1.) does not accept that the role is his but (2.) interprets the requirements of the group, inviting them to become an inquiring group. Then, the group, rather than get on with their responsibility, seeks another leader—that seems to be his narrative of this session.

Perhaps the two most striking things, which are taken into the following work with groups and then ultimately in his psychoanalytic work after 1953, are: (1.) the importance of introspection as a major source of evidence for his conclusions; and (2.) the emphasis on responsibility, the leader's and the members'. The group members are placed by Bion in a role in which they are expected to contribute to the investigation, even when they manifestly fail to take on this role effectively. This particular issue of responsibility had been key to Bion's challenge to the passive role of the patient in the hospital at Northfield.

Experiences in Groups I–VII

Bion produced a series of seven papers on the work he set up on groups between 1948 and 1951, although he left the Tavistock Clinic in 1948. In 1952 (revised in 1955), he wrote a paper reviewing much of what he had written in the original papers up to 1951. Consequently, there are several different methods of approach to the clinical material (see Gordon, 2011). Most of the clinical material he presents is in the first three of these papers (Bion, 1948b/2014, 1948c/2014, 1949/2014)—understandable since he left the Tavistock in 1948—and there is one significant piece in his revision in 1955 (not in the earlier 1953 version of that review).

Experiences in Groups I

The first of the papers (1948b/2014, pp. 121–129) is almost entirely an extended summary of an initial session of a group (probably a study group with professionals, rather than a patient group):

> At the appointed time members of the group begin to arrive; individuals engage each other in conversation for a short time, and then, when a certain number has

collected, a silence falls on the group. After a while desultory conversation breaks out again, and then another silence falls. It becomes clear to me that I am, in some sense, the focus of attention in the group. Furthermore, I am aware of feeling uneasily that I am expected to do something. At this point I confide my anxieties to the group, remarking that, however mistaken my attitude might be, I feel just this.

Bion finds himself in discomfort that, as in his previous work, he captures via an examination of his own experience of the moment. This leads him to perceiving a role in relation to the responsibility in the group. This he declines, in favour of an encouragement to discussion via verbal expression of the responsibility he has declined. He treats this as his most significant data and intervenes with it:

[T]here is some indignation that I should express such feelings without seeming to appreciate that the group is entitled to expect something from me. I do not dispute this, but content myself with pointing out that clearly the group cannot be getting from me what they feel they are entitled to expect. I wonder what these expectations are, and what has aroused them.

(Bion, 1948b/2014, pp. 121–122)

Bion pointed out their insistence that he needs to 'conduct' the group in a different manner. In the process, he places an expectation on them too and sticks to his developed method—the group is there to research their own experience. The group changed tack:

Mr. X, who has a likeable personality, has taken charge of the group, and is already taking steps to repair the deplorable situation created by myself. But I have given a mistaken impression if I seemed to suggest that we can watch this group in detachment, for Mr. X, who is anxious for the welfare of the group, quite rightly turns his attention to the source of the trouble, which, from his point of view, is myself.

(p. 123)

And Bion cannot enlighten him about the situation:

I can only apologize, and say that, beyond feeling that the statement that I want to study group tensions is probably a very inadequate description of my motives, I can throw no light on his problem; he has a good deal of sympathy from the group when he turns from this very unsatisfactory reply to question one or two others.

(p. 124)

The group is not entirely happy with Mr X's leadership, though some give some factual details about themselves. However, other members seem wary, and the attention returns to Bion himself, or so he thought:

Without quite knowing why, I suggest that what the group really wants to know is my motives for being present, and, since these have not been discovered, they are not satisfied with any substitute.

Bion has now relented and given his own understanding of what the group wants, rather than waiting for it to emerge:

> It is clear that my interpretation is not welcome. One or two members want to know why I should take curiosity, which would seem to be valid without any further explanation, upon myself. The impression I receive is that very little importance is attached to the view I express as a possible explanation of what is going on. It seems to me either to be ignored, or to be taken as evidence of a warped outlook in myself. To make matters worse, it is not at all clear to me that my observation, however correct, is really the most useful one to make at the moment. But I have made it.
>
> (p. 124)

When he does make a contribution to the investigation, it appears not wanted. Why, they seem to be protesting, is he talking about himself and not them and their problems? And maybe, anyway, the comment might have been less relevant than he thought. Indeed, perhaps he should have stuck to addressing their own lack of curiosity, investigation, and contributions.

One member then makes some explanation about logical argument not being the appropriate thing, and that Bion must have his good reasons. This changes the atmosphere, with a new friendliness—except that Bion realizes it is the same old friendliness aimed at seducing him into a more acceptable role:

> I point out that the group now appears to me to be coaxing me to mend my ways and fall in with their wish that my behaviour should conform more to what is expected or familiar to them in other fields. I also remark that the group has, in essence, ignored what was said by Mr. Q. The emphasis has been shifted from what Mr. Q intended to only one part of what he said, namely, that, after all, I was likely to know what I was about. In other words, it has been difficult for an individual member to convey meanings to the group which are other than those which the group wishes to entertain.
>
> This time the group really is annoyed.
>
> (p. 126)

He is indicating something that he will elaborate on more in the next paper. Here, he continues:

> I say that I think my interpretations are disturbing the group. Furthermore, that the group interprets my interpretations as a revelation of the nature of my personality. No doubt attempts are being made to consider that they are in some way descriptive of the mental life of the group, but such attempts are overshadowed by a suspicion that my interpretations, when interpreted, throw more light on myself than on anything else, and that what is then revealed is in marked contrast with any expectations that members of the group had before they came. This, I think, must be very disturbing, but quite apart

from any point of this sort, we have to recognize that perhaps members of the group assume too easily that the label on the box is a good description of the contents.

(p. 127)

He acknowledges that at this point a crisis has been reached. He does not try to present again the reality "that I am merely one member of a group possessing some degree of specialized knowledge" (p. 127), because the members would not accept it. The group in fact turns then to someone else who might perform as a leader, but without much conviction. He believes the members are unwilling to accept reality if it conflicts with the group's view of their need, and "critical judgement is almost entirely absent" (p. 129).

If we leave the process record at this point, we can see how Bion was focusing on roles in the group and, in particular, on the way he experienced himself in a role the group expected. He found himself in discomfort at 'failing' the group, but attributed that failure to the members' rejection of reality in favour of some assumption or phantasy they had come to share about him.

Inevitably, Bion had to choose between two alternative opportunities: to address either (1.) the way each member transferred their personal images or instead (2.) the role of the analyst, in the whole group space. His approach was to choose the latter. Eric Trist was at this time a co-therapist in one of these groups, and he gave his impression:

It became evident that he [Bion] was doing something different from what others were doing. He was neither applying psychoanalysis to groups nor was he just giving ego-support. He was searching for the equivalent of the psychoanalytic method in the group situation.

(Trist, 1985, p. 28)

He did not take the standard position of interpreting symbolic meanings in the material that individuals produced. Instead, his interest was in the process, and especially in the process of interaction between roles, between a role and the group (and not least, though not only, the interaction between the role of leader and the group). If he was looking for a group equivalent to a psychoanalytic method, he had the advantage that there were actually beings who could play the parts of some sort of unconscious phantasy. It is the group equivalent, perhaps, of the play technique with the individuals as the 'toys' to manipulate. He could focus on the process of this kind of interchange as the narrative of a phantasy.

He showed in the paper how he started from the familiar position of the commander of a group leading an investigation into group tensions. The discovery is that, without properly realizing it, the 'group' had other expectations, but then had great difficulties in paying attention to their own expectations.

Experiences in Groups II

In the second of his papers, he stressed how sensitive the individual member is to the group's opinion. Interestingly, he makes a point that will become extremely important 20 years later (Bion, 1970): "[T]his kind of assessment is as much a part of the mental life of the individual as his sense of touch" (Bion, 1948b/2014, p. 133). Bion stressed this sensitivity and the weight of its impact as having just as much importance as any ordinary sensory perception. This is a way of introducing his main theme—the group members have an unspoken kind of connection between them which is not explicit in words or in any of the ordinary senses. They must, he thought, be united with each other through channels other than the ordinary senses. Later (in 1970), he will use the expression 'non-sensuous' perception.

He gave the following sequence, as the moment of realization. At this point in a group session, Bion and the members seem to feel futile:

Mrs. X: I had a nasty turn last week. I was standing in a queue waiting for my turn to go to the cinema when I felt ever so queer. Really, I thought I should faint or something.

Mrs. Y: You're lucky to have been going to a cinema. If I thought I could go to a cinema I should feel I had nothing to complain of at all.

Mrs. Z: I know what Mrs. X means. I feel just like that myself, only I should have had to leave the queue.

Mr. A: Have you tried stooping down? That makes the blood come back to your head. I expect you were feeling faint.

Mrs. X: It's not really faint.

Mrs. Y: I always find it does a lot of good to try exercises. I don't know if that's what Mr. A means.

Mrs. Z: I think you have to use your will-power. That's what worries me—I haven't got any.

Mr. B: I had something similar happen to me last week, only I wasn't even standing in a queue. I was just sitting at home quietly when …

Mr. C: You were lucky to be sitting at home quietly. If I was able to do that I shouldn't consider I had anything to grumble about.

Mrs. Z: I can sit at home quietly all right, but it's never being able to get out anywhere that bothers me. If you can't sit at home why don't you go to a cinema or something?

Here is a group of patients in dialogue in which none seems to connect adequately with the others in cognitive terms. Ordinary speech makes no real contact:

> After listening for some time to this sort of talk, it becomes clear to me that anybody in this group who suffers from a neurotic complaint is going to be advised to do something which the speaker knows from his own experience to be

absolutely futile. Furthermore, it is clear that nobody has the least patience with any neurotic symptom. A suspicion grows in my mind, until it becomes a certainty, that there is no hope whatever of expecting co-operation from this group.
(Bion, 1948b/2014, p. 139)

However, reflecting on this experience, he thought: "[F]rom the way in which the group is going on its motto might be: 'Vendors of quack nostrums unite'" (p. 140). But then, at that point, he realized with surprise that he was expressing to himself not the group's visible disharmony but its unity! They all behave in this culture in the same apparently disconnected way—they co-operate in their uncooperativeness. There is a profound connection beyond the visible disconnection.

He elaborates on this. Another group is equally listless, with little apparent life going on:

I am inclined to think that the present leaders of this group are not in the room; they are the two absentees, who are felt not only to be contemptuous of the group, but also to be expressing that contempt in action. The members of that group who are present are followers. ...

I notice that one of the men who is asking the questions is employing a peculiarly supercilious tone. His response to the answers he receives appears to me, if I keep my mental microscope at the same focus, to express polite incredulity. A woman in the corner examines her fingernails with an air of faint distaste. When a silence occurs it is broken by a woman who, under the former focus, seemed to be doing her best to keep the work of the group going, with an interjection which expresses clearly her dissociation from participation in an essentially stupid game.

(p. 137)

Bion's impression was so strong he described:

The picture of hard-working individuals striving to solve their psychological problems is displaced by a picture of a group mobilized to express its hostility and contempt for neurotic patients and for all who may wish to approach neurotic problems seriously.

(p. 137)

What he was trying to convey is that there is an apparent commitment to the group, but it is a hidden group, one in a very negative state. This leads to a passage in which he describes a state which appears to be the equivalent of the dynamic unconscious in individual psychoanalysis:

Some contributions [a member] is prepared to make as coming unmistakably from himself, but there are others which he would wish to make anonymously.

> If the group can provide means by which contributions can be made anonymously, then the foundations are laid for a successful system of evasion and denial ... it was possibly because the hostility of the individuals was being contributed to the group anonymously that each member could quite sincerely deny that he felt hostile. We shall have to examine the mental life of the group closely to see how the group provides a means for making these anonymous contributions. I shall postulate a group mentality as the pool to which the anonymous contributions are made.
>
> (p. 138)

The disowned parts of individuals collaborate to create a group culture, so that: "Any contribution to this group mentality must enlist the support of, or be in conformity with, the other anonymous contributions of the group" (p. 138).

He has moved from a detailed description of the process of a group defined by his own personal experience to a conception that aligns with psychoanalytic observations of the unconscious in individual patients. The group has a disowned 'mentality.'

Having come to this recognition of the members' method of creating their own group context, its 'mentality,' the rest of this paper is a discussion of the relation of the individual to that group mentality. It disturbs the individual's need for a well-functioning group: "[E]very attempt I make to get a hearing shows that I have a united group against me. The idea that neurotics cannot co-operate has to be modified" (p. 140). This 'group mentality,' both created and suffered by the individual members, allows "the expression in a group of impulses which individuals wish to satisfy anonymously" (p. 141). This inferred abstraction means that individuals will use a group to pool those impulses which they do not wish to own. Membership of a group allows this deliverance from the unsavoury sides of themselves. Moreover: "If experience shows that this hypothesis fulfils a useful function, further characteristics of the group mentality may be added from clinical observation" (p. 49).

This second paper follows on the discovery of the first by creating a model of a 'part' of the group which no-one owns. This is a speculative entity, but in describing it to the group he provokes a crisis of resentment and opposition which he takes as evidence that the model has considerable validity.

Experiences in Groups III

He has left to the third of the papers his elaboration of the 'group mentality':

> How did the use of these three concepts, group mentality, group culture, and individual, as interdependent phenomena, work in practice? Not very well; I found that the group reacted in a tiresomely erratic manner.
>
> (Bion, 1949/2014, p. 146)

The limitations of the model of group mentality meant he had to conduct further exploration. He did find one result when he explored further; group mentality needs unpicking. And group mentality was revised to become three mutually exclusive cultures, each based on an emotional assumption. Somewhat apologetically he says, "The things that knocked holes in my theories were not words used, but the emotion accompanying them" (p. 147). And he confessed, as a result: "I wish I could give concrete examples, but I cannot record what was actually said" (p. 147). The guiding principle was not verbal content but, as usual, his own sensed emotional accompaniment. He is intent on the non-sensuous kind of communication he will eventually call "intuition" in 1970.

The lack of detailed material is therefore a limitation. But he gave an impressionistic account of the behaviour:

> [It] went like this: two members of the group would become involved in a discussion; sometimes the exchange between the two could hardly be described but it would be evident that they were involved with each other, and that the group as a whole thought so too.
>
> (p. 147)

He described the group sitting in attentive silence: "[He intuits] a basic assumption, held both by the group and the pair concerned, that the relationship is a sexual one" (p. 147). This is the first of the three well-known basic assumptions. This one is the paring assumption, and the others are the fight/flight and dependency assumptions.

In introducing the fight/flight group, he described:

> I had given interpretations showing how treatment had produced unpleasant feelings in members of the group. The effect of the interpretations had been to make members feel that I menaced the 'good' group. At one point my interpretation happened to hinge on remarks made by Miss Y. She listened to what I said and passed on smoothly as if I had not spoken at all. A few minutes later, when I gave another interpretation of the same kind, the same thing happened; a few minutes later, the same again. The group fell silent. At the moment when Miss Y had ignored my interpretation I was aware that the group had come together as a group; I had no doubt about this whatever. By the end of my third interpretation I was sure not only that the group had come together, but that it had done so to put an end to my interventions.
>
> (pp. 151–152)

Again, it is a powerful sense of his own feelings which gives him a conviction of certainty: "[It] is not easily conveyed by an account of the words used" (p. 153). These intuitions are very real, he says: "When the group has come together in this way it has become something as real and as much a part of human life as a family" (p. 153). This kind of conviction, not arising from ordinary communication, was a problem that occupied him 20 years later (Bion, 1967, 1970).

He has in this paper unpacked three elements of the 'group mentality,' the basic assumptions which reside innately within the human mind. I shall not consider the rest of the 'Experience in groups' papers (numbers IV–VII) as there is no clinical material, but will pass on to his subsequent radical review of his work.

The Review

As a contribution to a Festschrift for Melanie Klein's 70th birthday, Bion contributed a radical review of his model of three basic assumptions (Bion, 1952). This was subsequently expanded for a book of similar papers on Klein's work (Klein, Heimann, and Money-Kyrle, 1955). In that paper he did two things. First, he revised the basic assumption model, bringing it in line with Klein's paranoid-schizoid position:

> I think that the central position in group dynamics is occupied by the more primitive mechanisms that Melanie Klein has described as peculiar to the paranoid-schizoid and depressive positions. In other words I feel, but would not like to be challenged with my limited experience to prove, that it is not simply a matter of the incompleteness of the illumination provided by Freud's discovery of the family group as the prototype of all groups, but the fact that this incompleteness leaves out the source of the main emotional drives in the group.
> (Bion, 1955, p. 457)

This is now a more psychoanalytic model deriving the basic assumptions from Freud and Klein.

Second, he presents some clinical material that makes an important distinction in the way he, and Kleinians, approach the clinical encounter. This is a distinction in which the clinical material is seen in terms of process as much as symbolic representation. Or, to put it more accurately, it is a process in relation to what the context represents. Here is his material:

> A woman is talking in a group consisting, on this occasion, of six people and myself. She complains of a difficulty about food, her fear of choking if she eats at a restaurant, and of her embarrassment at the presence, during a recent meal, of an attractive woman at her table. "I don't feel like that," says Mr. A, and his remark is met by a murmur of sound from one or two others which could indicate that they were at one with him; could indicate it and does indicate it, but at the same time leaves them free to say, for this group had now become wily, if need arose, that they "hadn't said anything." The remainder looked as if the matter were of no interest or concern to them.
> (p. 238)

Bion explained that, in individual psychoanalysis, there are various possible interpretations that could be given to the woman's confidences to the group. None seemed appropriate, however, in the group situation. That is to say, the symbolic meaning is secondary to the process the woman elicited from the group. It is not so much the feeding with the beautiful 'mother' (whatever complex of feelings that evoked), but the quite different dismissive response of the contextual group:

> If a patient spoke in analysis as the woman had spoken, it is clear that according to the state of her analysis the analyst would not expect to have any great difficulty in seeing that a number of interpretations were possible. I cannot see how any of these interpretations, which are based on years of psycho-analytic study of the pair, can possibly be regarded as appropriate to the group; either that, or we have to revise our ideas of what constitutes the analytic situation. In fact the interpretations I gave were concerned almost entirely with pointing out that the material that followed the woman's confidence to the group indicated the group's anxiety to repudiate that the woman's difficulty, whatever it was, was theirs.
> (pp. 238–239)

Bion, of course, presented this material to make a point about the group mentality and how the splitting at a psychotic level leads to the individuals in a group sharing out, as it were, the characteristics of a personality among the group—around the restaurant table. That agreement to spread out the functions of a personality at the level of a group is the most original and profound of Bion's insights into group dynamics. It is the splitting, projection, and repudiation of parts of the self, and their being taken up by others which he is eager to communicate in this paper—that is the first point just alluded to. However, from the point of view of Bion's clinical approach, there is another important point.

The characteristic we must note is the process that occurs in the context of the group. The apparent symptom is dismissed as either alien or as of no interest. That process is what contributes so strongly to the powerful emotional experience—including the powerful experience in the analyst. Though it has been implicit previously, it is explicit here and can now be seen dramatically.

Later Manifestations of the Group Work

As mentioned at the outset of this chapter, Bion's dark experience as an active soldier probably clouded the whole of his career. However, his attempts to process his experiences, through his clinical work initially, as a psychotherapist, and through the influence probably mostly of Trotter and Rickman, stamped an indelible mark on the way he evolved his clinical approach with groups. That evolving approach then carried through into his work as a trained psychoanalyst. His book *Attention and Interpretation*, published in 1970, has the subtitle *Insight in Psychoanalysis and Groups*, putting psychoanalysis and groups on a level. And the late interview with Banet (1976/2014) demonstrated his enduring interest. That interest in group dynamics after he left the Tavistock Clinic in 1948 can be seen in his accomplishment in developing the idea of projective identification as an interpersonal phenomenon and, in particular, the familiar container–contained model that has informed clinical practice ever since.

However, we have seen clear indications in the work of this group period of elements of Bion's clinical approach that resurface later and are developed in his psychoanalytic work. These can be listed as follows:

- Introspection
- The emphasis on the patient's responsibility to enquire and investigate
- Intuition and non-sensuous perception
- Anonymized group mentality
- Problems of language in communicating the non-verbal
- Narratives and process involving roles and tensions rather than symbolic meanings.

Introspection

From his earliest recorded work, Bion was very attentive to his own experience within the clinical context and its potential use as evidence.

Responsibility

Bion cultivated a culture in his clinical work that laid responsibility on patients to accomplish the task (see the interview with Gooch, 2011).

Intuition

His own experience was used extensively, and often extremely confidently, as an indication for understanding and interpreting the dynamics of the setting of the immediate moment.

Group mentality

In groups, anonymized parts of the persons are denied, which becomes the collaboration of transference and countertransference in psychoanalysis, together with his later description of the genius (mystic) 'contained' in the group establishment. Perhaps this is the most significant of his conclusions, which carries forward and leads implicitly to his understanding of the transference in psychoanalysis (really the transference–countertransference) as a jointly created, anonymized form of anti-work. Not just a minus-link, but a collaborative attack on linking.

Language

Bion was explicit in confiding the difficulty in using language for describing the communications made intuitively and non-sensuously.

Process

Even before his analysis with Klein, Bion focused a great deal on narratives of the roles and tensions in the context of the clinical setting as expressing hidden dramas, rather as toys in play therapy do. Both patient and analyst are in a common context (Hinshelwood, 2018).

Conclusions

Bion became an accomplished psychotherapist before training as a psychoanalyst. Perhaps it was purely circumstances that directed him towards group dynamics as his particular entry into psychoanalytic training, as opposed to either the more usual interest in young children, as with Klein and Winnicott, or the experience of psychiatry.

The elements of Bion's approach echo forwards as it were to his later preoccupations, sometimes in exactly the same form, sometimes modified in a different context. The seeds that germinate later in other manifestations of his approach are quite visible in the early group period. This account has avoided excursions into the theoretical background and his wide readings in history and philosophy that helped him formulate both his wartime experiences and his experiences in groups. Such theoretical influences that intermeshed with his clinical experience will be approached elsewhere (Hinshelwood, 2023).

Notes

1 Alan Maberly (1903–1969) was analyzed by Stekel in Vienna. He was part of the Tavistock psychiatric contingent in the RAMC, but returned as temporary director of the Tavistock Clinic during the war. He was medical director of the Child Guidance Council after the war.
2 Leonard Browne (1887–1960) was one of the early group of psychiatrists at the Tavistock Clinic, serving in the RAMC in both world wars. In WWII, he was command psychiatrist of the Eastern Command.
3 Leopold Stein (1893–1969) was a refugee from Vienna, joining the Tavistock just before the war. He was one of the earliest originators of speech therapy in this country. He became a Jungian analyst and wrote a widely, though not well reviewed, book on "loathsome women."
4 Henry (H.V.) Dicks (1900–77) was an early psychiatrist at the Tavistock Clinic, who eventually wrote its history, *50 Years of the Tavistock Clinic* (1970).

References

Bion, W.R. (1943, 2014). On groups. In The Complete Works of W.R. Bion, Volume 4, pp. 23–30. London: Routledge.
Bion, W.R. (1946, 2014). Leaderless group project. *Bulletin of the Menninger Clinic* 10, 77–81. Republished (1996). Reprinted in *International Journal of Therapeutic Communities* 7817, 87–91. Republished (2014) in The Complete Works of W.R. Bion, Volume 4, pp. 35–40. London: Routledge.

Bion, W.R. (1948a). Group methods of treatment. In Flugel, J.C. (Ed.) *Proceedings of the International Conference on Medical Psychotherapy*: 106–109. Republished (2014) in The Complete Works of W.R. Bion, Volume 4, pp. 65–70. London: Routledge.

Bion, W.R. (1948b). Experiences in groups: I. *Human Relations* 1: 314–320. Republished (1961) in W.R. Bion, *Experiences in Groups and Other Papers*. London: Tavistock, pp. 29–40. Republished (2014) in The Complete Works of W.R. Bion, Volume 4, pp. 121–130. London: Routledge.

Bion, W.R. (1948c). Experiences in groups: II. *Human Relations* 1: 487–496. Republished (1961) in W.R. Bion, *Experiences in Groups and Other Papers*. London: Tavistock, pp. 41–58. Republished (2014) in The Complete Works of W.R. Bion, Volume 4, pp. 131–144. London: Routledge.

Bion, W.R. (1949). Experiences in groups: III. *Human Relations* 2: 13–22. Republished (1961) in W.R. Bion, *Experiences in Groups and Other Papers*. London: Tavistock, pp. 59–76. Republished (2014) in The Complete Works of W.R. Bion, Volume 4, pp. 145–157. London: Routledge.

Bion, W.R. (1952). Group dynamics: A review. In M. Klein, P. Heimann, and R. Money-Kyrle (Eds.), *New Directions in Psychoanalysis*, pp. 440–477. Republished (2014) in The Complete Works of W.R. Bion, Volume 6, pp. 207–245. London: Routledge.

Bion, W.R. (1955). Group dynamics: A review. Revised, in M. Klein, P. Heimann, and R. Money-Kyrle (Eds.), *New Directions in Psychoanalysis*, London, Karnac, pp. 440–477. And (1961) in W.R. Bion, *Experiences in Groups and Other Papers*. London: Tavistock. In The Complete Works of W.R. Bion, Vol 6, pp. 207–245. London: Routledge.

Bion, W.R. (1957). Differentiation of the psychotic form the non-psychotic parts of the ego. *International Journal of Psychoanalysis* 38: 266–275. Republished (1967) in W.R. Bion *Second Thoughts*, pp. 43–64. London: Heinemann. In The Complete Works of W.R. Bion, Vol 6, pp. 92–111. London: Routledge.

Bion, W.R. (1967). Notes on memory and desire. *Psychoanalytic Forum* 2: 271–280. Reprinted (1988) in E. Bott Spillius (Ed.), *Melanie Klein Today, Vol. 2: Mainly Practice*. London: Routledge, pp. 17–21. Reprinted (2013) in J. Aguayo, and B. Malin, *Los Angeles Seminars and Supervision*, pp. 133–149. London: Routledge.

Bion, W.R. (1970) *Attention and Interpretation*. London: Tavistock. In The Complete Works of W.R. Bion, Vol 6, pp. 221–330. London: Routledge.

Bion, W.R., and Banet, A. (1976/2014). Interview by Anthony Banet. In The Complete Works of W.R. Bion, Vol 10, pp. 147–164. London: Routledge.

Bion, W.R. and Rickman, J. (1943/1961). Intra-group tensions in therapy. *Lancet* ii: 678–681. Republished (1961) in W.R. Bion, *Experiences in Groups and Other Papers*. London: Tavistock, pp. 11–26. London: Routledge. Republished in The Complete Works of W.R. Bion, Vol 4, pp. 95–245. London: Routledge.

Freud, S. (1911). Formulations on the two principles of mental functioning. In *The Standard Edition of the Complete Psychological Works of Sigmund Freud*, Volume XIII. London: Hogarth, pp. 213–226.

Gooch, J. (2011). An analysis with Bion: An interview with James Gooch. Interview by JoAnn Culbert-Koehn. *Journal of Analytical Psychology* 56(1): 76–91.

Gordon, J. (2011). Some neglected clinical material from Bion's *Experiences in Groups*. In C. Mawson (Ed.), *Bion Today*. London: Routledge, pp. 340–346.

Hinshelwood, R.D. (2018). John Rickman behind the scenes: The influence of Lewin's field theory on practice, countertransference and W.R. Bion. *International Journal of Psychoanalysis* 100: 1409–1423.

Hinshelwood, R.D. (2023). *W.R. Bion as Clinician*. London: Routledge.
Trist, E. (1985). Working with Bion in the 1940s: The group decade. In M. Pines (Ed.), *Bion and Group Psychotherapy*. London: Routledge & Keegan Paul, pp. 1–46.
Vonofakos, D. and Hinshelwood, R.D. (2012). Wilfred Bion's letters to John Rickman (1939–1951). *Psychoanalysis and History* 14(1): 53–94.

2

Tracing the Clinical Trajectory and Technical Relevance of Bion's Cases and Theorizing from the 'Psychosis' Period (1950–1957)

Joseph Aguayo

Prelude to the Psychosis Papers

To address the technical and essential continuities and the context-specific discontinuities between the papers Bion wrote on groups and psychotic patients, there were obvious differences between the two types of populations that informed his implicit method of clinical inquiry: the treatment and assessment of soldiers at war and civilian outpatients vis-à-vis psychotic patients in individual psychoanalysis. In one respect, Bion had dealt with whole persons up to the time of his psychoanalytic training—what made for competent and optimally functioning officers as well as the rehabilitation of men suffering from combat fatigue so that they could be returned to the front. But, in his subsequent contact with seriously disturbed patients, he encountered the problems of those whose conflicts went beyond what they could articulate: psychotic patients faced severe challenges in the coherent expression of their self-experience, feeling more like partial personalities, subsumed and consumed by what the London Klein group would come to recognize as 'part-object' experience. The portal of entry into this world of personal sense of fragmentation and dissociation was Bion's treatment of "The Imaginary Twin," a case he presented for qualification at the British Psychoanalytical Society in November 1950.

The mentors and colleagues who mediated Bion's entry into the world of psychoanalysis became important to him as he began training at the London Institute of Psychoanalysis in the fall of 1945. Of central importance was Bion's own analyst, Melanie Klein, with whom he was in analysis from 1945 to 1953. Members and candidates at the British Institute had heard her seminars on technique, which went as far back as 1936 (Spillius, 2007; Klein, 2017). Klein's technique emphasized the patient's internal psychic reality as mediated through the ubiquitous operation of unconscious phantasy. Students in training learned how to analyze unconscious phantasies, such as: the infant's primal relationship of love and hate of the breast and the maternal body; attacks on it and the ensuing persecutory experiences of the paranoid/schizoid position; the Oedipus complex and the ensuing guilt and attempts at reparation in the depressive position; and splitting, projective and introjective processes, as well as attempts at integration (Spillius, 2007, p. 76). Students also learned how to link two aspects of unconscious phantasy as it pertained to the patient's 'remembered

DOI: 10.4324/9781003401926-3

past' (i.e., early relationships with parents and siblings) and the 'unconscious past' (or the remembrance of these universal phantasized experiences) (Aguayo, 2011). Graduated Kleinian analysts such as Hanna Segal and Herbert Rosenfeld were early advocates of Klein's technique when they demonstrated the operation of unconscious phantasy in the 'here and now' while linking it to early infantile situations. In John Steiner's assessment of Klein's technique seminars in 1936 as well as 1958, "Melanie Klein describes transference interpretations as feelers towards early situations" (Klein, 2017, p. 14). The next generation of analysts, such as Betty Joseph (who incidentally was a fellow candidate with Bion in the training cohort of 1945; Pick and Milton, 2001), also demonstrated how to make part-object symbolic interpretations, while linking the past to the present in the transference (Joseph, 1959).

Another important mentor was Paula Heimann, who likely served as Bion's first control case supervisor (Willoughby, 2006, p. 56). Her method of operating in the consulting room found a welcome reception in Bion, as she emphasized introspecting on direct emotional experience, especially in relationship to puzzling and disturbing subjective reactions to analytic work with patients. Heimann maintained that the analyst could use his subjective reactions as an "instrument of research" much as the wartime use of radar became an effective technology for detecting enemy planes at a distance.[1] Such ideas resulted in one of the most famous papers in our field, "On Countertransference" (Heimann, 1950) given, against Melanie Klein's counsel, at the IPA Congress at Zurich in 1949 (Grosskurth, 1986, p. 378). We start our exploration of Bion's method of clinical inquiry with his first analytic case, "The Imaginary Twin," moving through his subsequent papers on psychosis, some of which contained illustrative clinical material.

One guiding mode of orientation: this chapter reverses the usual figure–ground relationship between theory and practice. The approach here is from the clinical ground up—namely, how technical practices inform theory-building. Additionally, I think that Bion's group experience had a specific and organizing impact on his career as a Kleinian analyst. Some analysts politely marginalize the group work as a 'prepsychoanalytic' prelude to his enduring work. Hinshelwood takes exception here, asserting—and I support this basic position—that it is important and relevant to consider how the group period remained a vital (if not implicit) structuring background presence to Bion's subsequent analytic theorizing. In this instance, the work of John Rickman (Bion's first analyst and collaborator during his group period), who also emphasized the analysis of unconscious role-relationships in both groups and the individual analytic situation, was of enduring importance for Bion. Of course, there are the obvious differences involved in learning his craft as a workaday psychoanalyst, but there was also continuity with the group work in his clinical method of inquiry.

Bion's First Psychoanalytic Case: "The Imaginary Twin" (1950)

Bion's "Twin" paper complements the slew of group papers published during his training analysis, especially the focus on the different kinds of unconscious roles into which Bion's slippery and elusive patient recruited him. Seemingly whole objects related to one another—the patient as role-recruiting the analyst into a role of befuddled onlooker until the analyst drew upon his subjective reactions to muddle his way out of the recruited position. Bion's "Twin" paper occupies a place of special interest in his way of understanding how he worked with patients, as it segued at the very end of the paper into brief clinical vignettes regarding his work with psychotic patients, something that also reflected a formal Kleinian programmatic agenda when he began to publish on psychotic states of mind at the time of the IPA London Congress paper in 1953 (Aguayo, 2009).

While Melanie Klein had made her technique of child and adult analysis well known to the candidates and members of the British Society, it was less well known outside London. In fact, it would be during the 1950s that the London Klein group came to recognize that it had a distinctive technique, which in and of itself represented a shift in "novelty of content" in the analysis of psychosis becoming a "novelty of method" (Spillius, 1988). Within the Klein group of the 1950s, members proceeded as if they were practicing a standard psychoanalytic technique. Younger members who attended Klein's technique seminar in 1958 were all London Kleinians: Isabel Menzies, Oliver Lyth, Stanley Leigh, Brenda Morrison, Tom Hayley, and James Gammill (Spillius, 2007; Klein, 2017, p. 95).

To the analytic world outside London, the Klein group did not have an identifiably explicit clinical technique, so these factors help to establish a context for the inferences made here about Bion's *implicit method of clinical inquiry*, something of which, *at that time*, he gave no coherent account. Yet Bion's theoretical and clinical contributions have stood the test of time. How would we go about learning from his *clinical method of inquiry* based on textually close readings of his clinical examples, so we can trace how it developed and became elaborated throughout the course of his publications? If we stick to a close textual reading of Bion's clinical examples, what can we take away in our daily treatment of a wide range of patients—recalcitrant, psychotic, hard to reach, difficult to treat?

What does the "Twin" paper tell us about how Bion accessed the timeless truth of his patient's very disturbed condition? What did Bion imagine he was doing, and how did his efforts tally with what the patient thought he was doing in his own analysis? Is Bion's psychoanalytic method, even at this early date, identifiable as distinctive—and to what extent can it also be regarded as falling in a domain of technical practices recognizable at that time as 'Kleinian'? Was there a unique interpretative signature Bion drew upon? We start with the "Twin" paper and then look at Bion's other psychosis papers of the 1950s. Bion the Kleinian worked in the present moment, interpreting the patient's most urgent anxiety. With a background in war- and peacetime groups, where all emotional issues were dealt with in real time, it also suited Bion's analytic disinclination for taking or making active use of the patient's early history.[2] Like Freud and Klein, Bion ultimately formulated far-reaching clinical generalizations from a small body of patients (near-psychotic and psychotic).

The Twin's Early History

The "Twin" paper opens in a rather standard way—the analyst elucidates the patient's early history.[3] The reader hears about a tragic childhood filled with many losses. The patient's sister, older by just a year, died early in the patient's childhood. There were other tragedies and losses—the mother's death when he was 17, experienced against a bleakness of an austere childhood. It all had fallen apart when he was 13 and had a breakdown himself (Bion, 1950/1967, p. 3). Yet, despite these overwhelming early losses, Bion rarely refers to them at all during the rest of the paper. Now, it is probable that these early losses and trauma were listened to and worked with—and then not written about. However, more likely is that Bion, even at this early point in his career as an analyst, simply did not put much stock in directly factoring past experiences into active, present-tense work in the transference as a displacement from past to present, perhaps reprising his critique of his therapist from his Tavistock days, J.R. Hadfield, "Mr. Feel-It-in-the-Past" (Bléandonu, 1994, p. 41).

Bion's emphasis was recognizably Kleinian in some respects insofar as there was an accent on unconscious phantasy active and organizing in the present analysis (Isaacs, 1948). But what, in hindsight, appears distinctive and exceptional about Bion's approach here was his lack of emphasis on linking unconscious phantasies that were active in the moment with early childhood material that was otherwise abundant. Klein's concept of unconscious phantasy appeared ubiquitous in this instance, referring to *both* present ('deep') as well as past ('early') phantasies. In this instance, however, Bion omitted any evidence of his working with the patient's material from a remembered or unconscious past or linking interpretations of the patient's current material with it.

Bion's marginalization of the patient's early history may not have struck his Kleinian contemporaries as noteworthy—after all, Klein herself had written up so many child cases in which the analytic work occurred in real time, that of the present 'here and now,' while analyzing the unconscious phantasies tied to 'memories in feelings' associated with the distant past of hypothesized infantile conflicts. So, Bion's analytic approach was clear enough: he was flying under the Kleinian banner even though he bypassed linking past familial history with current conflicts. Where Bion could have hypothesized that the twin might have been some psychic manifestation of his feeling haunted or persecuted for having lived while his little sister had died, there is no mention of survivor's guilt. Indeed, there seems to be next to no mention of any event in the patient's past that could cast a persecutory shadow over his present life. In plain words, the patient's past conflicts, while listened to, were taken up exclusively in the 'here and now.' On the one side, Bion emphasized only the 'deep' aspect of unconscious phantasy, while Klein, Segal, and Rosenfeld took the 'deep' aspect as a jumping-off point for examining as well as linking to the operation of 'early' unconscious phantasy as well.[4]

The Emotional Atmosphere of the Twin Case

In the course of the present moment, Bion was left stymied and wondering, given the patient's listless and emotionally dull reactions, what in his interpretations might have felt valid to the patient. The patient's drained emotional tone, monosyllabic listlessness, and tendency to make very ambiguous statements left the analyst feeling preoccupied. With the Twin, Bion worked in earnest and tried to stay with his own direct emotional experience of a "stale, fetid" analytic atmosphere. It must have been quite emotionally trying for the analyst, as he allowed himself to be pulled away from what was happening in his own consulting room, leading him to become preoccupied excessively with the Twin's reports of his emotional life outside the analysis.[5]

This excessive preoccupation was also book-ended by another curious anomaly of this case: Bion never once mentions the transference in any explicit way, preferring instead to give a detailed narrative of the emotional atmosphere of the analysis. In other words, Bion, even at this early point, was so vigilantly preoccupied with the present moment that he gave no Freudian past-to-present transference interpretations despite the fact that he had outlined significant childhood material at the outset of the case write-up. This emphasis had endured from the group period: in 1948, he noted his concern primarily with his own direct emotional experience of groups before a consideration of the group's transference to him. In the "Twin" case, the writing was also more a narrative of a process than a static interpretation of symbols and their meanings. Bion shared his doubts with the reader in an unusual way: he admitted the possibility that the failure to connect sufficiently with the patient might be a shortcoming of the treatment, and perhaps another analyst might have been a more suitable choice. Ironically confident at the brink of despair and defeat, he scanned many possibilities in this stagnating analysis. If he was the wrong analyst, then so be it, as he endeavored to reveal the truth of the Twin's underlying disturbance.

A small movement occurred amid the boredom and depression: there was almost a jocular tone, as if the Twin was saying, 'Go on, it's your turn.' It was as if both men were playing at doing something serious, but it was all in vain. Bion interested himself in the stale emotional atmosphere, where flatness invited stale interpretations. When the analyst began to detect this false, pseudo-agreeable atmosphere, the Twin seemed to resent the usual rhythm being broken. Questioning this arrangement, Bion finally wondered if, when the patient reported talking with someone, it was not a factual report but merely his 'thought' or 'imagining' doing so. The startled patient agreed, as he made no real distinction between real and imaginary. So, as it turned out, there were four presences in the room—pseudo-patient with pseudo-analyst alongside a real patient with a real analyst.[6] When Bion brought this distinction to the patient's attention, it was one important point at which the potential for direct emotional contact was momentarily actualized: he had made a connection with an emotionally half-deadened-off patient living inside a sequestered emotional enclave (Bion, 1950/1967, p. 6). It was this deadened-off self that had lived inside the analyst's subjective experience; and it was this enduring experience which was now called to account.

As the analyst now activated his subjective experience of a patient unknowingly hiding in plain sight, the Twin reported a dream, where

> he was driving in a car and about to overtake another. He drew level with it and instead of passing it kept carefully abreast of it. The rival car slowed down and stopped, he himself conforming to its movements. The two cars were thus parked side by side. Thereupon the other driver, a man much the same build as himself, got out, walked round to his door and leaned heavily against it. He was unable to escape as, by parking his car near to the other, he had blocked egress from the far door, while the figure blocked egress from his door. The figure leered menacingly at him through the window.
>
> (Bion, 1950/1967, p. 8)

The patient awoke shaken from this dream and remained anxious throughout the next day. I think the crux of the patient's defensive anxiety was his self-depiction as an active agent in his own dream: he was driving a car and about to overtake another one, perhaps reflecting a competitive rivalry with the analyst, almost like a car race—only, in this instance, the patient reversed the role with the analyst as 'someone who comes up from behind' and takes the powerful position. After all, the analyst had emotionally calibrated to the Twin's internal phantasized lair, not the other way round. It was the Twin who had in fact been overtaken. Yet the patient depicted himself as pulling up in tandem with the other man. Nonetheless, the parallel emotional lanes of existence finally crossed. But now, the prospect of the analyst's proper emotional calibration left the patient feeling pinned in by the analyst/driver of the other car. A sense of suffocation, persecution, and claustrophobia now prevailed. It seemed that it was the Twin's turn to fear the analyst's retaliation in the form of pinning him in and suffocating him. This enlivened atmosphere now reflected the analyst becoming emotionally attuned to the patient's living state of mind.

One of the terrified patient's primary unconscious phantasies was now uncovered: he was living undetected *inside* a secret enclave and now feared reprisals, the sense of claustrophobically being 'pinned in' by a menacing, bad internal object in the form of an angry and threatening analyst. The immediate price for direct emotional contact was terror and persecutory anxiety. Bion interpreted that he was also the other driver, the 'imaginary twin' that the patient had created solipsistically over the long course of the analysis. Just as the patient felt he had prevented the birth of his twin, perhaps his sister, his own twin now determined that the patient should not be born (i.e., have either freedom or independence). Bion, (1950/1967, p. 8) wrote: "He was thus shut in, both by the twin and by his own act in parking his car so near to the twin's car." The other driver blocked the patient's escape from analysis, as the analyst personified the bad aspect of himself that had been dissociated (Klein, 1929).

The Twin could *look like and sound like* a patient, but hid unknowingly in plain sight, donning the role of 'pseudo-patient,' more adhered to a phantasized, emotionally deadened-off object world than a reality-oriented one with the analyst. The 'pseudo-patient' had self-deceptively led the analyst down a false trail—his linking interpretations had not emotionally touched the patient at all. The Twin had successfully recruited the analyst into the role of imaginary twin in the countertransference, rendering him into a phantasized extension of the patient's *imagined* but emotionally stultified object relational life, which was more real to him than the real one. Bear in mind Rickman's ideas about analysis as unconscious role assignment and its interpretation. It was as if patient and analyst were operating with two different models of the mind. An *as-if* patient was in analysis, playing at having contact—and one is also reminded of the role-plays and role reversals in Klein's (1932/1975) own play technique (Bléandonu, 1994, p. 110). Verbal communication was deployed by the patient as a mode of action, more charade than realistic encounter. The analyst's model of what was operative in the patient's mind, while it purported to be *about* the patient's mind, ran in a parallel track to the patient's own model of mind. The patient's own model of mind was premised on screening others out, all while appearing to be interested in emotional engagement. Psychic security was premised on non-detection. Interpretations geared by the analyst to be directed at the patient's maximum point of urgency were experienced by the patient within a safe, defensive enclave of rendering them non-urgent.

Emotional Urgency and Issues of Connection

But, at the point when real emotional contact was made, it was as if the analyst had been forced to swallow (or 'introject') the patient-as-twin and the 'poisonous family' he both staved off yet felt *living inside himself*. To secure his otherwise tenuous emotional safety, Bion (1967, p. 19) concluded that the Twin had to deny a reality different from his own internal construction. Bion thus located in the living analytic experience the origin of the Twin's pathology, in Bléandonu's (1994, p. 111) words, "in an excess of aggression, resulting in the introjection of bad objects." Staving off yet feeling toxified by a deadened-off object world obstructed his capacity to test reality. The problem posed to this patient resulted from the toxifying and endangering presence of damaged internal objects, which itself was a function of unacknowledged aggression directed at the self. It was these damaged bad objects that had been projected into the analyst. With the prospect of the patient's gradual acceptance of the imaginary twin, his analyst finally became a much more real person to him—and, one would suspect, more importantly, the patient became more real to himself. He could now begin to consider a slow transit from living inside a deadened-off, almost inanimate object world to an animated, if not terrifying and persecutory, one.

The 'Twin' had made himself comfortable within the analysis so as not to be disturbed. The 'pseudo-patient' had a complementary or 'imaginary' double, the 'pseudo-analyst.' He had not come to terms with reality, and the analyst had been led down a false trail—his linking interpretations had not touched the patient at all in the preceding months.

Analysts fear being taken in by their patients, and so it is good to ask: does the analyst's model of the patient's mind accord with the patient's own model of his own mind? Bion took his clinical experience seriously enough and spent much time in the dark about the patient's quite disturbed condition; he persisted until he grasped the patient's sequestered emotional experience. He focused on the Twin's emotional tone, his speech—and how these impacted his own state of mind, which had existed in an almost paralyzed state as he listened. The boredom was palpable, and it was his own enduring emotional reactions that the analyst ultimately privileged in guiding his way out of this maddening impasse.

The analyst's realization that he had a 'pseudo-patient' in his midst, one who relegated him to the role of 'pseudo-analyst,' began to clarify the imaginary situation for *both* patient and analyst. Emotional contact was now possible—and the analyst now personified a dreaded and persecutory internal figure. How to course-correct an interpretative line where each participant ran parallel to the other? How could the Twin face the light of a fully disturbing exposure when he had expended so much effort in keeping the analyst distracted, so as to remain undetected? It threatened the Twin with a loss of omnipotence, leaving him exposed to raw, aching splits in his own internal world. Direct contact with his analyst was unbearable, and the patient split his experience into external figures, such as the doctors who had not given him what he needed. Appreciating his analyst only made him feel entrapped by the longevity of their contact. Still, there was now some movement towards co-operation and collaboration with his analyst, integrating some of his unintegrated splits and split-off schizoid aspects.

Denouement

Some final words on this fascinating case: Bion added two more psychotically disturbed case examples at the very end of the "Twin" paper, which can initially strike the reader as extraneous and unnecessary supplemental material. So, why include them? Perhaps placing them at the end of the paper threw a darker, more disturbed hue over the Twin's pathology: the patient was dissociated and secured his safety against the fear of psychotic decompensation by pretending to interact. Ironically, the Twin's core unconscious phantasy seems like Freud's very definition of the psychotic patient: he is so autoerotically self-adhered that forming a libidinal attachment to others was his greatest psychological challenge. Real emotional exchange might precipitate another breakdown like the one he experienced in adolescence. Bion adduced some important speculations here: one referred to the personification of splits. He wrote (p. 20),

> Is it possible that the capacity to personify splittings of the personality is in some way analogous to a capacity for symbol formation to which Mrs. Klein has drawn attention in her paper on "The Importance of Symbol Formation in the Development of the Ego"?

In other words, was the healthier part of the patient's personality at the cusp of the depressive position, which, in Klein's understanding, would entail a capacity for symbolization, which could potentially lead to alternative understanding and fuller meanings? Bion no doubt initially thought so, and the text of the case study shows that the Twin was able to symbolize in a narrow sense but could not free-associate, let alone participate interactively in deciphering the meaning of his own dreams. The Twin presented anxiety-filled dreams that required another mind to receive, distill, and understand. Lastly, Bion repeatedly mentioned the term 'personification' in the text of the paper and, in all likelihood, had in mind Klein's (1929) paper, "Personification in the Play of Children" (Bion, 1967, pp. 8–9). In other words, whatever internal objects felt threatening to the Twin were personified in the fearful, dread-ridden transference responses exuded in the analyst's direction.

In anticipation of his emerging interests, the case of the Twin, with the endpiece of psychotic case examples, was linked to something else that was rapidly becoming Bion's enduring interest in the early 1950s—the understanding and analysis of psychosis. It is in this sense that the "Twin" paper had its darker and more disturbed shadowy side, and, thus, Bion's presentation of the two psychotic patients at the end of the paper became a meaningful prelude, a portal of entry to his work on psychosis proper in the papers from the 1950s.[7]

On Bion's Implicit Method of Clinical Inquiry with the Imaginary Twin

I offer conclusions here on Bion's implicit methods with the "Twin" case. Carrying on with what he had learned in the group period, Bion's implicit method of clinical inquiry seemed to have the following technical attributes as he now furthered his analytical experience with psychotic patients: introspection based on the analyst's direct emotional experience, and observations made in real time of the patient's internal, subjective, and phantasmic experience, all with a disinclination to make active transference links between past and present. It was 'deep,' not 'early,' unconscious phantasy that mediated the link between the present and deeply internalized object relationships. There was a necessary analysis of the unconscious roles into which the patient, via deep, unconscious phantasies, recruited the analyst (e.g., a self-deceived narrator and a befuddled, non-comprehending onlooker). The analyst drew upon countertransference as an 'instrument of research' to gather clues about the patient's unconscious experience, by which the analyst felt at times emotionally disturbed, identified with, and confused. Since Bion drew upon Heimann's wider notion of countertransference, it opened up more communicative possibilities in the present moment (i.e., the analyst had to differentiate his own personalized reactions to the patient from those patient communications that were more a matter of unconscious-to-unconscious ones). Further attributes included the need to establish co-operative contact with the patient's non-psychotic, object-seeking personality in order to analyze the disturbed, split-off psychotic part, and the capacity to bear being a sane, object-relating agent, the one who both interprets while remaining the object of destructive attacks via the patient's deployment of various mechanisms of defense (e.g., splitting, appeasing, emotional deadening-off). Yet, even at this early juncture, while Bion's methods would have passed as Kleinian—as he analyzed the Twin in real time just as children played and were analyzed in real time—he truncated his version of the 'here and now' by marginalizing the use of early unconscious phantasy in his analytic work.

Bion's Psychosis Papers: "Notes on a Theory of Schizophrenia" (1954), "Language and the Schizophrenic" (1955a), "Development of Schizophrenic Thought" (1956), and "Differentiation of the Psychotic from the Non-Psychotic Personalities" (1957)

Unlike "The Imaginary Twin" case, however, in the papers on psychosis from 1954 through 1957, Bion gave more truncated clinical examples, sometimes compressing bits of different analyses into a single vignette, at other times, simply compressing session material into a few sentences. In "Development of Schizophrenic Thought," Bion (1956, p. 36) mentioned that he had found presenting clinical examples of his work with psychotic analysands at the IPA Congress in Geneva in 1955 to have "produced more obscurity than illumination." As a result, the papers from this period were top-heavy in theoretical considerations regarding how Bion worked with and revised his understanding of Freud's and Klein's work on the psychoses. In keeping with the theme of this chapter, we focus attention on the longest single vignette provided by Bion in the 1954–1957 period, assuming that the maturing elements of his method of clinical inquiry will be found there.

In "Differentiation of the Psychotic from the Non-Psychotic Personalities," Bion (1957, pp. 52–59) provided ample clinical material from an ongoing analysis and started in an ironic fashion, stating that the clinical material he was presenting was "based on these theories rather than the description of an experience on which the theories are based." It raises the conjecture in the reader's mind that Bion may have chafed a bit and felt uneasy about some of the prevailing theories of psychosis, such as Freud's ideas about the reality principle or, to a lesser extent, Klein's (1946, 1952) programmatic agenda to deploy mechanisms she had defined, such as projective identification, splitting, and the paranoid/schizoid and depressive positions in the understanding and treatment of psychosis.

The analyst described a patient ("A") in analysis for 6 years, who arrived late at times, but never missed a session. "A" communicated in a fragmentary, elliptical, and disconnected way, almost as if he was talking to himself in the analyst's presence—first about not being able to do anything that day—and finally said, "I should have rung up my mother. ... No, I thought it would be like this," and, after a brief pause, "Nothing but filthy things and smells. ... I think I have lost my sight" (Bion, 1957, pp. 52–53). Bion here interjected that he had for some years noticed some odd-looking physical movements on "A"'s part while on the couch. Asking "A" if these movements had any meaning, he either said, "Nothing" or "I don't know," in a tone of voice that invited the analyst to mind his own business. The analyst was reminded of the tortuous motions made by the patient whenever he had to go to the lavatory, or down to breakfast, or to phone his mother (p. 53). But, as with some dreams he had had, the patient had "no idea" about the meaning of his physical movements. The analyst was left to his private conjecture—and, at this point, Bion thought it represented "mutilated attempts at co-operation, and this too was something to which I had drawn his attention."

Bion persevered in attempting to link sensory experience, which heretofore had existed in a non-representational realm, to the realm of psychological meaning, hypothesizing an "ideo-motoric activity … a means of expressing an idea without naming it." In this view, "A" had attacked his mind, damaging the communicative apparatus, so that he produced mutilated attempts at communication. The analyst here occupied the space of external reality, the sole meaning-maker and structural change agent. The analyst, however, was isolated as the sole meaning-maker insofar as his interventions were subject to "A"'s obstructive denials and rebuffs—dreams with no associations, no connection or interest in his physical movements on the couch. The analyst conjectured that he was watching a "series of miniature dramatic presentations, preparations for a baby's bath or feed, or a change of nappies, or a sexual seduction" (p. 54). He concluded that he was watching ideas that weren't being named. Did the patient feel punished for not calling his mother and, as a result, sense that he could not actually 'do' any meaningful work in analysis that day? Or that the analyst's interpretations would be mutilated in due course?

The analyst admitted to the reader that he really did not know 'anything' about the patient's real mother. She could have been a poor, working-class woman or a wealthy socialite—and it seemed here to appear far less psychologically consequential than the actual living experience of "A"'s mutilated, fragmented communication in the room (p. 55). One can say here that Bion allowed himself a momentary conjecture about the patient's mother, but then dismissed it as fanciful. He was too absorbed in the present circumstance of making sense of the patient's verbal bits and pieces as well as his motoric gestures—and would remain disinclined to make any sort of link between present behavior and its infantile roots.[8]

Klein's (1952) mature definition of projective identification, which now incorporated Rosenfeld's work on how psychotic patients concretely felt themselves forcefully entering their objects, now furthered Bion's absorption with the present clinical moment. It opened new explorations of the psychotic patients treating the analyst's mind in much the same way as he treated his own—all in real time. So, for example, as Rosenfeld (1947) had demonstrated, a patient's forceful entry into the analyst's mind could give rise to his paranoia and claustrophobic phantasies of imprisonment inside his mother's body (Aguayo, 2009). Another crucial distinction was the discrimination of the psychotic from the non-psychotic parts of the personality. Bion here demonstrated that the psychotic bits had to be taken up first, the ones particularly subject to concrete evacuation by means of projective identification, whereas the neurotic aspects were still governed by repression and other defense mechanisms outlined by Freud. In Kleinian parlance, the psychotic state of mind had to be analyzed before the non-psychotic, the vicissitudes of the paranoid/schizoid before the depressive position.

In taking up the understanding of the patient's utterance, "I should have rung my mother," Bion in effect regarded it as "A"'s attack on the connection to the analyst, all of which rendered him incapable of participating meaningfully in his own analysis. He also simultaneously regarded the array of descriptions "A" put forth of his own mother as therapeutically of little, if any, use:

> I may say that at the time of which I write I knew little more of his real mother than would be known by a person who had rid himself of his ego in the way I have described as typical of the psychotic personality.
>
> (Bion, 1957, p. 55)

The analyst's interventions were either dismissed as wrong-minded by "A" or, when close to the mark, jealously denied. In an atmosphere of excessive projective identification, where self and other confusional states abounded, "A"'s experience of profound ineffectuality in understanding himself seamlessly became his felt experience of the analyst's interpretative inadequacy: "When the patient said, after a pause, that he knew it would be like this, I felt on fairly sure ground in assuming that it was I who was unlikely to do anything in that session" (pp. 55–56).

The enduring question preoccupying the analyst: how was he to effect some repair to the patient's ego, something represented by "A"'s claim that he had lost his sight? It was at this juncture that the analyst's articulation of what "A" felt internally overwhelmed by—and had projected into the analyst—proved somewhat helpful: "I told him that these filthy things and smells were what he felt he had made me do, and that he felt he had compelled me to defecate them out, including the sight he had put in to me" (p. 56). "A"'s abrupt and jerky convulsions, punctuated by his saying, "I can't see," confirmed that the analyst was on the right track. "A"'s ability to talk and see insightfully into himself was obstructed, then evacuated, all in the service of evading pain and frustration. As the analyst also recalled that "A" regarded the process as "memory torture," he achieved anesthesia by ridding himself of his memory. No wonder Bion thought "A" an unreliable narrator in describing his mother (p. 56).

The analyst's capacity to carry the emotional burden for such a long time, which now included memories evoked in him over the course of a long analysis, now made for more nuanced interpretations based on their long-standing work. To the next remark made by "A," "My head is splitting; maybe my dark glasses," Bion recalled "A"'s indifference to the fact that he himself had worn dark glasses several months earlier. Perhaps "A" was seizing this long-ago fact as an "ideograph" suitable for communication purposes. In other words, momentary contact with the non-psychotic part of the personality had been made—and perhaps the dark glasses were now implicated in a very rudimentary attempt at symbolic communication. Again, while no links were made between present and early infancy or unconscious 'early' phantasies, the analyst could and did play in his evoked memory of the history of the analysis, for which he did have direct sensory evidence.

Nonetheless, the analyst here carried the burden of being object-related, one who could remember that the original use of the 'dark glasses' had no meaning for "A," but now, months later, figured in a rudimentary communication—an "ideograph" in Bion's terms—in which he was attempting to relate and be in contact with an analyst as a representative of the external world that might assist the patient in making some repair to a mutilated ego. In this instance, Bion shared with the reader the various meanings he attributed to the 'dark glasses': they hinted at a baby's bottle; the two glasses resembled two breasts (p. 57); their darkness offered him cover as he spied on the parents having intercourse; their darkness also reflected the toxified 'bad' stuff in the milk. Of course, there were the inevitable retaliatory fears that resulted from his toxifying projections. The momentary movement into the depressive position, complete with a capacity to tolerate more varieties of representational meaning here, occurred.

When "A" then followed by expressing his apprehension about the weekend break, "The week-end; don't know if I can last it," Bion linked it to himself as a missed maternal figure, wondering if "A" felt he could not contact him at a distance, just like "A" feared he couldn't do with his own mother. "A" no sooner admitted that this was a "brilliant" connection before he began to convulse. The analyst shifted the emotional meaning of 'brilliance' onto light shed on a chronic problem, all of which led to a clenched-fist expression of hatred for the analyst. Again, this was a rudimentary exploration of an unconscious wish to peek into the analyst's sexual life over the weekend. "A" was envious, destructive, and jealous—and wanted to gain access to the analyst's coupling or linking capacity while remaining undetected himself (p. 59).

Bion's work here adhered to the Klein line of elucidating the patient's internal, phantasmic, and subjective state of mind, but, again, there were no transference interpretations that linked early infantile phantasies with current behavior. This was an account of a narrative journey in the present moment. Bion attempted to understand and articulate fragmented bits of psychotic states of mind that lay scattered about in session work. Bion (1954/1967, p. 24) increasingly was now able to conceive of how the psychotic split his internal objects in real time by a more dexterous use of projective identification. He had written:

> At the moment I want to consider only his use of it as a mode of action in the service either of splitting the object or projective identification. It will be noted that this is but one aspect of schizophrenic object relations in which he is either splitting or getting in and out of his objects. The first of these uses is in the service of projective identification.

In effect, Bion endorsed Klein's formal definition of projective identification as a defining feature of a psychotic state of mind, as when the patient forced himself hostilely into his objects, then felt trapped inside, and then faced the problem of extrication. In this, the patient concretistically would use words as 'things' or as split-off parts of himself which he pushed forcibly into the analyst. Put differently, when the patient is constantly 'disintegrating' his objects, or splitting them up, *he is mired in part-object experience and unable to meaningfully deploy symbolic thinking*. It will be more symbolic equations than anything else. Klein had pointed out that verbal thought was an act of integration, and that the depressive position was one of active synthesis and integration, but, with Bion's patients, it was more a matter of psychic disintegration and extreme constriction, punctuated by moments of rudimentary symbolic thinking.

The attainment of verbal thought could be felt as catastrophic by the patient, something so depressing that he resorted to projective identification, split it off, and pushed it back into the analyst. Without a mind to assist in understanding, the patient felt insane, yet re-introjection of this capacity was felt to be overwhelmingly depressive because he would realize he had been acting insane. The patient dreaded and at times hated the analysis now because he realized that it demanded of him the verbal thought which he dreaded. Violent disintegration could and did occur as the patient trickled in and out of the depressive position.

A Theoretical Side of the Method of Clinical Inquiry: Bion's Questioning of Existing Analytic Theories

The most immediate reason for taking up Bion's reworking of existing psychoanalytic theories of psychosis is that it illustrates another aspect of his clinical method of inquiry: the capacity to draw upon his clinical experience to clarify his theoretical understanding of existing psychoanalytic theories of psychosis. For instance, in Bion's "Language and the Schizophrenic" (1955a), he elaborated upon Heimann's wider understanding of countertransference, something he had merely mentioned *en passant* in the "Development of Schizophrenic Thought" paper of 1956. His writing here made it clear that he was comfortable with Heimann's expanded understanding of countertransference, which goes back as far as his 1948 "Group Methods" paper, in which he wrote: "In psychoanalysis a means of investigation is at hand in the transference, but in the group situation I do not feel quite as happy about postulating a transference situation as I do about postulating a counter-transference" (Bion, 2014, Vol. IV, p. 65). Now in 1955, he regarded countertransference as sometimes the only evidence any analyst has for basing his interpretations—and this came at a time when Bion still participated as a member of Heimann's seminar (Grosskurth, 1986, p. 420).

Bion gave a clinical example of an analytic patient 6 months into analysis, one whose entry into his session left the analyst feeling emotionally quite uneasy—the patient lay in an ominous silence, and the analyst felt a tense, anxious feeling arising, then fantasized that the patient "was meditating a physical attack on me." Bion made an interpretation to that effect, at which point the patient clenched his fists. Bion concluded: "It will be noted that my interpretation depends on the use of Melanie Klein's theory of projective identification, first to illuminate my countertransference, and then to frame the interpretation which I give the patient." In one sentence, Bion here compressed the very ideas that Klein and Heimann had quarreled about; there was in fact no inherent contradiction embedded in Klein's refusal to publish publicly on Heimann's expanded use of countertransference, any more than there was justification for Heimann to avoid ever using the term 'projective identification' in any of her writings. And, in this instance, Bion deployed projective identification in a resilient way—to intuitively illuminate both transference and countertransference. Money-Kyrle (1956) soon followed with his own paper on countertransference that upheld both Heimann's and Bion's position on a topic that was increasingly becoming somewhat controversial within the London Klein group.[9]

Bion went even further when he defended the Klein group as a whole against a charge (e.g., Edward Glover back in the 1940s) the group had heard for some years, namely that Kleinians tended towards the creation of iatrogenic disorders in their patients by projecting their own organizing phantasies *into* the patient. This was a point that Bion (1955a, p. 225) implicitly referenced when he wrote about countertransference: "This mode of procedure is open to grave theoretical objections and I think they should be faced. ... The objection that I project my conflicts and fantasies on to the patient cannot and should not be easily dismissed." So, for the time being, it meant that Bion was extremely careful to differentiate the 'personal interference' version of countertransference from it as a form of unconscious-to-unconscious communication from patient to analyst. Recall here the other statement he made in the "On Group Dynamics" paper of 1955, namely that the analyst must differentiate those instances when he is the object of the patient's projective identification from those instances in which he is not. Bion's (1955b, p. 225) defense of the use of countertransference came with this statement: "I would not have it thought that I advocate the use of countertransference as a final solution; rather it is an expedient to which we must resort until something better presents itself." If Bion was more dexterous in the way he drew upon his countertransference, it derived from his experiences both with groups and with individual patients.

Another aspect of Bion's clinical method of inquiry was his capacity to draw upon his clinical experiences to integrate existing theories of psychosis, in this instance, Freud's and Klein's work. As Bion continued to rework the Kleinian theory of psychosis via the lens of a Freudian matrix, he felt increasingly freer to mix and match these ideas in an evolving theoretical signature that was becoming increasingly his own. One example from the "Notes on Schizophrenia" paper:

> It is therefore to projective identification that I now turn, *but my examination of it is restricted to its deployment by the schizophrenic against all that apparatus of awareness that Freud described as being called into activity by the demands of the reality principle.*
>
> (Bion, 1954, p. 345; 1967, p. 38; italics his)

To state in different terms the progression of Bion's thinking about psychosis at the crucial juncture of 1956–1957: he had worked quite co-operatively with both Herbert Rosenfeld and Hanna Segal in the programmatic implementation of Klein's agenda that proposed the psychoanalytic treatability of psychotic patients. He had robustly expanded upon and demonstrated the explanatory power of concepts such as projective identification in the understanding and treatment of psychosis. However, Bion also had a creative and fertile mind of his own. In 1945, when he started analysis with Klein, he even made it a condition of his treatment that he be able to retain his independence of mind as he underwent his analysis (Grosskurth, 1986, p. 487). It seems to me that he made good on this promise to himself because, at this precise juncture in 1956–1957, he slowly began to make his own distinctive contributions that advanced the Kleinian program to analyze psychosis, while simultaneously differentiating his own style of thinking.

Bion continued to engage with what little Freud had written about psychosis to stretch his own conceptions about what lay at the heart of this puzzling disorder. Here, Bion focused and returned to Freud's "Formulation of Two Principles on Mental Functioning" (1911a). He particularly questioned the idea that psychotic patients engaged only in a disregard of the reality principle. Psychotic patients, as Bion had seen, could evince a tendency to equate their thoughts with reality, and their wishes with fulfilment. Freud's own thoughts about psychosis were admittedly "preparatory, rather than expository," insofar as he had been looking at the "psychical consequences of adaptation to the reality principle" and how it came into being (1911a, p. 226).

Freud's project on psychotic disorders also fell to the side. Among the legacies of this fall-out, very few analysts expressed interest in taking up the arduous task of explicating the psychoses in a thoroughly systematic and psychoanalytic manner. One of the few who did, the gifted analyst Karl Abraham, died at an early age in 1925 and thus was unable to complete work he had done on psychotic states such as manic depression. One of his own students and analysands, Melanie Klein carried Abraham's wish that the psychoanalytic understanding of the psychoses was possible, and this was a kind of intergenerational agenda that the publishing trio of Rosenfeld, Segal, and Bion took up in the 1950s (Aguayo, 2009).

However, by 1956–1957, Bion had taken up the psychotic's disordered thinking, specifically their misuse of language as a mode of action. Where thought was required, the psychotic acted; where action was necessary, the psychotic could remain hopelessly trapped in an internal mental web in which they attacked their own mind. And, of course, the patient's own self-entrapment could induce inhibiting obstructive countertransference experiences in the analyst. When the patient forcefully intruded these primitive processes *into* the mind of the analyst, the analyst had to consider how they would extricate themself from such an imprisoning literality. How could the patient's actions be turned into food for thought? Bion came to regard the patient's projective identification as potentially illuminating his countertransference—as he felt literally put in the patient's shoes. Yet the analyst also carried the ego-discriminating activity of being the bearer of sanity, which often also aroused envious attacks on the patient's part. Bion wrote about how the analyst survived these bits of psychic shrapnel, especially when the psychotic split and attacked both their own mind as well as that of the analyst. The analyst had to be mindful of how the psychotic was gripped by omnipotent destructive phantasies, which they often treated as concrete 'facts.' Massive projective identification attacks left the psychotic with 'bizarre objects,' as they attacked the links to their mind and to others'. The analyst attempted to digest the psychotic's experience, so that metabolized understanding might indeed result (Aguayo, 2009).

Bion also revised and expanded upon Freud's rudimentary ideas about psychotic patients, emphasizing their internal experience. For instance, it was not that psychotics just hated reality and defensively altered it; they despised their *awareness* of it. Bion continued the analytic dialogue with Freud's writings on psychosis, differentiating his own views as he simultaneously expanded upon the Kleinian program of analyzing psychosis. Our aim here is to continue to trace Bion's clinical evolution through 1957.[10]

It was in "Differentiation of the Psychotic from the Non-Psychotic Personalities" (1957) that Bion also began to grapple substantively with aligning Freud's views on psychoses with both Klein's and his own. Very much in the spirit of Klein's work, which had filled in Freud's detailed map of the neurotic disorders in adults when she extended the range of analytic understanding into the actual analysis of young, pre-latency-aged children, Bion now attempted to reconcile Kleinian and Freudian views of psychotic states of mind. First and foremost, he accomplished this by a creative misreading of Freud's "Two Principles" paper. Bion effected what Fisher (2009, unpublished) termed a 'conceptual leap' in his discussion of Freud's reality principle when he extended Freud's analysis of the capacity to acknowledge the reality of the external world to the patient's capacity to acknowledge emotional/internal reality, a defining deficiency in the psychotic patient. I agree with Fisher here that Bion now became Freud's and Klein's heir in the development of the psychoanalytic understanding of psychosis.

Bion (1957) here began to define a process of thinking by means of which it became possible to incorporate emotions. So, in taking up Freud's descriptions of the 'ego functions' (attention, memory, judgment, thought, and action), aspects so crucial to Freud's view of adhering to the reality principle, Bion adduced clinical examples from his work with psychotic patients to demonstrate how this adherence to the reality principle was in effect attacked by the patient's own attacks on their ego functions. Yet the failure to adhere to the reality principle was only one aspect of the psychotic's profound dilemma: Bion also added that what the psychotic attacked were the organs of perceptions, thus mutilating their capacity to think, with the result of a profound distortion of their *awareness* of reality. So, at the heart of his deployment of Freud's "Two Principles" paper was a profound rethinking of some fundamental psychoanalytic assumptions about the relationship between the pleasure and reality principles. Bion reasoned that, if analysts could understand the capacity leading to the awareness and acknowledgment of *both* external and internal reality, then we could examine how psychotic states of mind resulted from a disruption of those processes.

In "Language and the Schizophrenic," Bion (1955a, p. 221) described in slightly different terms how the psychotic attacks their own mind by, in effect, attacking the ego functions associated with it. In effect, in their most regressed states, the psychotic patient attacks their ego functions in the form of "destructive attacks on all those aspects of his personality, his ego, that are concerned with establishing external contact and internal contact." Bion's (1956) phenomenological here-and-now approach was in turn augmented in his "Differentiation" paper when he proposed a different model for the psychotic's destructive attacks. Here, Bion drew upon Klein's notion of the 'splitting of the self or ego' and the projective evacuation of the ensuing fragments. Not only could the psychotic split off despised affective states, but, more importantly, they could attack, split off, and project the mental functions Freud associated with the institution of the reality principle. It was clear in Bion's thinking that projective identification and splitting were the defining mechanisms driving the psychotic's attacks on their own mind.

Initially, Bion (1957) regarded the environment as a sort of constant and maintained the Klein line of analyzing internal, subjective states of mind. We have already quoted what, in effect, may have been Bion's (1957, p. 44) response to Winnicott's critique of his clinical case of "A," that, while he acknowledged the 'environmental factor,' he chose not to elaborate on it. The 'inchoation of verbal thought' predominates in the paranoid-schizoid position. In Bion's rereading of Freud, he differs in the idea of the ego turning against reality by saying that the ego is never completely withdrawn from reality. Sparse though it may be, there is still a rudimentary object relationship, some reality sense left over, so that the analyst can facilitate a meaning-making contact with the sane aspect of "A"'s otherwise psychotic mind, so that his narrative capacity becomes more developed. Bion and Klein maintained that there are neurotic islands in psychotics just as there are psychotic islands in the neurotic. Bion the Kleinian here joined his work with Segal's (symbolic equations, where "A" equates, but does not symbolize) and Rosenfeld's (where 'A' profoundly confuses his internal experience with that of the analyst). Attacks on one's mind also represent an attack on one's links and attachments.

Conclusions Regarding Bion's Implicit Method of Clinical Inquiry (1950–1957)

We now take up the evolution of Bion's *implicit* method of clinical inquiry during this period. In terms of Bion's *privately held* theory of technique in 1950, a schematic of which was offered previously, the following list of interrelated attributes covers the main aspects of his approach during the period that evolved by 1957, during which he was part of the Kleinian program of analyzing psychotic and near-psychotic patients:

First, we start with a bedrock principle, one that provided a main point of orientation for his clinical work during this period and throughout the rest of his career: all psychoanalytic observations were made in the present moment. Bion continued his disinclination to tie current behavior, phantasies, and emotions to an early infantile or childhood history. This was now Bion's defining analytic/technical signature, and, unlike other members of the London Klein group, he would not tie current transference conflicts to past infantile states. In expanding his attempts to make meaning in work with his patients, Bion became more completely absorbed with detailed observations of fragmented, elliptical, and mutilated speech—all in the 'here and now.' Part of this evolving absorption now included psychologizing his observations of a new data stream during this time: sensory experience, physical movements and gestures, which he now added in his consideration of a total communicational gestalt.

If a psychotic communicated in a fragmented as well as elliptical way, the analyst would need some auxiliary method to make a communicative link with the meaning-making part of the patient's mind. Just as Klein had originally deployed the child's play with toys along with its rudimentary verbal associations, so that a more complete communicational gestalt might evolve, so Bion now played with the motoric gestures of his patients, all in the service of broadening the communicative potential with his patients.

Likewise, Bion expanded the notion of projective identification as well as countertransference, regarding them now as means of encompassing what the patient could not, as they were too disorganized as a function of incessant attacks on their ego functions, all of which resulted in profoundly disordered speech and an inability to communicate. They were profoundly deficient in articulating their self-experience. Bion now expanded the present moment to include fragmented speech and motoric gestures of a non-representational kind, thus broadening the net of potentially available meanings with patients who experience themselves as 'partial personalities.' Linked to a broader understanding of countertransference, Bion more fully embraced multiple communicative possibilities to expand the meaning from either side of the couch—for instance, in a more dexterous use of his own countertransference, which was first and foremost unconscious and could only be accessed through a careful tuning into his own disturbed emotional experience in the patient's presence—or away from it. Bion had the added flexibility of still being able to draw upon the older Freud/Klein view of the analyst's disturbed emotional state as reflecting some residual 'personal interference' on the analyst's conflictual side vis-à-vis unconscious-to-unconscious communications that, via projective identification, could also be informing.

Finally, during this period, particularly as the analyst's focus remained on the patient's internal, subjective, phantasmic as well as subjective experience, there was at times a certain strident attitude, almost as if, at times, the analyst regarded themself during this time as the sole epistemological agent in the consulting room. With severely compromised psychotic and near-psychotic patients, the analyst bore the curiosity for knowing the patient's enduring psychic reality, remaining the sane, meaning-seeking agent who observed the psychotic's attacks on their own mind that were, in turn, projected violently into the figure of the analyst.

Notes

1 Brown (2011, p. 53) links Heimann's discovery to work she did with her Berlin analyst Theodor Reik in the 1930s before she emigrated to London. In Brown's words, "'Reik was a flamboyant presence in the Berlin institute and a champion of the analyst's

spontaneity as well as of using one's intuition as an instrument of the analysis." Reik's theory of listening linked spontaneity, intuition, and empathic receptivity. Considering her work with Reik, Rolnik (2008) found Heimann's own seminar on technique in the early 1940s (after she had emigrated to London) particularly telling. In this seminar, she expressed her critique of Freud's (1912) "Recommendations to Physicians Practising Psycho-Analysis," in which he likened the analyst to a surgeon "who puts aside all his own feelings, even his human sympathy, and concentrates his mental forces on the single aim of performing the operation as skillfully as possible." Reading a letter Heimann wrote to Reik back in 1933, one can root Heimann's displeasure with Freud's "surgical" posture back to her Berlin years, and in particular her analysis with Reik. In Rolnik's (2008, pp. 420–421) words: "What started as an intuitive and personalized conception of the psychoanalytic encounter came to fruition in her seminal paper 'On Counter-Transference' (Heimann, 1950), which appeared at a critical period in Heimann's relationship, both personal and analytic, with Klein."

2 Most Bionian scholars accept Bléandonu's (1994, pp. 41–43) identification of J.A. Hadfield as Bion's first psychotherapist during his years at the Tavistock Clinic during the 1930s—and Bion's disdain towards the therapist he dubbed "Mr-Feel-It-in-the-Past" for the way in which Bion's painful early memories were politely dismissed. I am also not persuaded to take up the case of the "Imaginary Twin" as referring to Bion's treatment of Samuel Beckett during the mid-1930s. Aside from the evocative set of resonances between both men—and they are plentiful—there is no evidence to suggest that Anzieu's (1989) considerable work on the pair bears any resemblance to historical fact. Bion treated Beckett in 1935–1936 and he presented his control case of the Twin for qualification at the British Psychoanalytical Society in 1950. A case that he treated psychotherapeutically simply would not have been acceptable as a 'control case' that qualified a psychoanalytic candidate for graduation. In spite of this, Bionian scholars (e.g. Vermote, 2019, pp. 65–69) continue to discuss Bion and Beckett's thematic interrelatedness. However evocative those resonances might be, there is no historical evidence to suggest that the "Imaginary Twin" could in fact be Samuel Beckett. A more reasonable conjecture is that, while the Twin may have been disguised by Bion so that he appeared to be a schoolteacher, he seemed to act more like a physician insofar as he made references to physical problems of his "students" and a "locum" he appointed that would deal with their medical problems in his absence (Bion, 1950, pp. 11–12, 14–15). Unfortunately, the 1950 version of the "Imaginary Twin" paper has not been found (Chris Mawson, personal communication, April 9, 2016).

3 As a recently graduated analyst seeking membership in the British Society, Bion may well have been treading carefully here, especially with Freudian critics of Klein's theories, and so, with a nod towards Freudian conceptions of neurotogenesis, Bion demonstrated his awareness of the patient's early history. With the embers of the Controversial Discussions still burning, and considering Edward Glover's (1945, pp. 115–117) fierce critique of what he termed the "closed" Kleinian system, complete with what he thought were fantastical ideas about the infant's mental life in the depressive position between 3 and 5 months of age, Bion may have felt on safer ground by sticking to the patient's childhood years. Ironically—and despite Glover's criticism that Klein ignored core psychoanalytic concepts such as fixation and regression—Bion ended the "Twin" paper by discussing oral aggression, the eruption of teeth at 4 months of age, as possible validation for Klein's view of the earliest Oedipal phases (Bion, 1967, p. 22).

4 D.W. Winnicott attended the meeting where the "Twin" paper was read and, in a prescient letter to Bion (January 22, 1951; Winnicott, 2017, Vol. 3, p. 433), called attention to Bion's distinctive technical signature: "Whatever else I have got from the paper I get from it an insight into your doing analysis, and I feel very confident about the future of your analytic work. There is something essentially individual about whatever you do

and write, and eventually your contribution to the Society will be a big one. It is for us to gradually find out how to understand what you say." To the objection that perhaps Winnicott was engaging in a bit of flattery here with Bion, one can see that the compliment was sincere since Winnicott, at this time, was otherwise quite critical of the Klein group, as he relayed to Hanna Segal in a letter of February 21, 1952: "I am very genuinely concerned with Melanie Klein's contributions to psychoanalysis. This contribution of hers is steadily being made unacceptable because of the propaganda indulged in at every meeting, by Dr. Heimann and yourself in particular." Winnicott particularly objected to how fellow Kleinians formed what he termed a "paranoid organization" in defense of whatever Kleinian presenter was at the podium (Winnicott, 2017, Vol. 4, p. 30)

5 In reviewing the "Twin" case in 1967, Bion accentuated the distortions to which he felt subjected by the Twin. It led to an emphasis on trusting only what his senses would allow him to hear, see, touch, or smell vis-à-vis listening extensively to the patient's report of activities and people external to the analysis. It ultimately led him to question the very nature of the clinical report as a series of falsifications and distortions (Bion, 2014, Vol. 6, pp. 162–163). Another important point: as early as 1936, Klein herself had discussed the importance of the analyst's maintaining a balance between listening to the patient's reports of past and present experiences as mediated by unconscious phantasy (Klein, 2017, p. 71).

6 I have maintained that countertransference may have been to the back of Bion's mind at this point, especially since his supervisor, Paula Heimann (1950), had just written an important paper on the subject that she first gave at the IPA Congress in Zurich in 1949 (Grosskurth, 1986, p. 378). His middle-aged analysand had lived an unacknowledged pretend existence in and out of his analysis. Bion's belated understanding of his patient's counterfeit self was based on finally comprehending the nature of a maddening psychic quadrille that resulted in psychic stasis and therapeutic impasse. The uncovering of the *folie à deux* resulted in the analyst's awareness of existing as an 'imaginary twin' to the patient. In effect, the patient recruited the analyst in the service of defensive stasis—and this sort of 'role-recruitment' would have been a familiar idea to Bion since his group days and collaboration with John Rickman, who termed it 'social relations' in the group context—what sorts of roles do group members recruit the facilitator to enact or play out? In the case of the Twin, and in different terms, what *does* seem Beckettian about the patient was his existing also as an unreliable and self-subverting narrator. Once this point of collusion was grasped, Bion could extract himself from a countertransference web and feel like he was seeing his patient, not just a piece of a person, for the first time (Aguayo, 2009, p. 84, n. 9). Ironically, in giving credit to Bion for his use of countertransference with groups, Bléandonu, (1994, p. 280, n. 15) does not mention the decisive work of Heimann on the subject. In a letter to his wife Francesca (April 11, 1951; 2014, Vol. 2, p. 94), Bion referred to Heimann as the "best of the group, by far."

7 Again, another curious anomaly of the "Twin" case: in a collection of papers on psychosis, Bion included this case in which the patient is never described as psychotic. So, why include it in the collection? After all, Bion never described the Twin as evincing the kind of splitting Klein thought emblematic of the psychotic disorders. Of course, there is the position that Bion wanted to be considered part of a research group that was now setting out to analyze psychotic disorders, but, in my view, he included the "Twin" because of a continuity he was beginning to think about in terms of non-psychotic to psychotic. Segal (1956) subsequently pointed out that, just as there could be psychotic enclaves in otherwise neurotic personalities, the opposite also obtained: neurotic islands within psychotic personalities.

8 Winnicott again had attended the reading of this Bion paper and, in his letter to Bion (October 7, 1955), offered his impression of the clinical material. To "A"'s saying, "I should have telephoned my mother," Winnicott thought it was the heart of the matter.

He gave his own interpretation to Bion—it was about the patient's communication and his incapacity for making one. Winnicott here elaborated his perspective as an analytic observer of what was required of an actual external object, namely that of an attuned mother who would know from her baby's gestures what it needed—and that she, out of devotion, would have shown she understood. In the comment about the telephone, "A" reflected the "original failure from the environment which contributed to [his] difficulty in communication" (Winnicott, 2017, Vol. 5, p. 84). Winnicott here insisted that Bion, in fact, was implicitly talking about an environmental mother, a factor that Bion (1957, p. 44) brushed aside in the published version of the paper 2 years later: "There is the environment, which I shall not discuss at this time." Bion instead emphasized "A"'s internal, subjective, and phantasmic state of mind. Winnicott and Bion understood the role of the external object differently here: one emphasized its objective attributes, while the other was only concerned with the patient's enduring subjective view of it.

9 By 1958, there were further signs of tensions within the Klein group regarding the usefulness of countertransference (Klein, 2017). In a seminar with young students, Klein came down on the side of countertransference as mainly the analyst's unresolved personal interferences that required further analysis or supervision. While she recognized that very disturbed patients could project in a dysregulating way into the analyst, these views remained private and not the subject of publication (Hinshelwood, 2008).

10 It is a bit curious that, while Bion took up Freud's views on psychosis, he ignored Freud's (1911b) Schreber case. In all his published writings, he refers to Schreber only once—and that was in his late autobiographical novel, *Memoir of the Future* (Bion, 1977/2014, pp. 35–36, 216). Melanie Klein, on the other hand, was quite aware of the Schreber case, writing an appendix that reinterpreted Freud's understanding in "Notes on Some Schizoid Mechanisns" (Klein, 1946, pp. 108–109). On the other hand, she ignored Freud's "Formulation of Two Principles" paper (1911a). Klein's view seemed to be that, while Freud (1914) came down on the side of the debate that held that the analytical understanding and treatment of psychotic patients were not possible, he then contradicted himself by producing an extensive psychoanalytical understanding of Daniel Schreber. She also reinterpreted some of Schreber's key dynamics in terms of her own concepts of splitting of his objects and the vicissitudes of object-libido.

References

Aguayo, J. (2009). 'On Understanding Projective Identification in the Treatment of Psychotic States of Mind: The Publishing Cohort of H. Rosenfeld, H. Segal and W. Bion, (1946–1957),' *International Journal of Psychoanalysis*, 90: 69–90.

———. (2011). 'The Role of the Patient's Remembered History and Unconscious Past in the Evolution of Betty Joseph's "Here and Now" Clinical Technique: (1959–1989).' *International Journal of Psychoanalysis*, 92: 1117–1136.

Anzieu, D. (1989). 'Beckett and Bion.' *International Review of Psychoanalysis*, 16: 163–169.

Bion, W. (1950/1967). 'The Imaginary Twin,' in W. Bion, *Second Thoughts: Selected Papers on Psycho-Analysis*. New York: Basic Books.

———. (1952). 'Group Dynamics: A Review.' *International Journal of Psychoanalysis*, 33: 235–247.

———. (1954). 'Notes on a Theory of Schizophrenia.' *International Journal of Psychoanalysis*, 35: 113–118; also in: *Second Thoughts* (New York: Basic Books), pp. 23–35.

———. (1955a). 'Language and the Schizophrenic,' in M. Klein, P. Heimann, and R. Money-Kyrle (Eds.), *New Directions in Psycho-Analysis* (London: Tavistock), pp. 220–239.

———. (1955b). 'On Group Dynamics: A Re-View.' In M. Klein et al. (Eds.), *New Developments in Psychoanalysis* (London: Tavistock), pp. 22–239.
———. (1956). 'Development of Schizophrenic Thought.' *International Journal of Psychoanalysis*, 37: 339–343; also in: *Second Thoughts*, pp. 36–42.
———. (1957). 'Differentiation of the Psychotic from the Non-Psychotic Personalities.' *International Journal of Psychoanalysis*, 38: 266–275; also in: *Second Thoughts*, pp. 43–64.
———. (1967). *Second Thoughts* (New York: Basic Books).
———. (1977/2014). *Memoir of the Future*. In The Complete Works of W.R. Bion, Vol. 14 (London: Routledge).
———. (2014). The Complete Works of W.R. Bion. Edited by C. Mawson and F. Bion, 16 volumes (London: Routledge).
Bléandonu, G. (1994). *Wilfred Bion, His Life and Works, 1897–1979* (London: Free Association Books).
Brown, L. (2011). *Intersubjective Processes and the Unconscious: An Integration of Freudian, Kleinian and Bionian Perspectives* (London: Routledge).
Fisher J.V. 'The Emotional Experience of the Container-in-K' (Unpublished paper from the Bion in Boston Conference, July 2009).
Freud, S. (1911a). 'Formulation of Two Principles of Mental Functioning,' in *The Standard Edition of the Complete Psychological Works of Sigmund Freud*, Volume 12, pp. 215–226.
Freud, S. (1911b). 'Psychoanalytic Case Notes on an Autobiographical Account of a Case of Paranoia,' in *The Standard Edition of the Complete Psychological Works of Sigmund Freud*, Volume 12, pp. 3–83.
Freud, S. (1912). 'Recommendations to Physicians Practising Psycho-Analysis,' in *The Standard Edition of the Complete Psychological Works of Sigmund Freud*, Volume 12, pp. 109–120.
Freud, S. (1914). 'On Narcissism: An Introduction,' in *The Standard Edition of the Complete Psychological Works of Sigmund Freud*, Volume 14, pp. 67–102.
Glover, E. (1945). 'An Examination of the Klein System of Child Psychology.' *Psychoanalytic Study of the Child*, 1: 75–117.
Grosskurth, P. (1986). *Melanie Klein: Her World and Her Work* (New York: Knopf).
Heimann, P. (1950). 'On Countertransference.' *International Journal of Psychoanalysis*, 31: 81–84.
Hinshelwood, R.D. (2008). 'Melanie Klein and the Countertransference: A Note on Some Archival Material.' *Psychoanalysis and History*, 10: 95–113.
Isaacs, S. (1948). 'The Nature and Function of Phantasy.' *International Journal of Psychoanalysis*, 29: 73–97.
Jacobson, E. (1967). *Psychotic Conflict and Reality* (New York: International Universities Press).
Joseph, B. (1959). 'An Aspect of Repetition Compulsion.' *International Journal of Psychoanalysis*, 40: 213–222.
Klein, M. (1929). 'The Personification of Play in Children.' *International Journal of Psychoanalysis*, 10: 193–204.
Klein, M. (1932/1975). *The Psychoanalysis of Children. The Writings of Melanie Klein*, Vol. 2. Edited by R. Money-Kyrle et al. (London: Hogarth).
———. (1946). 'Notes on Some Schizoid Mechanisms.' *International Journal of Psychoanalysis*, 27: 99–110.
———. (1952). 'Notes on Some Schizoid Mechanisms,' in M. Klein et al. (Eds.), *Developments in Psycho-Analysis* (London: Hogarth), pp. 292–320.

———. (2017). *Lectures on Technique by Melanie Klein*. Edited with Critical Review by John Steiner (London: Routledge).
Money-Kyrle, R. (1956). 'Normal Countertransference and Some of its Deviations.' *International Journal of Psychoanalysis*, 37: 360–366.
Pick, D. and Milton, J. (2001). 'Memories of Melanie Klein: Part 2. Interview with Betty Joseph.' November 23, 2001. Melanie Klein Trust.
Rolnik, E.J. (2008). '"Why Is It That I See Everything Differently?" Reading a 1933 Letter from Paula Heimann to Theodor Reik.' *Journal of the American Psychoanalytic Association*, 56: 409–430.
Rosenfeld, H. (1947). 'Analysis of a Schizophrenic State with Depersonalization.' *International Journal of Psychoanalysis*, 28: 130–139.
Segal, H. (1956). 'Depression in the Schizophrenic.' *International Journal of Psychoanalysis*, 37: 339–343.
Spillius, E. (1988). *Melanie Klein Today, Volume II: Mainly Practice* (London: Routledge).
———. (2007). *Encounters with Melanie Klein: Selected Papers of Elizabeth Spillius* (London: Routledge).
Vermote, R. (2019). *Reading Bion* (London: Routledge).
Willoughby, R. (2006). Entry on 'Wilfred Bion.' In *Edinburgh International Encyclopaedia of Psychoanalysis*, Edinburgh: Edinburgh University Press.
Winnicott, D.W. (2017). *The Collected Works of D.W. Winnicott*. Edited by L. Caldwell and H.T. Robinson, 12 Volumes (Oxford: Oxford University Press).

The Psychosis Papers (1958–1959)

Sira Dermen

Introduction: General Remarks

Bion's early papers, published in *Second Thoughts*, contain more clinical material than his later theoretical works. It is natural to assume they will be easier to read than his dense theoretical writings. Surprisingly, they are just as difficult. They are not case studies in any ordinary sense of the word: they are not stories, nor are they organized around an overarching theme. Even the "Imaginary Twin," the earliest and closest to a case study, is not the story of an analysis. It is an exploration of *episodes* in the journey of the clinical situation. The protagonist is neither the patient nor the analyst. The protagonist is the *clinical situation* which moves along of its own accord, with its own generative core. Bion treats the failure of movement—and negative therapeutic reactions—as potentially revelatory of what he has failed to understand. My aim in this chapter is to illustrate how Bion's implicit method of clinical inquiry enabled him to *discover* his most innovative ideas about early mental development—ideas he went on to articulate in abstract terms.

Bion shows us in detail how insight into this core emerges unpredictably and retrospectively. Previously revealed features of the patient's mental functioning and elements from the current material suddenly combine into a pattern. The loose system of linkages moves into a *temporary* coherence: the analyst articulates the meaning of this occurrence. One reason the clinical papers are difficult is that Bion is writing experimental prose—he is looking for a form that will do justice to the complex movements of the clinical situation. Another reason is that, when things come together and cohere, his prose becomes correspondingly condensed. We are in the domain of systemic rather than direct causation.

Bion thinks like a mathematician: he goes back and forth between the particularities of emotional experience and corresponding abstract formulations at the same time. He is attuned to the primitive origins of the patient's mind—its development in the clinical encounter and its failure to develop—from which he abstracts to conditions which facilitate and conditions which distort the development of the infant mind. He has no inhibition in generalizing from a handful of clinical cases, or even one. If every case is a dense system, then every case, provided it is studied in depth, will illuminate all others (the universe in a grain of sand).

These are some of the features of Bion's mind. But why do I find his method of inquiry clinically so useful? He shows in practice how to avoid foreclosure. His fundamental presumption is: "I am missing something." He does not treat *any* insight, however hard gained and temporarily illuminating, as a resting place. What matters is what happens next. His capacity to live with the uncomfortable premise that every gain in analysis will come at a cost—to patient and analyst alike—is remarkable. Insight is a way station on the stormy journey of therapy.

"On Arrogance"

I take Bion's paper "On Arrogance" (1958a, p. 166; 1967, 92) first as it is more clearly illustrative of his *implicit* method of clinical inquiry (i.e., before "On Hallucination"). In this paper, his method bears fruit not only in a new understanding of his patient, but in a new clinical generalization, and finally in his ground-breaking theoretical speculation that projective identification is a "primitive mode of communication that provides a foundation on which, ultimately, verbal communication depends" (Bion, 1958a, p. 92). The thesis is by now so familiar that we might not recognize it as Bion's *clinical* discovery.

"On Arrogance" opens with a bald claim: the analyst should take the appearance, in the material of a certain class of patient, of references to curiosity, arrogance, and stupidity as evidence of a psychological disaster (Bion, 1958a, p. 144; 1967, p. 86). He emphasizes that these references will be so dispersed and separated from each other that their relatedness may escape detection—a fact which in itself he takes as evidence that the disaster has happened. He approaches his subject first theoretically, then clinically. He uses a particular period from the analysis to show *how* he came to discover the relatedness of the initially separated qualities of arrogance, curiosity, and stupidity, and *how*, in stages, he worked out the nature of the disaster.

The theoretical section opens with Bion's innovative rereading of the Oedipus myth, where the sexual crime is peripheral, and the central crime is the arrogance of Oedipus in vowing to lay bare the truth at whatever cost. The clinical usefulness of this reading of the Oedipus myth emerges later, when he describes a particular quality of transference he encounters with such patients: it is to "the analyst as analyst." The analyst's very commitment to psychoanalytic inquiry, which requires curiosity in the service of revealing truth, will make them, from the patient's perspective, an accessory to the crime they feel to be perpetrated against them. The analyst is felt to be blind, stupid, suicidal, curious, and arrogant. Bion uses his previous understanding of psychotic mechanisms—the mutilating attack not only on reality but on the very organs of awareness which apprehend reality—to ask: what is there in reality that makes it so hateful to the patient that they must destroy the ego which brings them into contact with it? He says, a plausible answer would be the sexually oriented Oedipus situation. Plausible, but not true to his clinical experience with these patients. "There is evidence that *some other element* is playing an important part in provoking destructive attacks on the ego and its consequent disintegration. The key to this is the references to arrogance" (Bion, 1958a, p. 88; my italics).

Bion uses intuition coupled with rigorous reasoning to see that "I am missing something": there must be some other element at play. He does not know what it is. And he has the patience to wait. Most of us would stay with the plausible, the true and tried. Later in the paper, he shows how he persisted with his ignorance about the "something else," and how he worked out, step by step, the nature of the disaster the patient is intent on getting their analyst to understand. In this endeavor, he shows a capacity to hear a part of the patient who is intent on collaborating in the analysis, however obscured this part is by the noisier phenomena—a bit of the patient that is communicating with the analyst, albeit in its own way (Bion, 1958a, p. 91).

Who, then, are these class of patients? First, they are not diagnosable as psychotic. The analysis seems to follow patterns familiar in the treatment of neurotic patients, except that there is an absence of improvement one would expect from the work done and, Bion adds, the presence of references to curiosity, arrogance, and stupidity. He offers no familiar diagnostic terms. He simply calls them patients in whom psychotic mechanisms, chiefly projective identification, are active and have to be analytically uncovered (Bion, 1958a, p. 146; 1967, p. 91). This is only a step away from what he will come to conceptualize as the psychotic part of all of us. Bion here seems to be asking himself: is the psychotic part always announced by this triad of qualities?

The clinical section of the paper starts at a point where the patient is behaving in a way he himself recognizes as mad. The only background to this change we're given is that the previously scattered references to curiosity, arrogance, and stupidity had become frequent, and that Bion had given his patient some insight into their relatedness. The patient could, at times, express his anxiety that he cannot use the analysis in a productive way. The analyst is also impressed by the fact that, for sessions on end, his patient is devoid of a capacity for insight and judgment which he knows, by experience, the patient to possess. The material is now almost entirely of the kind with which Bion is familiar from the analyses of psychotic patients. Projective identification is extremely active. Bion does not rehearse how he worked with this material; he implies it would not add anything new to what he has already communicated in previous papers. "There is nothing new here" is another feature of his clinical method. He summarizes the clinical situation as one where it is impossible to establish an analytically potent couple through *verbal communication*. They have to be a frustrated couple (Bion, 1958a, p. 145; 1967, p. 90). He discovers that interpreting the sexual anxiety underlying this situation, far from lessening the patient's anxiety, increases it. He then makes one of his creative deductions: something has changed, but he has failed to observe it. So he waits for a clue and goes on feeling at a loss. The situation continues unabated. Eventually, there is a clue. In a lucid moment, the patient wonders how the analyst can "*stand it*." Bion reasons: at least I know there is *something* I can stand which my patient apparently cannot. He still doesn't know what this is, but he considers it pivotal. It links in his mind with previous work done, where they had established that the patient felt *obstructed* in his aim to establish a creative contact with his analyst. The obstructive force, or object, could reside in the patient or the analyst or somewhere else; and the patient felt it was out of his control (Bion, 1958a, p. 146; 1967, pp. 90–91).

What follows is the gradual emergence of understanding the nature of the obstructive object. I quote a whole paragraph, as it is so condensed and illustrates briefly what I have been at pains to point out about his clinical method—abjuring the familiar explanation because it does not advance understanding and waiting.

> The next step forward occurred when the patient said that *I* was the obstructing force, and that my outstanding characteristic was "that I could not stand it." I now worked on the assumption that the persecuting object that could not permit any creative relationship was one that "could not stand it," but I was still not clear what 'it' was. It was tempting to assume that 'it' was any creative relationship which was made intolerable to the persecuting object through envy and hate of the creative couple. Unfortunately this did not lead any further because it was an aspect of the material which had already been made clear without producing an advance. The problem of what 'it' was still, therefore, awaited solution.
> (Bion, 1958a, p. 146; 1967, pp. 90–91)

While waiting, Bion is learning more about the relations between arrogance, stupidity, and curiosity. For example: the stupidity is purposeful; the arrogance is sometimes an accusation, sometimes a temptation, and sometimes a crime; if curiosity increases, so does stupidity. This persuades him that their relatedness depends on their association with the obstructive object.

Then comes the creative leap:

> in so far as I, as analyst, was insisting on verbal communication as a method of making the patient's problem's explicit, I was felt to be directly attacking the patient's methods of communication. ... when I was identified with the obstructive force, what I could not stand was the patient's method of communication.
> (Bion, 1958a, p. 146; 1967, p. 91)

And that's the final step, containing the solution, namely: the patient's link with the analyst is his ability to employ projective identification. Bion concludes that the disaster stems from mutilating attacks made upon this extremely primitive mode of a link, made by an object that can't stand projective identification. *The obstructive object is a projective identification-denying object.* He goes further than concluding that the denial of projective identification is a disaster for this patient. He generalizes to this class of patients. Within 2 months, in the "Attacks on Linking" paper (1959), we have the unqualified version: normal projective identification is the very first mode of communication; it must be distinguished from projective identification in the service of evacuation. To miss the communicative aspect of the patient's projective identification is to deny the patient's *need* for bits of himself to be modified by their "sojourn" in the analyst's psyche.

These statements are by now very familiar, a cornerstone of Bion's container–contained model of mental development. I have tried to identify some of the features of his implicit method of clinical inquiry which led him to his theoretical model.

There is scarcely any need these days to argue that Bion's theoretical contributions have stood the test of time. I add that clinical Bion has also stood the test of time. I have focused on what there is to be learned from his implicit method of clinical inquiry. I could have stressed that I find his clinical insights applicable to a wide range of patients, especially those we regard as recalcitrant, hard to reach, difficult to make emotional contact with. Personally, I gain a great deal of *practical* help from rereading his clinical papers: how to keep on questioning my own understanding of the intransigent clinical situation, how to find a new direction which could open up a fruitful line of inquiry, and how to listen for a bit of collaboration from the patient when all I can hear is obstruction.

"On Hallucination"

While "On Arrogance" is an account of the clinical journey which led Bion to discover an extension to the established concept of projective identification, in "On Hallucination" (1958b) he is establishing a psychoanalytic understanding of the concept of hallucination which will be clinically useful.

I think the paper is underpinned by Bion's belief that the subject of hallucination has not received the psychoanalytic attention it deserves. He starts by saying "Descriptions of hallucination with which I am acquainted lack the precision necessary to afford material for psycho-analytical interpretation" (Bion, 1958b, p. 341; 1967, p. 65). He goes on to tell us that, in this paper, he will "describe some detailed observations" of hallucination, and that he aims to persuade the reader these are "essential and rewarding." This raises the question, essential to what? We get the answer in the concluding paragraph of the paper: hallucinations are much more frequent than we realize. Again, why "rewarding"? He does not say so, but I think he must have found it rewarding that his understanding of hallucinations led him to his discovery of the nature of psychotic dreaming (Bion, 1958b, p. 346; 1967, p. 78).

Bion gives scarcely any background to the patient whose clinical material he will use in the paper. He launches straight into a session. This highlights one element of his clinical method: evidence will come entirely from the clinical situation between patient and analyst. The few facts he gives emphasize what is relatively *new*. The patient had previously been certifiably diagnosed as a schizophrenic. When called to the session he "appears without further ado," and his rapid glance at the analyst is one of "frank scrutiny," which has been a development of the past 6 months.

The paper is difficult to read for many reasons. One reason is that, though Bion calls his observations of the patient "descriptions," they are much more than descriptions. Or rather, close observations of the patient's movements are mixed in with those which have a psychoanalytic meaning for Bion. A vivid image is of the patient and himself as "both parts of the same clockwork toy" (Bion, 1967, p. 66). More to the point, his capacity to make some of his observations depends on theoretical understandings already established in the analysis. The most striking example, in this opening sequence of minute observations of the patient's movements from the door to lying on the couch, is of the "shudder of his head and shoulders." Bion notes the exact moment of the shudder—where the patient was looking, where he himself was, how it followed a pause of a second when the patient was gazing at a particular corner of the room. The shudder "is so slight and rapid that I might suppose myself mistaken." "Yet it marks the end of one phase and the start of the next"—a claim we are not yet in a position to understand. We have more minute observations of how the patient makes his way to the couch, where he looks. Eventually, he lies on the couch, is still, and speaks: "I feel quite empty. Although I have eaten hardly anything, it can't be that. No, it's no use; I shan't be able to do anything more today" (Bion, 1967, p. 66).

We have to wait for another paragraph before the relevance of the observation of the shudder is explained. For Bion, the shudder was a *sign* that at this moment the hallucination was complete. It is only a sign because of his understanding of how hallucinations are formed, an understanding which has emerged out of the psychoanalytic process, put to the patient as interpretations which the patient has confirmed, so that it is now established as an illuminating theory. The lynchpin of the theory is, in shorthand, "the double meaning of verbs of sense." *The patient feels and uses his sense organs to expel as well as to receive.* Thus, when the patient glanced at the analyst early in the session, he was taking a part of the analyst into him, into his eyes, as if he could suck something out of the analyst. It was then expelled, again through his eyes, and deposited into the particular corner of the room where he could keep it under observation while lying on the couch.

> This I put forward as the first step in the comprehension of hallucinatory phenomena: if a patient says he sees an object it may mean that an external object had been perceived by him or it may mean that he is ejecting an object through his eyes; if he says he hears something it may mean he is ejecting a sound—this is not the same as making a noise; if he says he feels something it may mean tactile sensation is being extruded, thrown off by his skin.
> (Bion, 1958b, p. 342; 1967, p. 67)

Thus an understanding initially about one sense organ is generalized to all senses. The important thing to note here is that it is an understanding that a psychoanalyst can offer to his patient in the form of an interpretation. The paper contains many examples of interpretive work done using close observations of what the patient is doing with his organs of sense and the mental states which follow, such as confusional states. At this point, he claims that appreciation of the double meaning of verbs of sense can make it possible to detect a hallucinatory process before it betrays itself by more familiar signs. Might he be suggesting that detection of hallucination by these subtler signs might have prophylactic value? It is also true that his theoretical understanding relies on his capacity to observe very closely. There is a back-and-forth between observation and clinical generalization, eventually resulting in theoretical formulation.

Having addressed the mechanism of hallucination, Bion moves on to the content. Based on evidence from this session and the way the previous session had ended, Bion works out that the object the patient is ejecting out of himself is a hostile part of himself. Yet, even in a situation where the patient is in a psychotic state of mind, Bion can recognize a more benign motive in the patient: he is using hallucination in the service of ingesting cure. This is *new*, it was not the case earlier in the analysis. Even his treating the analyst and himself as the same part of a clockwork toy is an attempt to bring two objects together, albeit denuded of life (Bion, 1958b, p. 342; 1967, p. 68).

Such recognition of change in the patient makes Bion's interpretations even-handed. I note here another element in his implicit method of clinical inquiry: his capacity to intuit and to acknowledge in his interpretations the minute shifts in the patient's movements towards collaboration with the analyst. He is very intuitive and very disciplined.

Bion moves on to use his observations of developments in the analysis to make theoretical generalizations: he discriminates between different forms of splitting, and between splitting and dissociation. The earlier form of splitting is such that any attempt to bring objects together is done with great "violence" and produces "minute fragmentation," whereas the latter is effected with a "degree of gentleness and a regard for psychic structure and function." The former splits are under the dominance of the wish to destroy, they arise from the psychotic part of the personality; the latter contain creative impulses and arise from the non-psychotic part of the personality. He proposes to use the term splitting (as explored by Klein) for the former and dissociation (as in Freud's hysterical paralysis) for the latter. He adds here one of his pithy thoughts: "the patient who dissociates is capable of depression." We will hear more in the paper about the achievement and the dangers of the approach to the depressive position, especially if the dangers are not analyzed (Bion, 1958b, p. 342; 1967, p. 69).

To return to this session, Bion says it achieved a degree of integration. The patient called such sessions "good." But there was a pattern of "good" sessions followed by "bad" ones, which was the case in the following session.

The patient starts the next session in a toneless voice: "I don't know how much I shall be able to do today. As a matter of fact I got on quite well yesterday." His attention begins to wander. He goes on: "I am definitely anxious. Slightly. Still I suppose that does not matter." He then becomes incoherent. "I asked for some coffee. She seemed upset. It may have been my voice, but it was good coffee too …" and so on. Such incoherence early in a session is familiar to Bion as a feature of a "bad" session. He feels he will have to give all interpretations he has ever given his patient all over again, but also that it will tell him nothing new. Nevertheless, he tries out an interpretation: he says the patient is showing him how "much" he can do but without regard to quality. The patient's response confirms Bion's suspicion: he says he has placed his gramophone on the seat. Bion understands this as the patient telling him the interpretation "combines the characteristics of a recording familiar to him and a defection." I have chosen to give this sequence in detail because I am impressed by what Bion tells us next. "I had reason, very shortly after that, to suppose that this response was far more than a mere criticism." At this point, though, he uses the patient's response to debate with himself whether there is any point in giving the patient interpretations he could make for himself. Nevertheless, sometimes one has to repeat the familiar, but he discovers this is not such a situation.

> I felt I had exhausted my supply of explanations and was more exercised with the possible causes of the patient's return to a pattern which seemed to disprove the efficacy of any analytic approach to his problems. *Something must have happened, but what?*
>
> (Bion, 1958b, p. 342; 1967, p. 74; my italics)

This question is, I think, central to Bion's implicit method of clinical inquiry. He does not resort to a default position of the patient's resistance. He stays with his belief that something must have happened, and that he himself doesn't know what it is. So he draws the patient's attention to the fact he was having what he often called a "bad" session and that there must be a reason. The patient seems to accept the fact but offers no explanation, nor can the analyst detect any in the material. Then comes Bion's surprising statement: "The one reason that did not occur to me but which, in the light of later events, might have led me to some illumination of the material, was the possibility that he had had a dream." I thought, why did his mind go to a dream? Why should he have thought the patient might have had a dream? It isn't clear; except that this is the way he chooses to signal his theory of the nature of psychotic dreams, namely by his own *failure* to have seen something (Bion, 1958b, p. 344–345; 1967, pp. 73–74).

But, again, we have to wait to get the theory. At this point, he only tells us that the patient had begun to report dreams. This was a recent development. But he did not associate to them, and Bion felt in no position to do anything with them, except to say some obvious things, such as the patient felt it was important to tell his analyst, or that he felt the analyst was the kind of person who understood dreams.

Having said that, he moves on to an account of the rest of the session, where there is nothing more about dreams. But it seems that something has changed: patient and analyst do some productive work together. In fact, at some point, Bion is able to understand something *new*, which surprises him: the sense organ through which the patient ejects may not be the same as the one through which he has received. And, on this basis, he interprets: you "are feeling that your ears are chewing up and destroying all that I say to you. You are so anxious to get rid of it that you at once expel the pieces out of your eyes" (Bion, 1958b, p. 345; 1967, p. 76).

The patient confirms the interpretation; he is much more amenable; he can convey his fear. The sequence culminates with the patient demonstrating his capacity for insight. "Then everything around me is made by me. This is megalomania." He cannot stay there long. His associations become less coherent. Bion listens and detects a pattern: interspersed among the incoherent associations there are phrases which report the patient's emotional states, such as "definitely a bit anxious," "Yes, slightly depressed," "a bit anxious now." While Bion finds this striking, the session ends with his not being able to formulate any clear idea of what was going on.

> I said that we did not know why all his analytic intuition and understanding had disappeared. He said "Yes" commiseratingly, and if one word can be made to express "and I think that your intuition must have gone too" then his "Yes" did so on this occasion.

Again, I'm impressed by Bion's openness to being corrected by his patient—through the meaning he hears in the single word "yes" (Bion, 1958b, p. 346; 1967, pp. 76–77).

The patient starts the next session by speaking rationally and coherently. He says: "I had a peculiar dream, it was a day or two ago." His voice becomes depressed. He adds: "You were in it." It's clear to Bion that he is not going to hear more about this dream at this point, and that there will be no associations. He is not unduly disturbed, he tells us, as he had already been led to some conclusions about the nature of psychotic dreams. He had noticed that much work had to be done before a psychotic patient reported a dream at all, and that when he did so he felt he had said all that was necessary in reporting the fact (Bion, 1958b, p. 346; 1967, p. 77).

And now we get Bion's theory of the nature of psychotic dreams. Central to his understanding are the close links he traces between hallucination and psychotic dreaming. His account is brief and schematic. He starts with the questions he asked himself. Why does the patient call his experience a dream? How does he distinguish it from other experiences which seem to be hallucinations? He concludes that a dream, for the patient, means something that happened to him at night when he was in bed and asleep. "I felt that the 'dreams' shared so many characteristics of the hallucination that it was possible that actual experiences of hallucination in the consulting room might serve to throw light on the psychotic dream." The next step, given what he has already understood about hallucination, is that, when the psychotic patient speaks of having a dream, he thinks his perceptual apparatus is expelling something, and that "a dream is an evacuation from his mind strictly analogous to an evacuation from his bowels." It follows that he feels he must have taken something in. "In short, to the psychotic a dream is an evacuation of material that has been taken in during waking hours." He concludes this theoretical section with "Bearing this in mind, an approach to understanding the patient's dream becomes simpler" (Bion, 1958b, p. 346; 1967, pp. 77–78).

Returning to the specific session, Bion still has a question: Why does the patient call his dream *peculiar*? (Again, a question to himself.) He hopes the session may illuminate this. But meanwhile, he has an interpretation he can offer the patient. He says that this dream, together with the "good" session, had been the cause they had not found for the reactivation of the state of mind in the "bad" session. The patient replies, "I was mad." The term "mad" has been elucidated sufficiently in the analysis for Bion to use it as a shorthand in his interpretation. He says to the patient: "You seem to feel that you are mad when you are denying my interpretations by taking them in and getting rid of them at once. You must have felt that they have something to do with the peculiar dream." The patient's response is to go through a series of convulsive twitchings of the chest. Bion immediately asks, "Why are you moving like that?" The patient says he does not know why. "My thoughts go too quickly" (Bion, 1958b, p. 346; 1967, pp. 78–79).

Bion's thoughts go to Freud's description of motor activity, before the establishment of the reality principle, as an unburdening of the mental apparatus of accretions of stimuli. He adapts Freud's thesis to the current clinical situation in a surprising way. He tells the patient it is his way of showing his feelings. "Like smiling," replies the patient. His movements stop. He associations revert to the pattern Bion had observed at the end of the previous session: incoherent associations interspersed with reports of "anxious" and "depressed." But now, oriented by his question about why the patient thinks his dream is peculiar, Bion can make more precise observations. He thinks the patient's report of anxiety is associated with the more fragmented material, while his report of depression is associated with articulated wholes. On this basis he says:

> Your dream has frightened and upset you because when I came into it you felt I was a real person whom your mind had swallowed up and was losing while you slept. It made you think that during your analysis you must have been greedily destroying a real person and not just a thing.

The patient at once starts to talk quite rationally. But he cannot stay there. His response to the next intervention alerts Bion to the fact that he has got rid of his awareness of his dream. Nevertheless, a little later, he returns to a point of sufficient self-awareness to tell his analyst that "he felt he had made some progress, but felt very depressed, he did not know why" (Bion, 1958b, p. 346; 1967, p. 79).

Work done during the next fortnight convinces Bion that his understanding of the significance to the patient of his dream was substantially correct. He doesn't give us clinical material from this work. He tells us his conclusions in the form of clinical generalizations.

> I was confirmed in my impression that the appearance of whole objects in dreams ... is at one and the same moment a sign of progress and a forerunner of depression which may reach a dangerous intensity if the source is not elucidated. The peculiarity of the dream to the psychotic is not its irrationality, incoherence,

and fragmentation, but its revelation of objects which are felt by the patient to be whole objects and therefore fit and proper reason for the powerful feelings of guilt and depression which Melanie Klein has associated with the onset of the depressive position. Their presence is felt to be evidence that real and valued objects have been destroyed. The immediate oscillation to fragmentation, however, does not, as I have shown in my account of the stream of associations with a running commentary of the patient's feelings, afford any true relief, because it merely substitutes persecutory anxiety for the dread depression.

(Bion, 1958b, p. 347; 1967, p. 80)

From this point on, to the end of the paper, we do not get any more detailed sessional material. We get Bion's clinical generalizations and theoretical links he makes with Klein and Freud and his own previous publications.

Clinically, he is exercised, above all, to explore the dangers of the psychotic patient's approach to, and retreat from, the depressive position. The danger is of the possibility of suicide, or a secondary fragmentation and minute splitting.

It seems as if the patient, regressing from the depressive position turns with increased hatred and anxiety against fragments that have shown their power to coalesce and splits them with great thoroughness; as a result, we have a danger of fragmentation so minute that the reparation of the ego becomes impossible and the prospects of the patient correspondingly hopeless.

Unless, he adds, this is detected and interpreted (Bion, 1958b, p. 347; 1967, pp. 80–81).

He returns briefly to the patient he has been discussing to tell us that his patient, at this point, had started to complain that he could not distinguish between what is real and what is unreal, that he did not know whether something is a hallucination or not. But Bion does not say anything about how he worked with this material. I find this omission puzzling and somewhat frustrating. Given his emphatic descriptions of the dangers of this period, I would have welcomed some samples of interpretive work. One is left dangling about how the interpretive work contained the dangers.

Bion is more concerned from this point on to give a comprehensive account of understanding of how the different elements of the psychotic patient's mental state reinforce each other, and how nothing in his experience prepares him to tolerate a painful state—frustration above all. In this account, he makes links between his Kleinian conceptualizations and Freud's, particularly the difference between the pleasure principle and the reality principle where the capacity for judgment develops. He draws on Freud's view of the function of delusions as attempts at explanation and cure. At this later period, the patient's delusions were more in the service of cure. The explanatory element of delusions becomes more purely curative at a later point. He suggests the later hallucinations are more like Freud's hysterical hallucinations, whereas the earlier ones are psychotic hallucinations, their purpose being to unburden the psyche of accretions of stimuli, in Freud's terms. They do not aim to alter the environment.

Bion goes on to give a rich and original description of what happens when the patient feels the impulse to express feelings of love and feels obstructed because of feelings of impotence and hatred and envy of the parents whom he feels deny him the potent breast and penis. "Overall is the sense of obstructed love." In brief, the patient resorts to projective identification and creates bizarre objects. He now feels free to love without conflicting feelings.

> Such relief is short lived. This description is an approximation to the state of mind of which the patient is dreadfully aware in the non-psychotic part of his personality. It contributes to his fear of any progress that might lead him to form loving attachments which would give rise to desires to express his love, and from that to intolerance of the frustration preserved by the destructive impulses, and from that to being overwhelmed by the psychotic part of his personality in which only he can find mechanisms that hold promise of instantaneous solution of the problems presented by the existence of unwanted emotions. The danger which the patient fears is, therefore, one he has good reason to fear.
> (Bion, 1958b, p. 348; 1967, pp. 83–84)

I feel this understanding, with its poignant conclusion, is one which gives the analyst dealing with this hopeless situation empathy for the patient. Although I don't have personal experience of psychiatrically psychotic patients, I recognize the combination of the sense of obstructive love, dread of progress, and a conviction that they can provide themselves with instantaneous cure in a number of my patients. It is Bion's way of articulating how the central elements of the personality interrelate and, in effect, create a closed system, which I find clinically so useful.

Bion concludes the paper with a statement that he hopes he has made a case for the close and detailed observation of hallucinations, adding that they indicate possibilities for further research. One possibility of research I think of is the application of his understanding of hallucinations and delusions to patients who have found a modicum of sanity and stability through their perverse solutions.

"Attacks on Linking"

Introduction

In the opening paragraph of "Attacks on Linking," Bion (1959) refers to the thesis he put forward in his paper on "The Differentiation of the Psychotic from the Non-Psychotic Part of the Personality": the psychotic part of the patient makes destructive attacks on anything which they feel to have the function of linking one object with another. He says his intention in this paper is "to show the significance of this form of destructive attack on the production of some symptoms met with in borderline psychosis." Why does he single out borderline psychosis, a term he employs for the first time in this paper? Is it to suggest that what he has discovered by working with psychotic patients is of more general applicability? Or is it that, in this paper, he will use material from borderline psychotics to amplify his developing understanding of what motivates attacks on linking (Bion, 1959, p. 308; 1967, p. 93)?

What soon becomes clear is that this will not be a clinical paper. There will not be a sustained clinical narrative. The brief clinical vignettes he gives are to illustrate the variety of ways the patient—actually a composite of two patients—destroys whatever links two objects together, and the variety of ways the attack is mounted. Bion proceeds to use these vignettes to articulate his theoretical understandings. The paper is synthetic. He brings together concepts and theses from his own previously published papers with his further elaborations of them. Equally, he brings together his own new elaborations with theories of Klein and Freud.

While the paper is not clinical, it is clinically highly applicable. What he is aiming at is complex and initially perplexing. The complexity is due to the fact that Bion approaches any claim he makes, any understanding he offers, from a variety of points of view. The paper is perplexing because these different points of view are scattered throughout the paper. The paper appears, and to an extent is, formless. If there is a form, it is dictated by his aim to show how all these different claims are connected. One could say there is method in the apparent formlessness. The way in which the paper hangs together has to be discovered in a back and forth way; it acquires density with each rereading.

All of which makes for a paper which is not suitable for illustration of Bion's implicit method of clinical inquiry. And yet, even in the brief vignettes, one can hear familiar elements of his method. First, I will briefly discuss two such elements from his vignettes. I will go on to discuss developments in his previously advanced theories and new ways he uses the theories of Klein and Freud. Finally, I will discuss the central contribution he makes in this paper: a systematic discussion of the relations between the innate and the environmental contributions to disturbed states the hallmark of which is the excessive use of projective identification.

Examples 1 and 2 from the "Clinical Examples" Section

1. Bion interprets the patient's feelings of affection and his expression of them to his mother for her ability to cope with a refractory child. The patient attempts to express his agreement, but his expression is interrupted by a very pronounced and long-drawn-out stammer. The sounds he emits are like a gasping for breath, interspersed with gurgling, as if he were immersed in water. These descriptions were actually supplied by the patient when Bion drew his attention to his stammer. I surmise from Bion's report of the vignette that he is making contact with the co-operative part of the patient: although the patient indicates he agrees with the interpretation, his stammer intervenes, but even then he co-operates by producing the descriptions of the sounds. I hear this as Bion's capacity never to lose sight of the co-operative part of the patient, however dominated he is by the destructive part of his personality (Bion, 1959, p. 308; 1967, p. 94).

2. The patient complains that he cannot sleep. "It can't go on like this," he says, showing signs of fear. Bion has the impression that he feels superficially some catastrophe will occur, perhaps insanity. He suggests the patient fears he would dream if he were to sleep. The patient denies this and says he cannot think because he is wet. Bion reminds him of his use of the term "wet" as an expression of contempt for someone he regards as feeble. The patient disagrees and says the state he is referring to is the exact opposite. Bion tells us that, from what he knows of his patient, he feels that his correction at this point is valid. He weaves the patient's correction into his subsequent interpretations. He takes up the wetness as urinary attacks, and the fear as the oozing away of his mind. The patient says, "I am dry now." Bion's response is to hear the patient's agreement but also to take up how precarious this good state is. We have here Bion's openness to being corrected and also his capacity to interpret in an even-handed way (Bion, 1959, p. 309; 1967, pp. 94–95).

"Features Common to Above Illustrations" Section

Bion starts this section with: "The episodes have been chosen by me because the dominant theme in each was the destructive attach on a link." In the first example, the attack is expressed through the stammer and is designed to prevent patient and analyst using language as a bond between them. In the second example, sleep was felt by the patient to be projective identification he could not control. So, sleep for the patient meant that "his mind, minutely fragmented, flowed out in an attacking stream of particles" (Bion, 1959, p. 310; 1967, p. 98).

Bion seamlessly proceeds to give us the developed version of the theory of psychotic dreaming he had advanced in the "Hallucinations" paper. His current view is that the apparently dreamless state of the early years in analysis is, in fact, "a phenomenon analogous to the invisible-visual hallucination." I am presenting this material more schematically than it is in the paper. In his description of clinical example 3 in the previous section, Bion has already given the clinical evidence for his idea of "invisible-visual hallucinations." The clinical context is as follows: when Bion interprets some associations as the patient having felt that he had been and was still witnessing an intercourse between two people, the patient reacts as if he has received a blow. He sits up and stares intently into space. Bion says he seems to be seeing something. The patient replies that "he could not see what he saw." So, the idea of not being able to see what one sees actually comes from the patient. Bion's theoretical formulation of invisible-visual hallucinations derives from clinical experience that is repeated over time, as he tells us (Bion, 1959, p. 309; 1967, p. 95).

To return to Bion's developed theory of psychotic dreaming, having previously noted that psychotic patients don't report dreams till late in their analysis, he now says his current understanding is that "this apparently dreamless period is a phenomenon analogous to invisible-visual hallucination. That is to say, that the dreams consist of material so minutely fragmented that they are devoid of any visual component." Dreams can only be reported when they contain visual objects. When they do, the patient regards these objects as solid (equated with feces), in contrast to the continuous stream of the previous state (equated with urine; Bion, 1959, p. 310; 1967, p. 98).

In the following paragraph, we're told that the attack is not illustrated by the selected sessional material, but rather the consequences of the attack previously made. The patient feels bereft of a satisfactory relationship with his bed because he has made a destructive attack on the state of mind of his coupling parents. The patient is therefore left with a double anxiety: one that he was being rendered mindless, and the other that he could not control his hostile attacks. "Sleep and sleeplessness were alike unacceptable" (Bion, 1959, p. 310; 1967, pp. 98–99).

In his discussion of the second clinical example, we are not shown the attack, but rather the consequences of the attack. Further, Bion uses the clinical example to illustrate the development in his theory of psychotic dreaming. We could say we see here something more than Bion's implicit method of clinical inquiry: we see how his mind works—clinically and theoretically at the same time. He goes seamlessly from one to the other.

The exposition illustrates the clinical applicability of Bion's thinking. It is not unusual for an analyst to say the patient does not bring dreams to the analysis. Bion's developed theory opens up new possibilities of clinical inquiry. We can ask new questions. Is it that the patient cannot report their dreams because the dreams do not contain visual objects? (This is very different from seeing the not bringing as a matter of withholding, for example.) Is this an indication of the patient's psychotic functioning? Something we have not been alerted to?

I have found Bion's thesis applicable to a patient, Ms A, who is not obviously psychotic. She brought dreams and appeared to associate to them. Yet, what I thought of as work done could not be built on. There were persisting elements in the way she reported her dreams. The objects which populated them would slip and slide, they seemed endlessly replaceable—a phenomenon which felt different from free association. She would move to past dreams, which did not illuminate the current dream. I found this confusing. Thinking about Bion's theory made me consider the possibility that something I had hitherto seen as my own problem was clinically significant: namely, that *I could not visualize* the objects in her dreams. The subsequent work became much more disturbing and much more meaningful—the split-off, disturbed part of her came to life in the analysis.

Central Contribution of the Paper: Relations between the Innate and Environmental Contributions of Disturbed States

Bion approaches his central contribution in a way which defies schematization. He builds on themes from previous papers. For example: from "On Arrogance" he takes curiosity, arrogance, and stupidity and the primitive catastrophe implicit in this triad. He revisits Melanie Klein's theory of part and whole objects, to make the point that a part-object relationship is not only with anatomical structures, but with function: not only with the breast but with feeding, poisoning, loving, hating.

He also explicitly revises (though he had implicitly done so in "On Arrogance") Klein's position on the importance of excessive employment of splitting and projective identification in disturbed infantile development. "I shall suppose that there is a normal degree of projective identification ... and that associated with introjective identification this is the foundation on which normal development rests" (Bion, 1959, p. 312; 1967, p. 103).

Bion goes on to elaborate clinically his grounds for positing the importance of normal projective identification. The patient resorts to projective identification with persistence, suggesting it was a mechanism of which he had never been able to avail himself sufficiently. In some sessions there was some object that *denied* him the use of projective identification. The patient felt that parts of his personality that he wished to repose in his analyst were refused entry by him. When the patient felt his fears of death, which were too powerful for him to *contain*, he split them off and put them into his analyst, with a view that, were they allowed to repose there long enough, they would undergo modification by his psyche and could then be safely re-introjected. If the patient felt that the analyst evacuated them quickly, they became more painful. In such sessions, he strove to force them into the analyst with increased desperation and violence.

All this is, by now, so familiar that I wonder why I'm describing it in detail. Except that it is how Bion gets to what is *specific* to this paper. *It is his reconstruction of the early situation between the infant and his mother.* "I felt that the patient had experienced in infancy a mother who dutifully responded to the infant's emotional displays. The dutiful response had in it an element of impatient 'I don't know what's the matter with the child.'" He says that, in order to understand what the child wanted, the mother should have treated the infant's cry as more than a demand for her presence. She should have taken into her, and thus experienced, the fear that the child was dying. "An understanding mother is able to experience the feelings of dread, that the baby was striving to deal with by projective identification, and yet retain a balanced outlook."

> This patient had had to deal with a mother who could not tolerate experiencing such feelings and reacted either by denying them ingress or alternatively by becoming a prey to the anxiety which resulted from introjection of the infant's feelings. The latter reaction must, I think, have been rare: denial was dominant.
> (Bion, 1959, p. 313; 1967, p. 104)

Bion here gives us two new elaborations. One, a detailed deduction, based on his clinical experience, of what the *actual object* was contributing to the patient's disturbance. Two, a new description of the ingredients of *containment*, a term he uses here as an ordinary English word, but it will soon become the basis of his most influential theoretical contributions (Bion, 1959, p. 314; 1967, p. 106).

He also makes the point that the "reconstruction" he has made may seem fanciful. But, he says, it is his reply to the objection that too much stress is put on the transference to the exclusion of the elucidation of "early memories." But, even as he acknowledges the importance of early memories, there is no indication that he will take up the reconstruction of the early experience of the mother with the patient. I think his reasons emerge in "the complex situation" he will go on to discuss (Bion, 1959, p. 313; 1967, p. 104).

Bion proceeds to describe the complex situation that can be observed when the patient feels he is being allowed, in the analysis, an opportunity of which he had been cheated in the past.

> The poignancy of his deprivation is rendered the more acute and so are the feelings of resentment and deprivation. [...] Gratitude for the opportunity coexists with hostility to the analyst as the person who will not understand and refuses the patient the use of the only method of communication by which he feels he can make himself understood. [...] Thus the link between patient and analyst, or infant and breast, is the mechanisms of projective identification. [...] The destructive attacks on the link originate in a source *external* [my italics] to the patient or infant. [...] The result is excessive projective identification.
> (Bion, 1959, p. 313; 1967, pp. 104–105)

On the basis of his clinical experience, Bion finds that, even as the patient comes to appreciate the opportunity his analyst has given him, nevertheless the analyst will also be experienced as the primary object who deprived him. The denial of projective identification is real in external reality, and the denial will inevitably be lived as real in the transference.

This is my understanding of Bion's reasons for *not discussing reconstruction and early history with the patient*. As this is, I think, an invariant feature of Bion's implicit method of clinical inquiry, it is interesting that the rationale emerges in this paper.

Bion then says that the account he has given is "the central feature of the environmental factor in the production of the psychotic personality." But he is not putting forward this experience as the *cause* (my italics) of the patient's disturbance. "That finds its main source in the inborn disposition of the infant." Inborn characteristics, such as primary aggression and envy, play their part in producing attacks by the infant on all that links him to the breast. He articulates his position on the environmental and inborn factors: "The seriousness of these attacks is enhanced if the mother displays the kind of unreceptiveness which I have described, and is diminished, but not abolished, if the mother can introject the infant's feelings and remain balanced." Diminished but not abolished. He refers to his experience with a patient who insisted he go through it with him, yet he was filled with hate when he experienced Bion as able to do so without a breakdown. His conclusion is that "attacks on the link are synonymous with attacks on the analyst's and originally the mother's peace of mind."

> The capacity to introject is transformed by the patient's envy and hate into greed devouring the patient's psyche; similarly peace of mind becomes hostile

indifference. At this point analytic problems arise through the patient's employment ... of acting out, delinquent acts and threats of suicide.
(Bion, 1959, p. 313; 1967, pp. 105–106)

(I am not persuaded that Bion has made a convincing case for his conclusion that attacks on linking are "synonymous" with attacks on the analyst's, and originally the mother's, peace of mind. The attack may be so motivated in the consulting room, but it is less obvious that this was the case with the mother of infancy. What about the mother who is in a highly anxious state of mind, as Bion himself has described?)

In the concluding sections of the paper, Bion reviews what he has already said about attacks on linking, as well as adding new thoughts. He looks at the subject from different perspectives. His overall aim, I think, is to demonstrate the momentous consequences of relating on the basis of attacking the link with the object—consequences for life, growth, development. His procedure is to describe a vicious circle, each anti-developmental element reinforcing the others. In each perspective, he singles out and elaborates on the consequences of one element (Bion, 1959, p. 313–314; 1967, pp. 108–109).

He starts with curiosity, and projective identification as *the* mechanism for the exercise of curiosity. He reiterates his view of the contributions of internal and external factors which produce severe early disturbance: the infant's inborn disposition to excessive destructiveness, *and* the environmental contribution, at its worst, of denying the infant's use of splitting and projective identification. He adds the qualification that, on some occasions, the destructive attacks have their origin in the patient, on others, in the mother. But he still holds to his view that, in psychotic patients, it can never be the mother alone. "The disturbances commence with life itself." The problem that confronts the patient is: what are the objects of which they are aware? He means functions rather than morphological structures. The nature of these functions that excite the patient's curiosity he explores by projective identification. "Projective identification makes it possible for him to investigate his own feelings in a personality powerful enough to contain them." Denial of the use of these mechanisms of projective identification, by either party, "leads to a destruction of the link between infant and breast, and consequently to a severe disorder of the impulse to be curious on which all learning depends. The way is therefore prepared for a severe arrest of development." "Further, the denial of the main method open to the infant for dealing with his too powerful emotions, the conduct of emotional life, in any case a severe problem, becomes intolerable." Feelings of hatred are therefore directed against all emotions, including hate itself, and against external reality which stimulates them. "It is a short step from hatred of emotions to hatred of life itself" (Bion, 1959, p. 314; 1967, pp. 106–107).

Bion then takes up how the superego is affected by this kind of mental functioning. The understanding object is transformed into one whose devouring greed aims to introject the infant's projective identifications in order to destroy them. We can see this in clinic in the patient's belief that the analyst strives, by understanding them, to drive them insane. The result is, in short, "a severe and ego-destructive superego" (Bion, 1959, p. 314; 1967, p. 107).

He then turns to clinical method with such patients. He suggests a line of interpretation that could be helpful to a patient who cannot use their curiosity, now described as a patient who cannot ask "why" or appreciate causation. The patient "will complain of painful states of mind while persisting in courses of action calculated to produce them." Elucidating the limited scope of their curiosity, Bion says, leads to some modification of conduct which otherwise prolongs their distress.

In his conclusions, Bion summarizes and also changes his earlier formulations enough to pave the way to new thoughts.

> The main conclusions of this paper relate to that state of mind in which the patient's psyche contains an internal object which is opposed to, and destructive of, all links whatsoever from the most primitive (which I have suggested is a normal degree of projective identification) to the most sophisticated forms of verbal communication and the arts.
> [...]
> In this state of mind emotion is hated; it is felt to be too powerful to be contained by the immature psyche; it is felt to link objects and it gives reality to objects which are not self and therefore inimical to primary narcissism.
> (Bion, 1959, p. 314; 1967, p. 108)

Note Bion's use of the concept of primary narcissism here: not a concept one associates with him.

He continues to add new thoughts right up to the end.

> These attacks on the linking function of emotion lead to an over prominence in the psychotic part of the personality of links which appear to be logical, almost mathematical, but never emotionally reasonable. Consequently the links surviving are perverse, cruel, and sterile.
> (Bion, 1959, p. 315; 1967, pp. 108–109)

Thus he ends with making a link with perversion dynamics.

References

Bion, W.R. (1958a). 'On Arrogance.' *International Journal of Psychoanalysis*, 39: 144–146. In: W.R. Bion (1967). *Second Thoughts* (New York: Aronson), pp. 86–92.

Bion, W.R. (1958b). 'On Hallucination.' *International Journal of Psychoanalysis*, 39: 341–349. In: W.R. Bion (1967). *Second Thoughts* (New York: Aronson), pp. 65–85.

Bion, W.R. (1959). 'Attacks on Linking.' *International Journal of Psychoanalysis*, 40: 308–315. In: W.R. Bion (1967). *Second Thoughts* (New York: Aronson), pp. 93–109.

Bion, W.R. (1967). *Second Thoughts* (New York: Aronson).

Clinical Restlessness
The 1960s

Nicola Abel-Hirsch

What was happening in Bion's clinical work during the years he wrote *Learning from Experience* (1962), *Elements* (1963), *Transformations* (1965b), and *Attention and Interpretation* (1970)?

In the early 1960s, Bion took the format in which he wrote into his own hands. Instead of scientific papers (to be given at IPA congresses and published in the *International Journal of Psychoanalysis*), he wrote the four books listed above. He also focused his reading on works from outside the analytic tradition. These included the writings of the philosophers Plato and Descartes, mathematicians Poincaré and Frege, and the work of mystics Meister Eckhart and St John of the Cross. My impression is that he wanted to look at psychoanalysis through new and various perspectives. Through the 1960s, Bion developed new concepts, many of which would become of notable importance in psychoanalysis: container–contained; beta and alpha elements, and alpha function; the Grid; transformations and invariants; eschewing memory and desire; and "O". But what was happening in his clinical work during this time?

Our access to his 1960s clinical work—the focus of this chapter—is mainly through the clinical examples published in *Learning from Experience*, *Elements*, *Transformations*, and *Attention and Interpretation*. For reasons of confidentiality, the clinical work from this period recorded in his personal notes was largely left out of the publication of his *Cogitations* after his death.[1]

We do, however, also have an account written by one of his patients (Frances Tustin) and a number of comments made by people in supervision with him during the 1960s, from which I have included quotes later in the chapter.

Outline

- Book 1, *Learning from Experience* (1962)
    - Introduction
    - A clinical illustration from Bion's own practice
    - Bion imagines himself in the position of an infant
    - Psychoanalytic instrumentality

- Book 2, *Elements of Psychoanalysis* (1963)
  - Introduction
  - Bion's illustration of his own use of the Grid
  - Reversible perspective

- Book 3, *Transformations Change from Learning to Growth* (1965b)
  - Introduction
  - Detecting invariance through a breakdown
  - From different points of view (vertices)

- Book 4, *Attention and Interpretation: A Scientific Approach to Insight in Psycho-Analysis and Groups* (1970)
  - Introduction
  - The pander and the whore
  - I scream/Ice-cream
  - A clinical illustration of eschewing memory, desire and understanding

- Notes from a patient and from two candidates supervised by Bion in the 1960s
- Where does Bion get to by the end of the 1960s in relation to his method of clinical inquiry?

Book 1, *Learning from Experience* (1962)

Introduction

Learning from Experience, the first of the four books Bion wrote during the 1960s, addresses the process through which human beings move from what is 'unthought' (undigested experience) to what is 'thought.' Bion explores and develops his new concepts of beta and alpha elements, alpha function, and container–contained. He revisited the site of the battlefields he had fought on during World War I at the same time as he was formulating his concept of alpha function (Brown, 2012). It may have been not only his patients' material that he was working from, but also his experience of trauma.

The first clinical illustration below is from Bion's clinical practice. Two other clinical developments can also be noted in *Learning from Experience*. The first is Bion's imaginative illustration of an infant's experience from within that experience, rather than observed from the outside. He is careful to describe the baby as a hypothetical infant, but his capacity to put himself into such a primitive scene is notable. This approach went on to have an increasing place in Bion's exploration of the vertex of the patient. A second development seems very different. I am going to call it his development of psychoanalytic instrumentality. Bion gives a clinical illustration of the choice of whether the 'key' to a session is 'K' (knowing), 'L' (loving), or 'H' (hating). He refers to the illustration as an "an imaginary episode," adding that what he says about it "is hardly less true to say just that about a real session." I include it because it gives sight of Bion's interest in looking at the same material first one way, then another, and so on.

A Clinical Illustration from Bion's Own Practice

In a clinical illustration from his own practice, one senses Bion restlessly testing what kinds of understanding actually make a difference to the patient. The account sounds traditionally scientific (based on observation and hypotheses). Bion appears unusually clear about the effect (or non-effect) of an interpretation on the patient. He talks in terms of days and weeks for a hypothesis to be tested or something to become more evident. The experience of analysts more generally, and probably of Bion more generally too, may well be of a much longer process and a less conscious one than how Bion describes it here. I have added emphases in the quote below to draw attention to his summations of there being no change.

Bion begins by saying that he will discuss a small number of patients who have "symptoms of disordered capacity for thought." He has tried orthodox transference interpretations, but the patient (he now goes to the singular) hasn't seemed to learn from the experience. Referring to a patient's stream of disjointed associations, he interprets this from the point of view of anal erotism; the patient improvising a personality; theories of splitting, projective identification; defence against assault and more. These interpretations, he says, have had little effect. He continues:

> Sometimes I could visualize the situation, unfolding in the analysis, as one in which the patient was a foetus to whom the mother's emotions were communicated but to whom the stimulus for the emotions, and their source, was unknown. ... At other times he seemed to have a rudimentary idea of what was going on, but no idea how he felt.

Bion visualises the situation in terms of a foetus and mother. In the years prior to this, he visualised the patient in "On Arrogance" (1958) as an infant with an unavailable mother and went on to abstract from that particular situation the universal significance of container–contained. Visualising clinical situations in terms of foetus/infant and mother is becoming part of his clinical method. He continues:

> The theory of functions offered a prospect of solving this problem by assuming that I contained unknown functions of his personality and from this to scrutinize the sessional experience for clues of what these might be. I assumed that I was "consciousness." Freud's theory that consciousness is the sense-organ of psychic quality, allowed an assumption that a separation was being effected between consciousness and psychic quality. *This assumption proved fruitful, but only for a session or two* and then I found myself in the same situation as before, or nearly so. I was still thinking of the problem as one that could be solved in terms of transference theory and projective identification, that is to say, that I could

assume that patients felt under scrutiny by me and the parts of their personality I was supposed to contain. In the light of theories of transference and projective identifications the material poured out could be seen as the link between patient and analyst and I could interpret in the way described in "Attacks on Linking." *Interpretations had some success, but I did not feel that changes necessarily related to illumination received from interpretations.* It then occurred to me that he was doing what I earlier described as "dreaming" the immediate events in the analysis—that is to say, translating sense impressions into alpha-elements. *This idea seemed to be illuminating sometimes, but became dynamic only when I related it to defective alpha-function, that is to say, when it occurred to me that I was witnessing an inability to dream through lack of alpha-elements and therefore an inability to sleep or wake, to be either conscious or unconscious.*
(Bion, 2014, Vol. 4, p. 288; emphasis added)

In this quote, Bion refers to "the theory of functions." The reference is to his own "theory of functions" as laid out in the opening chapter of *Learning from Experience*, where he introduces his term 'alpha-function.' In the clinical illustration above, we hear of him testing this concept in his work with patients, although we don't see the detail of it.

Bion 'Visualises' in the Position of an Infant

In the example above, Bion speaks about visualising a clinical situation in terms of a foetus/infant and mother. In *Learning from Experience*, he also begins to visualise situations from within the infant's experience:

> Suppose the infant is fed; the taking in of milk, warmth, love may be felt as taking in a good breast. Under dominance of the, at first unopposed, bad breast, "taking in" food may be felt as indistinguishable from evacuating a bad breast. Both good and bad breasts are felt as possessing the same degree of concreteness and reality as milk. Sooner or later, the "wanted" breast is felt as an "idea of a breast missing" and not as a bad breast present.
> (Bion, 2014, Vol. 4, pp. 301–302)

From his imagined position inside the baby's experience, one can see how the repeated movement backwards and forwards gradually leads to noticing a difference in psychic quality between the present good breast and not-present breast—the difference that lies at the base of becoming able to think. Venturing into the imagined experience of the infant can also throw more light on what kind of thing can go wrong. Bion differentiates, for example, between the "actual milk" and the "psychical quality of the milk" and goes on to explore the splitting between the two in a disturbed relationship:

> We must now examine enforced splitting associated with a disturbed relationship with the breast or its substitutes. The infant receives milk and other creature

comforts from the breast; also love, understanding, solace. Suppose his initiative is obstructed by fear of aggression, his own or another's. If the emotion is strong enough it inhibits the infant's impulse to obtain sustenance. ...

Fear of death through starvation of essentials compels resumption of sucking. A split between material and psychical satisfaction develops ... its object and effect is to enable the infant to obtain what later in life would be called material comforts without acknowledging the existence of a live object on which these benefits depend.

(Bion, 2014, Vol. 4, pp. 278–279)

Bion describes a patient who demanded more and more material comforts in the consulting room, as well as more and more interpretations, but these were treated as if they were inanimate objects, like the number of pillows. The patient lacks a psychical quality to the attention he demands. Bion's imaginative conjecture into the experience of the infant and his formulation of a patient's difficulties would appear to deepen into each other.

Psychoanalytic Instrumentality

In the first two books of the 1960s, *Learning from Experience* and *Elements of Psychoanalysis*, we also see a different kind of clinical illustration. They illustrate what I am going to call Bion's 'psychoanalytic instrumentality,' 'tools of the trade,' for all analysts' use. At the same time as expanding the spectrum on which he works (including imaginative conjecture), Bion also wants to introduce more clinical discipline. The tools by which to achieve this include the use of specific questions. In *Learning from Experience*, Bion advocates asking what the 'key' to any session may be and, in *Elements* (1963), he introduces the Grid.

On the question of the key to a session, Bion comments that the analyst must "allow himself to appreciate the complexity of the emotional experience he is required to illuminate and yet restrict his choice to these three links." The links are K (knowing), L(loving), and H (hating). Bion is adding the vicissitudes of 'knowing' to Freud's understanding of the Oedipus complex in terms of loving (one parent) and hating (the other). Like Klein before him, he views the epistemological instinct as a primary instinct in its own right.

The movement between appreciating complexity and the identification of a recurring pattern (constant conjunction) or underlying relationship (i.e., that between container and contained) is very much part of Bion's work generally.

Bion refers to the clinical illustration as an "an imaginary episode," adding that what he says about it "is hardly less true to say just that about a real session." While rather dry in comparison with some other of his clinical illustrations, it does give access to a way he thinks clinically. We first hear of the co-operation and friendliness of patient Smith. Smith then begins to talk about a psychotherapist called Jones (Smith and Jones are two of the most common surnames in the UK!). Jones is "stupid" and treated a friend, Mr May, with shocking results. Bion comments that there are various links:

> The patient says he knows Jones. Is this to be recorded as Smith K Jones? He says he dislikes Jones. Should it be Smith H Jones? The patient says "his friend" Mr May. Should this then be Smith L May? Or is there some previous material in the analysis, or some manner or intonation that suggests a link, Smith L Mrs May? But perhaps there is some material that suggests there is a homosexual relationship between Smith and Mr May? There need be no end to the questions stimulated by an imaginary episode or limit to the number of answers for each question. But it is hardly less true to say just that about a real session. Yet on the answers to the questions, which the analyst begins to entertain, will depend his interpretation of the direct evidence of the nature of the transference.
> (Bion, 2014, Vol. 4, p. 310)

Bion experiments with looking one way and then another. The whole question of how we can scrutinise what we are thinking and see something that we have not seen so far is occupying Bion both epistemologically and, as we see here, clinically too.

Book 2, *Elements* (1963)

Introduction

Elements was published the year following *Learning from Experience* and contains Bion's most concentrated effort to develop a psychoanalytic instrumentality, specifically the Grid. He doesn't talk about how he initially came to the idea of the Grid or the stages he may have gone through in devising it. I suspect that he's 'gridifying' (my term) how he already works. He has long been sensitive to the level of development of any material (which is now formalised by the 'rows' on the Grid) and the use to which it is put (now formalised by the 'columns'). He likens the use of the Grid to a musician practising scales between concerts. The practice is done outside the concert and, for the analyst, outside the session, but is an essential discipline underpinning the concert's work. It is often pointed out that Bion did not continue with the Grid. This is not quite right. He continues to make references to its usefulness in his later work (see the Los Angeles Seminars and Supervisions and those in São Paulo and Brazil). The clinical illustration below is Bion's example of his use of the Grid. A second clinical illustration is from a complex clinical discussion of 'reversible perspective' later in the book.

Bion's Example of His Use of the Grid

> Suppose the patient had said "I know that you hate me."
> (Bion, 14, Vol. 5, p. 62)

Where would this be logged on the Grid? Bion first considers its possible place on the vertical axis: the rows (the level of development of any material). The first row is that of the most primitive material, what Bion calls beta elements. If "I know that you hate me" belongs on this row, although words are used, the material is not symbolic, and the words are being used instead as an action, possibly an attack: "a disguised fart." Bion then takes the same statement and considers it as relating to a dream, or part of a phantasy. In this case, it would belong in Row C (dream thoughts, dreams, myths).

He then turns to the horizontal axis—the columns ("the function that a statement is being made to perform"). He suggests that "I know you hate me" may be:

> an oracular pronouncement, an announcement of the theme of the session, a definition in the light of which the remainder of the session is to be understood. In short it may fall in the category represented by column 1.
>
> (p. 60)

Column 1 is called "Definitory Hypothesis." In suggesting that "I know you hate me" could be an "oracular pronouncement," Bion makes reference to the oracle at the beginning of the Oedipus myth (he thought it possible to map the Oedipus myth on to the Grid). From this point of view, "I know you hate me" is a predictive description of what is to happen in the session. Bion then experimentally places the statement in Column 2 (statements known to be false but used defensively), Columns 3, 4, 5 (notation, attention, and inquiry), and finally Column 6, where the statement becomes a warning of an acting out, including using analysis as a form of acting out.

Bion wants to give himself the widest of possibilities to choose from. He also wants a means of checking his work, a method of self-supervision.

Reversible Perspective

In Chapter 11 of *Elements*, Bion begins a clinical discussion that runs through three chapters. The clinical material starts with an illustration of an apparent cooperation between patient and analyst. However, the patient is actually rejecting the premise that the analyst is the analyst and the patient is the patient. This results in stasis, and Bion explores the means by which the patient maintains the stasis, including hallucination and delusion.

Bion then introduces someone who seems to be a different patient. This patient is talking in such a way that Bion is offered material for familiar transference interpretations (he asks how an ill patient could be doing something of such complexity). He suggests that the patient may want analyst and patient to agree that there is a familiar known transference in order to obscure how "utterly incomprehensible" the patient is actually finding things to be:

> It was not till I was able to suggest that he made this class of communication because he felt that the episodes he mentioned were utterly incomprehensible that he made a response showing that this was indeed the case.
>
> (p. 50)

In Bion's view, the stasis maintained by the patient is to defend against unbearable pain. "The lesson to be drawn from this discussion is the need to deduce the presence of intense pain and the threat that it represents to mental integration" (p. 53).

As we have seen in Aguayo's chapter on the 'Imaginary Twin,' at the beginning of the 1950s, Bion was already cognisant of what we now call enactment taking place between the analyst and patient. In the 'Imaginary Twin,' Bion observed the patient speaking and then pausing, implying it was now Bion's turn. There was stasis in the work while this pattern went unnoticed. The clinical illustrations of reversible perspective in *Elements* are a continuation of this earlier work and have the level of detail found in Bion's 1950s papers.

Book 3, *Transformations: Change from Learning to Growth* (1965b)

Introduction

Bion describes the content of *Transformations* (1965b) as "a method of critical approach to psychoanalytic practice" (p. 131). Indeed, this densely theoretical book is intended to be an approach to practice and does contain the largest number of clinical illustrations of all four publications.

One intention of Bion's work during the 1960s is to draw analysts' attention to their being in more unknown territory than may be thought. He attempts to develop new instruments to assist us (the question of K, L, or H, and the Grid), perhaps somewhat like a compass, and now, in *Transformations*, he illustrates how we can avoid being swept from the clinical position if and when we reduce our defensive use of psychoanalytical theory.

Bion's discussion of 'memory and desire' is very much a part of *Transformations*. He advocates a radical putting from one's mind any memories and desires that do not evolve spontaneously in the session itself. He gave his paper "Memory and Desire" (1965a) in the same year *Transformations* was published. However, there is notably little mention of eschewing memory and desire in the clinical illustrations in *Transformations*. For example, in the second, detailed clinical illustration below, we hear only "But beyond preserving an awareness of such a background of theory I allowed myself to be as open to clinical impressions as possible." Does this indicate a lag in Bion's clinical use of his developing concept of eschewing memory and desire? Perhaps not; when he talks about eschewing memory and desire, it certainly sounds like he is talking from his own clinical experience. So, he may well have been making use of the approach clinically, but has not included the detail of it in the clinical illustrations in *Transformations*.

Detecting Invariance through a Breakdown

The first clinical illustration in the book is one of Bion's best known. The patient is described as a borderline psychotic. The analysis has been proceeding slowly, but then there is a "sudden deterioration": the patient is morose and appears to be hearing voices and seeing things. Relatives and the family doctor are alarmed.

> Change from an analytical experience, confined to the consulting room, to a crisis that involves more people than the pair is remarkable for a number of features. It is catastrophic in the restricted sense of an event producing a subversion of the order or system of things; it is catastrophic in the sense that it is accompanied by feelings of disaster in the participants; it is catastrophic in the sense that it is sudden and violent in an almost physical way. This last will depend on the degree to which analytical procedure has produced a controlled breakdown. ...
>
> In this situation the analyst must search the material for invariants to the pre- and post-catastrophic stages. These will be found in the domain represented by the theories of projective identification, internal and external objects. Restating this in terms of clinical material, he must see, and demonstrate, that certain apparently external emotionally-charged events are in fact the same events as those which appeared in the pre-catastrophic stage under the names, bestowed by the patient, of pains in the knee, legs, abdomen, ears, etc., and, by the analyst, of internal objects. In brief, what present themselves to the outward sense of analyst and patient as anxious relatives, impending law-suits, mental hospitals, certification, and other contingencies apparently appropriate to the change in circumstances, are really hypochondriacal pains and other evidences of internal objects in a guise appropriate to their new status as external objects. These then are the invariants or the objects in which invariance is to be detected.
>
> (Bion, 2014, Vol. 5, pp. 133–134)

Bion is drawing on Klein's understanding of internal objects, particularly in hypochondriasis. Together with this, we see Bion's understanding of the behaviour of groups in relation to the relatives, family doctor, and potential lawyers. We hear about a patient's 'breakdown,' which could have caused Bion to stop thinking as an analyst and become instead a man under legal scrutiny (how could he have let it happen?), a medical doctor managing the case, or an auxiliary member of the family. His identification of what is invariant between the pre-breakdown and post-breakdown states, by contrast, supports his analytic position.

From Different Points of View (Vertices)

In a second clinical illustration in *Transformations*, we hear some detail of what Bion may be thinking in a session. As I comment above, this is particularly interesting because Bion wrote the clinical illustration around the same time as he presented his thoughts on eschewing memory and desire to the British Society (1965a). What I think we see most clearly is how he views the material from a number of perspectives. To assist in observing this, I have added the subheadings.

What the Patient Said and Did:

> The patient came in, but, though he had been attending for years, seemed uncertain what to do. "Good morning, good morning, good morning. It must mean afternoon really. I don't expect anything can be expected today: this morning, I mean. This afternoon. It must be a joke of some kind. This girl left about her knickers. Well, what do you say to that? It's probably quite wrong, of course, but, well, I mean, what do you think?" He walked to the couch and lay down, bumping his shoulders down hard on the couch. "I'm slightly anxious ... I think. The pain has come back in my knee. You'll probably say it was the girl."
>
> (Bion, 2014, Vol. 5, pp. 143–144)

Bion further describes the events observed and the atmosphere of "depression, fear, anxiety, confidentiality, and others." His report of what he sees, hears, and senses of the mood is "verbally nearly correct" and yet a "misleading record." He begins again, but from a different point of view.

Bion's Conception of the Events

This time, we hear Bion's conception of events:

> After his pause of uncertainty he whispered his good mornings as if he were pre-occupied with an object he had lost but expected to find close at hand. He corrected himself in a tone that might imply a mental aberration that had led him to think it "good morning". The speaker of the words "good morning", I gathered, was not really the patient, but someone whose manner he caricatured.
>
> (p. 144)

Bion is describing thoughts he had during the session. He describes the patient as "pre-occupied with an object he had lost but expected to find close at hand." The patient acts as though Bion must already know the girl, and much else besides, possibly omnipotently, but also as a conspirator. Bion, from what he reports, hasn't yet said anything. He then adds another level to his account, moving his point of observation further inside the patient: the patient looking out on Bion, with his own model of Bion's functioning.

What the Patient Might Assume Bion to Be Feeling and Thinking (According to Bion)

> When he lay on the couch he did so as if trying to express surreptitiously his wish to damage my property. ... he hazarded a guess that I was anxious at his violence ... "The pain in my knee, which I now experience, is what you as analyst think is really the girl inside me." Such a statement meant that despite

evidence to the contrary he had knowledge of my analytic theories and that he was now having an experience which I would explain by that particular theory.

(pp. 144–145)

Bion goes on to talk about what "theoretical pre-conceptions" he has in his mind, identifying classical analytical theory, the Kleinian theories of splitting and projective identification, and his own understanding of hallucination. By "preconception," Bion means theory held in the form of a template that can be matched with actual experience. He adds that, "beyond preserving an awareness of such a background of theory I allowed myself to be as open to clinical impressions as possible" (p. 145).

This is Bion's only reference to 'openness.' However, as I comment in the introduction to this section, *Transformations* was published in the same year as Bion's "Memory and Desire" paper, and, in both publications, Bion advocates a radical putting from one's mind of any memories and desires that do not evolve spontaneously in the session itself. Do we see this in his clinical example above? His mind seems very full of thoughts. What we see more clearly is his looking at the material from different points of view, or perspectives. I have suggested we see some of the roots of this approach earlier in the 1960s (and before), specifically Bion's interest in putting himself inside an infant's experience (drawing on his own primitive experience?); inside a patient's experience; and in his development of the psychoanalytic instrumentality necessary to train oneself in considering material from different perspectives.

Dermen has drawn attention to Bion's question (in "On Arrogance," 1958) of "what am I missing?" I think we see another question evolve in his clinical method during the 1960s: "how can I see the analysis from as many different points of view as possible?" (what he comes to call vertices).

Re Bion's 1967 Commentary on His Papers of the 1950s

In the Commentary, Bion gives a detailed discussion of the clinical papers written in the 1950s from the point of view of his current thinking about analysis. I have decided not to include it because it doesn't contain 1960s clinical illustrations and I want to keep our attention on these.

Book 4, *Attention and Interpretation: A Scientific Approach to Insight in Psycho-Analysis and Groups* (1970)

Introduction

For Bion, the 1960s began with a change from writing papers to writing short books of his own design; it ended with a change of country. In 1968, the Bions moved to California. Regarding his clinical work in *Attention and Interpretation*, he comments:

this book has been concerned with the formulation of a theory, the few "facts" mentioned being illustrative models intended to give body to what might otherwise be an exercise in the manipulation of abstractions.

(Bion, 2014, Vol 6, p. 294)

The illustrative models that are clinical include a patient who represented her parents' relationship as that between a pander and whore, the patient who makes references to ice-cream, and an account of a married patient who is emotionally unmarried.

The Pander and the Whore

In Chapter 2, "Medicine as a Model," Bion discusses the difference between medicine and psychoanalysis. He then continues:

I shall now give three different formulations of the same episode occurring in the psychoanalysis of a woman. More could easily be given to demonstrate the problem of communication and publication that faces the psychoanalyst.

The patient produced an association to express, though in a disguised manner, her hostility to parents whose relationship to each other she represented as that between pander and whore. She intended also to evoke a response from the analyst such that he would be wrong whatever facet of a multi-dimensional association he selected for interpretation. Choice of dimension and interpretation could be "proved" to reflect the analyst, not the analysand; he could hesitate impotently before the wealth of alternatives presented to him.

(Bion, 2014, Vol. 6, p. 226)

Bion does not provide any further details. Hinshelwood commented that the three different formulations are, first, a classical Freudian symbolic interpretation of hostility to the Oedipal parents. The second formulation would seem to be Kleinian in its focus on the attack on the analyst's potency, and the third formulation a deeper layer, explored by Bion, of an explosion in a vast mental space—an explosion of time and space (Hinshelwood, personal communication).

Bion presents different perspectives on the same material. The clinical instrumentality of the Grid comes to mind in the sense that Bion is attempting to determine the level of development of the material (vertical axis) and what it is being used for (to undermine the analyst's potency—horizontal axis).

I Scream/Ice-cream

The events of an analysis, spread out over what to the analyst are many years, are to A but the fragments of a moment dispersed in space. The distance in time separating one statement from another can be taken as a measure of the distance in space of one element from another in which all are contemporary. Thus A says he

could buy no ice-cream. Six months later he says he cannot even buy ice-cream. Three days later he mentions his being too late to buy ice-cream: there was no ice-cream left. Two years later he says he supposes there was no ice-cream. Had I known, when the topic was mentioned first, what I know now I might have noted the time and place of the reference, but I did not know and therefore could not attend to this statement or note it. When I did, it was because of the obtrusive 'I scream' theme. It was later still that I grasped the significance of 'no–I scream.' ... I now know that a violent attack had been delivered on a relationship in which the link between the two personalities had been 'I scream.' This had been destroyed and the place of the link 'I scream' had been taken by a 'no—I scream.' The 'I scream' link had itself previously been food, 'ice-cream,' a 'breast,' until envy and destructiveness had turned the good breast into an 'I scream.'
(Bion, 2014, Vol. 6, p. 231)

Bion comments that what he is seeing clinically is an intense catastrophic emotional explosion 'O.' This event "is then transformed, in the medium of acting-out and by virtue of beta-elements." With this illustration, we may see the close interrelation between what is on the very edge of Bion's clinical understanding being put together with what is on the edge of his capacity to conceive of phenomena that do not fall within our usual spectrum of understanding. It was once said to me that Hanna Segal could see the wood as well as the detail of the trees. This is also true of Bion, and, in this instance, the wood (the whole personality of the patient and his history) is the site of an explosion, and one that has previously lacked an observer.

A Clinical Illustration of Eschewing Memory, Desire, and Understanding

In the first place [eschewing memory, desire and understanding], the analyst will soon find that he appears to be ignorant of knowledge which he has hitherto regarded as the hallmark of scrupulous medical responsibility. ... Thus an analyst may feel, to take a common example, that his married patient is unmarried; if so, it means that psychoanalytically his patient is unmarried: the emotional reality and the reality based on the supposition of the marriage contract are discrepant. ... If the analyst does not remember that his patient is married, the fact that he is is irrelevant until the patient says something that reminds the analyst of this fact. ...

What matters is that to statements of a particular category [of the Grid] the patient begins to add statements of a different category. The patient whose statements have at no time suggested to the analyst that he, the patient, is married, now, at a particular point in his analysis, introduces statements that indicate that he is.
(Bion, 2014, Vol. 6, pp. 261–263)

The first stage will not be unfamiliar to the reader. A person may be legally married, with children, without actually being emotionally married. This thought is not an unusual one. We are arguably prone at this stage to assume we know about people's unconscious or hidden motivations and leave it there. Bion, however, is saying something more: not just that we should put the fact of the legal marriage aside in considering the person, but that we should put it aside and observe if and when 'being married' makes its presence known, and, second, what other kinds of material appear around the same time. We may see something similar to this back in his 1950s paper, "On Arrogance" (Bion, 2014, Vol. 6, pp. 131–137). Bion observed that references to "arrogance," "curiosity," and "stupidity" emerged around the same time as each other and went on to explore the meaning this conjunction might hold. The fact that we can make a link to his earlier work does make me wonder to what extent—in his new conceptualisation (of eschewing memory and desire)—Bion was managing to name, as well as hone, an observational state of mind he had long known to be valuable.

Patients and Supervisees in the 1960s

Francis Tustin, a Patient in the 1960s

Tustin recounts being able to see into "dark corners of her mind she never really knew existed." In her comments, we see Bion's attention to the patient finding his or her own mind—in contrast to the patient being told in an 'authoritative' way about themselves by the psychoanalyst. There is also reference to what she describes as "Bion's respect for the organic process of analysis." Bion was attempting to get greater access to something that has a life in its own right—the organic process of analysis—he was not intending to fabricate a new kind of process.

> Some years ago Dr. Bion suggested that I might write a book for the general reader about my personal experience of psycho-analysis. I am not yet ready to do that but, when the Editor of this Journal approached me to write a short article about the experience of analysis with Dr. Bion, I remembered the title I had thought of for such a book—'A Modem Pilgrim's Progress.' Inevitably, this title arises from the religious background in which I was reared. Although I value this, I now conceive of it in somewhat different terms. For the modem pilgrim, the final goal is not the Heaven which Bunyan envisaged, but a step into the unknown which Bion so eloquently and disturbingly placed before us. The purpose of this article is to try to give fellow travelers a brief glimpse of the pilgrimage I embarked upon under his auspices which led into dark comers of the mind I never realised existed.

Tustin also talks about Bion's never talking about her past: "He talked about the present." One point to make about this—and we see it, for example, in the detailed clinical illustration "From Different Points of View" in the section on *Transformations* above—is how much Bion was able to see in the present. If one focuses on the present, it may magnify what is there, but often unseen.

> He didn't talk about my past ever. I kept thinking, he's never hearing about my childhood. He never talked about it. He talked about the present and I don't

know that I went into the past. Perhaps I did—but he didn't. I know he never talked about the past. It was all to do with the present and awful silences!

Dr. Bion had a good sense of humor and that was important to me.

He was always brief, to the point and extremely simple and clear. But he was very disturbing.

Dr. Bion aroused in me the courage to see things from a different perspective from the current and accepted ones, and also different from his. He provoked me to think for myself—to have a mind of my own. He did this by asking challenging questions and by making unexpected remarks rather than by imposing a rigid interpretive scheme on what I said and did. In so doing, he made me think about what was happening to me in my own terms.

It was Bion's respect for the organic process of analysis, which he allowed to take its course, and which he never tried to manipulate that made me feel so safe.

(Tustin, 1981)

J. Hill, a Supervisee in the 1960s

My experience was that Bion's technique as a supervisor differed sharply from others; in particular from those supervisors who combined an insistence that their students should not take notes during sessions with a requirement that in supervision they should attempt rigorously to reproduce the minute by minute, word by word detail of the session. Whether this is still widely practised I do not know but even then it seemed to me that such a requirement was perhaps impossible to the point of absurdity. In contrast Bion would sometimes say: "Don't take notes, keep a diary and on those days when you curse the day you ever heard of psychoanalysis put that down in your diary." He reminds me of a lecturer in philosophy at Oxford (Gilbert Ryle) who would tell his students that if he caught anyone taking notes in his lectures he would send them out for inattention.

Very early on I remember being startled when he remarked almost casually in a social setting: "The trouble is that there is so much bad analysis around."

He said that analysts shared with doctors, sailors and miners an awareness of the presence of death and would sometimes recall his childhood experiences in India and the sound of the tiger in the jungle at night, "when your blood literally runs cold and the same thing can happen when listening to a patient."

Bion's personal presence was clear to all who met him and expressed in various ways. Eric Trist, for example, would describe how anyone meeting Bion for the first time would experience this as a "massive encounter," while Tommy Wilson defined him as "the mother of all father figures." Ken Rice said that he was a man who "sat further behind his face than any one I have ever known," and many felt that he was secretly enjoying the disconcerting ambiguity that his originality provoked in his fellow analysts. "Only Bion," it was said, "could make interpretations like that."

Yet again he pointed out that in the course of an analysis, as integration proceeds, the bad parts of the self become stronger as well as the good and progress is, therefore, endangered. "Even Melanie," he added, "has not spotted this one."

Was he a good analyst? I don't know but am reminded of his own comment to me once that it would need three linked generations of analysands before one could be sure that analysis was really doing any good. Yet he also said that even in one generation it was possible to gain certain convictions.

(Hill, 1991)

Irma Brenman Pick, a Supervisee in the 1960s

Irma Brenman Pick describes Bion as opening up new possibilities in her thinking in a "non-intrusive way." This seems to echo what Tustin says about his helping the patient to think about what was happening on their own terms. We might want to say that all analysts hope to do this. I suspect, however, that Bion had an unusual capacity to promote thinking in others.

> The other was Bion, who was my second supervisor, but with whom I had earlier had attended his clinical seminar presenting this first case that Rosenfeld supervised. And I was in a bit of a different place than the rest of my year. ... I presented the case, and there was just a terrible silence, just awful. Nobody said a word. And I became very—Bion didn't say a word either. And I became anxious and anxiously said, should I be offering more? Should I be giving you more material? And Bion said, I think this may be what you're meant to feel. That was all he said. But it was very important, actually, because it allowed me to think about whether this feeling I should be giving more was coming from the patient demanding more, coming from the group that I wasn't giving them what they wanted, or coming from someplace inside me.
> ... he had this capacity in a very non-intrusive way. He wasn't going into my private world of what might drive me to feel I had to give more, but ... opened up the possibilities [of] thinking across these different spectras.
>
> (Pick, 2015)

Elizabeth Bott Spillius, a Supervisee in 1965

One of the interesting points in the following comment from Elizabeth Bott Spillius is that what Bion said "was ... seemingly obvious." I think that, in his clinical work, he did try to identify that which is closest-in, 'under our noses,' most taken for granted.

> I had a year's supervision with Bion in 1965, which was deeply important to me. I expected him to be as obscure as I had at first found some of his writings to be, but found that everything he said was straightforward and seemingly obvious,

except that it hadn't been obvious before he said it. He was not at all judgmental, and he had a way of communicating, largely by example I think, that whatever gifts one had as an analyst, it was one's duty to use them as best one could for one's patients and for psychoanalysis.

(Spillius, 2009)

Where Does Bion Get to by the End of the 1960s in Relation to His Method of Clinical Inquiry?

Bion, in his clinical method, has an unusual capacity to facilitate another person's thoughts. Tustin and the people he supervised in the 1960s talk about this, and the reader of his books of the 1960s may also discover this (if he or she perseveres with more difficult sections!).

Bion often comments that the observations the analyst makes sit at the heart of any analysis. Through the 1960s, I think we see him restlessly and determinedly working to improve his observational capacity. Dermen has drawn attention to Bion's question in "On Arrogance" (1958) of "what am I missing?" In addition to this question, I think we see another question evolve in his clinical method in the 1960s: "How can I look from different points of view?" (what he comes to call vertices). Involved in this endeavour are both sense-based observation and intuition. He seems freer to use his imaginative conjectures—perhaps particularly in opening up very early, even fetal, functioning to the possibility of our noticing it in sessions.

At the same time as an opening up of his clinical observations, Bion is also intent on developing an increased clinical discipline. The Grid, in particular, formalises the requirement to experiment with different ways of looking at the same material. I have suggested a continuity between the Grid and the discipline of memory and desire. The Grid represents a more concrete instrumentality evolving through the 1960s into the discipline of memory and desire; Bion moving from what analysts should do (the Grid) to how they need to be (discipline of memory and desire). I feel some confidence that, in relation to both the Grid and the discipline of memory and desire, Bion is developing something he was already doing clinically. He is engaged in what he classifies as a Column 1 activity—managing to name something already in existence (i.e., 'gridifying' the attention he already paid to the developmental level of any material and the use to which it is being put) and thus making it available for further exploration.

Did Bion's conceptual thinking through the 1960s go ahead of his method of clinical inquiry? I have drawn attention to the fact that *Transformations* (1965b) contains a radical discussion of the eschewing of memory and desire, but not overt clinical illustrations of its use. What we do see clinical illustrations is the maintenance of the analytic position through the observation of invariants (in contrast to a more theory-based analytic identity) and Bion's attention to the different perspectives possible on clinical material.

I am aware that I have not referred to 'O' in relation to his clinical illustrations. What is clear in the illustrations from the beginning of the 1960s (and before) is his attention to what does and doesn't have a clinical effect. I think his work on 'O,' and 'being' rather than 'knowing about,' is in this tradition. By the mid-1960s, he comes to the view that change is achieved at the level of being. Tustin refers to "Bion's respect for the organic process of analysis." My own impression too is that he is attempting to get greater access to something that has a life in its own right (the organic process of analysis) and was not intending to fabricate a new kind of analysis.

There is an urgency to Bion's clinical work of the 1960s. In his quickness and restlessness, we see him under clinical strain. He wants to make sure that his newly developing models are based on evidence and tested clinically, and to give specificity to his theoretical generalities, but I suspect he may not be wholly able to keep up with the rapid development of his own thought. He does, however, arrive at the end of the 1960s deeply convinced of the direction he is moving in.

Note

1 From the Editor's Introduction to "Cogitations" (1992): "Cogitations comprises notes, edited by Francesca Bion, made between February 1958 and April 1979. Notes that contained references to patients were omitted, although on later reading it seems clear that at least some of them might have been published with some disguising alterations. Some notes were judged to have been too personal to include" (Bion, 2014, Vol. 11, p. 3).

References

Bion, W.R. (2014). The Complete Works of W.R. Bion [Book series]. C. Mawson & F. Bion (Eds.). London: Routledge.

Bion, W.R. (1958/2014). On Arrogance. In The Complete Works of W.R. Bion, Volume 6. London: Routledge.

Bion, W.R. (1962/2014). Learning from Experience. In The Complete Works of W.R. Bion, Volume 6. London: Routledge.

Bion, W.R. (1963/2014). Elements of Psycho-Analysis. In The Complete Works of W.R. Bion, Volume 5. London: Routledge.

Bion, W.R. (1965a/2014). Memory and Desire. In The Complete Works of W.R. Bion, Volume 6. London: Routledge.

Bion, W.R. (1965b/2014). Transformations: Change from Learning to Growth. In The Complete Works of W.R. Bion, Volume 5. London: Routledge.

Bion, W.R. (1967/2014). Second Thoughts: Selected Papers on Psycho-Analysis. In The Complete Works of W.R. Bion, Volume 6. London: Routledge.

Bion, W.R. (1970/2014). Attention and Interpretation: A Scientific Approach to Insight in Psycho-Analysis and Groups. In The Complete Works of W.R. Bion, Volume 6. London: Routledge.

Bion, W.R. (1992/2014). Cogitations. In The Complete Works of W.R. Bion, Volume 11. London: Routledge.

Brown, L.J. (2012). Bion's Discovery of Alpha Function: Thinking under Fire on the Battlefield and in the Consulting Room. *International Journal of Psychoanalysis* 93: 1191–1214.

Hill, J. (1992). Recollections: A Brief Personal Memoir of Wilfred Bion. *British Journal of Psychotherapy* 9(1): 70–73.

Spillius, E.B. (2009). On Becoming a British Psychoanalyst. *Psychoanalytic Inquiry* 29: 204–222.

Pick, I.B. (2015). Irma Brenman Pick on "Working through in the Countertransference" (IJP, 1985). PEP/UCL Top Authors Project Video Collection 1:1.

Tustin, F. (1981). In Memoriam W.R. Bion. A Modern Pilgrim's Progress: Reminiscences of Personal Analysis with Dr. Bion. *Journal of Child Psychotherapy* 7(2): 175–179.

5

Wilfred Bion's Clinical Seminars in North and South America and Europe, 1967–1978

A Clinical Method of Inquiry as an Implicit Theory of Psychoanalytic Technique

Joseph Aguayo and Sira Dermen

Introduction (Joseph Aguayo)

Between 1967 and 1978, while residing, practicing and lecturing in Los Angeles, Wilfred Bion gave a series of clinical seminars to various analytic audiences on three different continents (Bion, 1975, 1980, 1990, 1994, 2013, 2014, 2018; Bion and Bion, 1987). Our aim here is to take some of these seminars in hand—with the exception of work Bion did in Brazil, which will be covered in Chapter 6—so we can investigate the question: did Bion have an *implicit* method of clinical inquiry that he disseminated in the form of analytic technique in these seminars? Our focus here is on both the presentation of his own analytic case material as well as selected supervisory consultations done along the way. The publication of so much of Bion's own clinical work in recent years makes possible this kind of research insofar as he provided so few examples of his clinical work in the epistemology monographs of the 1960s. After 1967, he more or less departed from his practice of writing dense, difficult-to-understand, theory-driven monographs and now instead gave many clinical examples of his work to new audiences less familiar with it—all in rather plain, direct and intelligible English.

Depending on the different audiences' familiarity with his ideas, he presented his work in a way that required no previous familiarity with it and did so, for example, in Los Angeles in 1967 to a group of medically trained male American Freudian analysts who had a keen interest in the treatment of both borderline and hospitalized psychotic patients. Speaking clearly and simply, Bion also implicitly appealed to colleagues on whom he would rely for referrals once he settled in Los Angeles a few months later, in January 1968.[1] He continued this traditional format in the same year in Buenos Aires—giving seminar material before the floor was opened up to question and answer periods. The notable exception here was that Bion assumed— probably on the basis of his contact with Léon Grinberg, his host in Buenos Aires on this occasion—that his audience in Buenos Aires was more familiar with his

DOI: 10.4324/9781003401926-6

recent ideas than were his colleagues in Los Angeles—for example, the Grid, on which he gave an entire seminar (Bion, 2018, pp. 29–46). Indeed, within a few years of Bion's visit, Grinberg's small group produced the first book-length introduction to Bion's ideas (Grinberg, Sor and Tabak de Bianchedi, 1975).[2]

A few years later, in the four discussions at the Veteran's Administration, Brentwood, California, in 1976, Bion continued his custom of fielding questions from the audience, which in this instance consisted of a group of psychiatric residents, clinical psychology interns and other mental health workers. He established from the outset a question-and-answer format and answered the numerous queries put to him in a respectful and thorough manner, taking into consideration that he was speaking to an audience of individuals at the outset of their careers. Yet, at the same time, Bion (1994, p. 266) also made it clear that the question-and-answer format itself needed to be interrogated. Here, he drew upon a French aphorism by Maurice Blanchot that André Green had passed along to him at the Menninger's Borderline Disorders Conference earlier that year: "La réponse est le malheur de la question" (The answer is the question's misfortune) (Hartacollis, 1977, p. 508; Bion, 1994, p. 307).

So, for example, when the young interns repeatedly asked Bion (2014, Vol. 10, p. 72–73) about how he actually worked in the psychoanalytic setting, he demurred, refusing to give clinical examples of 'how-to-do-it.' On this point, Bion had long been consistent, feeling reluctant to answer questions of technique because it would put him in an explicit leadership position vis-à-vis the group. Better that each individual think for themselves and receive a senior colleague's considered 'second opinion.' The point here was for any analyst to become their own practitioner and develop their own unique style. At times, Bion also seemed interested in interrogating the very nature of the 'question-and-answer' format so as to not appear as the unquestionable 'expert' to the group. He contrasted basic assumptions that "kill curiosity" with genuine inquiry that was "a disciplined and informed curiosity" (2014, Vol. 10, p. 80). When his work is compared with that of other Kleinians, such as Hanna Segal (1964), she appeared more systematizing in her intentions, beginning to publish on questions of 'Kleinian technique,' and, within a few years, other Kleinians, such as Betty Joseph, (1971, 1975) would follow suit and establish a systematic account of Kleinian technique (Aguayo, 2011).

As plain and direct as Bion appeared in Los Angeles and Buenos Aires, his mode of group presentation varied with the circumstances. In other American conferences, such as the Menninger's Borderline Disorders Conference in Topeka in March 1976, he appeared quite different, veering off the topic of borderline states, a topic on which he was otherwise quite expert, and at points jarring and shocking his audience. The majority of the main conference presenters thought in terms of structural/diagnostic characteristics of the borderline patient, treatment plans and indications for hospitalized and out-patient treatment paradigms, as exemplified by Kernberg's (1975) increasingly popular paradigm. Bion's discourse did not take up any of these nodal points in either of his presentations. Perhaps at these presentations, Bion's less conventional manner, along with what by now had become a customary reluctance to cite his analytic sources, may have given rise to a feeling that one was in the midst of a guru or a wild man, who in Hinshelwood's (1994, p. xi) terms was "linked in with 'truth' in a way that ordinary mortals were not."[3]

The presentation style was not much different at the New York IPTAR seminars in 1977, where Bion again appeared distinctly less conventional. Rather than deliver lectures in the traditional format, stopping to take questions directly linked to his presentations, he here favored a less structured and more impromptu, free-form style of presentation. He free associated in a rather enticing fashion and essentially invited participants to do the same. The resulting atmosphere at times became chaotic and unpredictable: at one moment, he might get a question about supervising a case on the spot, the next instant, a process comment from an attendee about what was happening in the group (2014, Vol. 8, 297, 275)—or repeated requests to cover what at that point had become old ground, such as the technical advisory of 'abandoning memory and desire.'[4]

If one traces these clinical seminars in a comparative context during the 1970s, one sees that Bion increasingly varied his rhetorical practices, experimenting with the traditional seminar format, especially its question-and-answer aspects. He seemed to clearly assess how sophisticated his audiences were in terms of their acquaintance with his ideas—and, at times, was amused by being feted as the 'grand old man' by his hosts—as he evinced in his letters to wife Francesca, who did not accompany him on some of these trips (Bion, 1951).[5] Yet, in demonstrating an ease and sophistication in varying the way in which he approached groups, this factor probably assisted him in keeping fresh material that had to be repeated (e.g., 'no memory and desire') to audiences new to his work. Hinshelwood (1992, p. 124) thought that Bion was experimenting with communication itself and, at times, seemed to "use the audience as a participating group." In this rather free-wheeling, free-associational style of discourse, the emphasis was often theoretical and less often clinical.

Taking a different look at Bion's rhetorical practices with different groups in his 1977 Italian seminars (2014, Vol. 9), given just a few months after the New York seminars, Bion sounded more at ease with his audience and—perhaps with the mediating influence of daughter Parthenope, who served as the seminars' Italian translator—presumed a greater familiarity with his ideas. Proceeding in an orderly fashion, Bion would pause for a question or comment from the audience, and there was a mixture of reactions from attendees who at times felt compelled to give unsolicited and quite compressed clinical examples that they thought might best exemplify some of his ideas (2014, Vol. 9, pp. 106, 114). His own responses involved so much intricate detail that it strained attendees who had to overly rely on the translator's efforts (2014, Vol. 9, pp. 107–109). To further complicate matters, Bion continued with his now customary mode of responding that tackled the underlying emotional tonality of the question, at times regarding it as reflecting some systemic tension in the group itself. Since his visit to Rome was sponsored by two groups—the Società Italiana Psicoanalitica and the Via Pollaiolo Research Group (the latter of which consisted of group psychotherapists)—Bion's addressing of group themes would have fallen on receptive ears.[6]

From these examples of how Bion varied his rhetorical practices as a function of how he addressed the overall structure of the groups, his long-term experience with groups was at the back of his mind. In a seldom-quoted interview with Bion on his group work conducted by Anthony Benet in 1976, he was clearly at ease discussing basic assumptions and the turbulent unpredictable nature of the group experience—and he said at much:

> I sometimes think that an analyst's feelings while taking a group—feelings while absorbing the basic assumptions—are one of the few bits that scientists might call evidence, because he can know what he is feeling. ... In real life you have an orchestra: continuous movement and the constant slither of one feeling into another. You have to have a method to capture all that richness.
> (Bion, 2014, Vol. 10, p. 156)

So, to the main question addressed in this chapter is: was there in fact an implicit theory of clinical technique embedded in Bion's late seminar presentation of his analytic work? Was he casting about for some alternative way of presenting his own distinctive clinical technique, and, if so, can this technique be deciphered from his clinical examples? From the perspective of clinical technique, was Bion attempting to differentiate his own method of clinical inquiry from the systematizing efforts of his London Kleinian colleagues? Alternatively, did Bion retain aspects of Kleinian technique while moving onto a style that was distinctly his own?

Examples of Bion's Clinical Method of Inquiry in his North and South American Seminars

Since we now have copious examples of both Bion's own clinical work as well as supervisions he did in his many clinical seminars, there is the question of which examples to select. In bypassing the plentiful but short supervisions conducted by Bion, we present his own analytic work with longer clinical examples: first, a distraught borderline female that he discussed both in Los Angeles and Buenos Aires in 1967–1968.[7] The other example is a prolonged supervision conducted with Horatio Etchegoyen as the main presenter in Buenos Aires in 1968. Since both these experiences are quite extensive, detailed and, in the instance of Etchegoyen, subjects of further publications, we have the materials that make it possible to provide a rather intricate analysis.[8] By this late point in his career, Bion was quite a seasoned analyst, and we think that a detailed examination of his work reveals the implicit technique guiding his interventions, first as a treating psychoanalyst and, second, as a clinical supervisor.

Bion's Analytic Understanding of a Stormy Borderline Patient

To set the context for this case presentation: since the main theme guiding so many of Bion's clinical and supervisory presentations in Los Angeles in 1967 dealt with near-psychotic borderline as well as psychotic patients—all treated with an unmodified psychoanalytic technique of treatment five times a week—Bion emphasized his specialty in this area to colleagues on whom he would soon depend for referrals. Since the majority of the Freudian analysts attending these seminars were psychiatrists with hospitalized psychotic patients, they were keen to learn about Bion's work and less exercised about the ways in which his method was 'Kleinian' or some other mix of ideas of his own.[9] Since he had reprised his paper on memory and desire on the occasion of his visit to Los Angeles, it became a dominant theme in the clinical discussions. The Los Angeles attendees would have not been aware that Bion had not been accustomed to presenting examples of his clinical work for some time as he now proceeded to directly describe the fundamental stance of the analyst as a tranquil and openly receptive receiver of the patient's total communications in the 'here and now.'[10]

Bion accentuated the present moment in the analytic encounter, making clear that the analyst who abandoned memory and desire could make crisp observations about his patient, which in turn could lead to a creative evolution. The analyst's true trajectory was towards the unknown, which, in Los Angeles, he referred to as "the infrared part of the spectrum," where more light needed to be shed. It was important to forget what one knows in the immediacy of the current session, so that some new (and heretofore unknown) pattern might be allowed to evolve. Bion (2013, pp. 5–6) emphasized issues of desire as well, such as not distracting oneself by looking at one's watch during a session, or desiring the session's end or the end of the analytic week.

Bion here differentiated a relaxed receptivity from the actual analysis of countertransference—the latter was a process, or an ideal state in which one has the time, awareness and resources to handle it. The workaday reality is that analysts don't often have time for such measured reflection. He pointed to what might be possible in an uncommon way: the analyst will often, for good or ill, enter the next session as he or she is, so it is better for the analyst to aspire to patience and security because he or she will, in his or her workaday practice, sometimes feel persecuted and depressed (Bion, 2013, pp. 21–25). Lastly, Bion linked the abandonment of memory and desire to Freud's own topographic aphorism about technique: "To put it in a formula: he must turn his own unconscious like a receptive organ towards the transmitting unconscious of the patient" (1912, p. 115). In Bion's (2013, p. 85) own words:

> Now I'd like just to mention the term 'free-floating attention.' The idea being that this is the term for the appropriate state of mind of the psychoanalyst. No countertransference, no nonsense of that sort, free-floating attention. Or, as I

have just put it, get rid of your memory and your desire, so that you expose yourself to the full treatment.

In the case of a young borderline woman, it began with a description of her verbal attacks and reviling the analyst the moment he opened the door to the waiting room:

> And she started by expressing her doubts about analysis—about me personally, about the relationships with father and much the same about her mother, what had been going on in the office, which made her have doubts about the efficacy of analysis—and all this between the waiting room and the couch. By the time she got to the couch, a woman of about thirty, she had really warmed to the job [audience laughter]. To say that she seemed to be hostile was putting it very mildly indeed. The abuse became much more violent and in the course of this, she slithered off the end of the couch onto the floor, appeared frightened by the fall, which led to still further abuse and violence. She then proceeded to slap herself on the thighs, still generally pouring out hatred against analysis, with a parting swipe at Kleinians generally, of which she regards me as one, but made it clear that this wasn't to the exclusion of all other forms of analysts; that the whole lot were equally bad, but some more equal than others.
> (Bion, 2013, pp. 81–82)

In the midst of all of the patient's hateful screaming and ranting, when he could not get a word in edgewise, Bion told his colleagues in Los Angeles that he literally could not hear himself think. He again presented himself as unable to understand the immediate dynamic meaning of what had been communicated to him.[11] Had his patient destroyed the communicative link with her analyst, so that no interpretation was possible, all to such an extreme extent that he had also lost a link with himself (Bion, 2013, p. 82)?

Bion then told his Los Angeles audience how profoundly lost he felt, despairing that he could make no satisfactory interpretation let alone think of an explanatory theory after the patient left the session. At this juncture, he invoked his newer ideas about memory and desire—if he approached such intensely grueling experiences, having exposed himself fully to the onslaught presented by the patient, how was he to make sense out of such a sheer cacophony? At this point, there were those in the audience, Ralph Greenson among them, who stated that perhaps such seriously disturbed patients presented "an untreatable situation by analysis" (Bion, 2013, p. 87).

But here Bion disagreed, subtly stating that his analysand was untreatable *at that moment*, and, as a result, he persisted with making sense out of what he had experienced as a "climactic affair." He viewed the analyst's task as to withstand such emotional assaults, as the patient relied on the analyst's capacity to make sense eventually of what was bothering her. So, with the patient's 'beta-screen' attack in mind, Bion thought after the session about what might be the invariant here, the unalterable something that remains undetectable in a variety of different situations.

After having recovered his capacity to think, he concluded that his analysand was dominated by feelings of omnipotence and greed of the breast because she created "such a situation in that session that you proceed to bother about that patient when you're supposed to be seeing another one" (Bion, 2013, p. 94). In different words, she attempted to appropriate more than her fair share of the analyst's time and mind. When the analyst was with his next patient, he found himself instead wondering if he should have called the police or hospital. After having felt the full force of the "ideo-motor activity," the analyst may have realized that the organizing fact was that he was not being fair to the rest of his practice, in effect cheating the next patient out of his full and undivided attention. Yet the nature of psychotic bombardments was such that, inevitably, there would have to be moments when such dramatic enactments remained unmetabolizable and thus uninterpreted. Bion (2013, p. 96) then linked this bombardment to a phantasy of omnipotence, a kind of visual "hallucination in reverse," when the patient attempted to force her way into the analyst's mind through the medium of the analyst's eyes; it was an attempt at a hostile takeover of his mind. In Bion's words (2013, p. 99), the patient in effect said: "Well, if you won't take in what I am telling you, I will jolly well make you."

In this example, Bion drew upon a notion of disciplined receptivity when he exposed himself to the full onslaught of the patient's violent projective evacuations, causing him momentarily to lose his mind before he was able to recover it. In essence, then, Bion deployed a wider notion of projective identification and countertransference, realizing that he needed to metabolize the beta-elements in order to make alpha-function sense of what had happened, which in turn would lead to a satisfactory and apposite interpretation.

Another outstanding feature of this presentation: Bion shared more of his own personal subjective reactions—and how he processed and understood them—with his audience of listeners, and these sorts of self-disclosures are of a kind that we do not have evidence for in previous presentations in London. Is it possible that he felt freer and more at ease in the springtime climate of Southern California?

Bion's Continued Treatment of the Stormy Borderline Patient

In the Buenos Aires seminars (fifth seminar) in 1968, Bion again presented the same borderline female patient that he had discussed the previous year in Los Angeles. We say this because of so many repeated details of the patient's make-up that sound so strikingly similar. In opting for the idea that this is the same patient, this case represents the longest single continuous case presentation recorded by Bion, something quite unusual insofar as he was generally disinclined to present extensively on his own case material.[12]

To set a brief context for Bion's 1968 case presentation in Buenos Aires: from the time of the founding of the Argentine Psychoanalytic Association in 1942, Melanie Klein's theories were studied, her papers were translated and published in Argentine analytic journals such as *Revista de Psicoanálisis* —and she generally had held sway for 30 years. Jewish refugees who fled Nazi Germany, such as Heinrich Racker, added distinction with their contributions to Argentinian psychoanalysis (Etchegoyen and Zysman, 2005). In 1949, at the IPA Congress in Zurich, Argentinian analysts were introduced to Melanie Klein as their group became a component society of the IPA. And, by the 1950s, London Kleinians such as Hanna Segal and Donald Meltzer went on teaching and supervision trips to Buenos Aires. Horacio Etchegoyen, like other Argentinian analysts, went to London for further training, and Etchegoyen himself had a re-analysis with Donald Meltzer in 1966. Other illustrious Argentinian analysts such as Pichon-Rivière also did a lot to promote Klein's work in Argentina thereafter.

There was a symposium on Melanie Klein held in 1961, honoring her life and contributions during Léon Grinberg's presidency of the Argentine group. Analysts from all over South America came to hear of how the Rio de la Plata group had integrated her findings into their own work (Etchegoyen and Zysman, 2005, p. 876). So much of this psychoanalytic work also occurred during a time of intense political turmoil—from the Peron dictatorship in the 1940s right up to the political dictatorship of General Onganía during the mid-1960s when students at the university—and this included members of the Psychology Department—were beaten during the brutal "night of the long sticks" (28 June 1966) by General Onganía's police thugs.

So, it would seem that Bion's arrival in Buenos Aires in July 1968 was amid both political turmoil and robust enthusiasm among his Argentine colleagues. He was regarded as one of the best-known members of the London Klein group, and analysts from far and wide attended his seminars in Buenos Aires. In contrast with the interested but somewhat critical reception Bion received in Los Angeles the year before, Argentinian analysts involved with Kleinian ideas gave Bion a warm and generous reception—as evinced by the variety and types of questions posed to him at the end of each seminar (Pistiner de Cortinas, in Bion, 2018, p. xxviii). In the wake of his 1968 visit to Buenos Aires, a group of well-known Argentinian analysts—Grinberg, Bianchedi, the Barangers and Mom—organized day-long seminars and supervisions, all to further discuss the clinical implications of Bion's new theoretical ideas (Pistiner de Cortinas, in Bion, 2018, p. xxx).

To Bion's treatment of the patient herself: from the outset of the analysis, there were profound difficulties in the form of two previous failed analyses that had left the patient in what she described as a "deplorable state." She insisted that Bion now treat her, and he asked the obvious question of why she thought he might do any better with him. Having given analysis a try, perhaps she should just set it aside. Bion confessed that perhaps another mistake, one of many, occurred when he talked with a member of her family—as the patient had merely written to Bion and requested an interview. One explosive reaction came with his suggesting the possibility of setting the idea of analysis aside—the patient became violent and even threatened suicide. It was either analysis with Bion—or death.[13] So, in this rather extorted atmosphere, he embarked on an analysis with her. As reported in Buenos Aires, all proceeded more or less smoothly for 3 months—she turned up, he interpreted, and the work went on (Bion, 2018, pp. 67–68).

Then, 3 months into the analysis, at one session, she mentioned that she had a urinary tract infection, something that would necessitate her going to the lavatory during her session. After her return, she seemed embarrassed, anxious—and the analyst wondered if she had to leave for "psychological reasons," a point to which she was initially non-responsive. This behavior continued, as did the interpretations of the patient's unconscious motives to continue to leave the consulting room. The analyst repeated and interpretatively addressed her need to leave—and all his interventions fell on non-responsive ears. Bion then became more specific: was there a 'voice' she was hearing when she left the room? She denied that, and it then seemed that he in turn became a bit insistent that she was hearing some sort of 'voice.' At this point, the patient became emotionally disruptive, denying the validity of what he was saying. The emotional atmosphere devolved into emotional recriminations and interpretations that left the patient feel misrelated to (Bion, 2018, pp. 69–70).

After the patient protested that the only 'voices' she heard were his and hers, she became quite emotionally distraught, as if she was being told that she was delusional and 'hearing voices.' She reproached the analyst: how could he think she was not in touch with 'reality'? He persisted with the interpretative line of her hearing some sort of 'voice,' and she in turn counter-provoked him, accusing him of not taking his work seriously. He then pointed out that she kept returning to the room even though she experienced him as an 'inadequate' analyst. He couldn't seem to say anything right, even about the transference. She then became so upset that she stood up and threatened him with her bag (Bion, 2018, pp. 69–70).

These episodes persisted, and finally the analyst concluded that her behavior was making analysis impossible. His tone sounded stern:

> I told her that she found it really difficult to put up with the fact that she owed something to the analytical interpretations and to myself as an analyst, but that, in truth, she owed part of her improvement to my insistence on keeping some sort of discipline.
>
> (Bion, 2018, p. 72)

He felt that his words were "unimportant or insignificant." He thought he was being put into a position of being just a 'bad analyst' who didn't know what he was doing. He reprised the 'angry voices in the room' interpretation, ones that seemed engaged in a heated argument that she was dramatizing.

Then, he was surprised that she calmed down for the moment. When he took a different interpretative line—that, from a time in infancy, she had been accustomed to hearing her parents argue—she commented on how much better things went when he analyzed her correctly. He should have done so earlier! To the analyst, it seemed that, even when he was right, he was still in error. She seemed "superior, hostile and contemptuous." There was always something to criticize. This kind of session alternated with the more usual sessions. When he then voiced the feeling that these were not the conditions under which analysis could continue, she became violently angry. More angry arguments ensued, as the analyst was again intermittently pummeled as the "inadequate partner." The analyst felt that he had had enough, and that what he termed his "minimum work conditions" had been violated.

But, after he unilaterally interrupted her analysis, she called him, sounding contrite, and asked him to take her back—to which he said, "I would think about that." Bion then offered to continue, but only if the necessary conditions to carry out the analysis remained in place—if these didn't obtain, the analysis would again be interrupted. When the analysis was restarted, the arguments resumed: when she reproached him and said he should act like a good analyst, Bion (2018, p. 73) retorted "that I had no obligation to be so as I was just forced to try to act like one." He tried then to get behind the noise of all the enactments—on the one hand, he needed to be informed about what was happening—and, yes, she was "anxious," but she couldn't decide whether to help him or to deceive him. He thought she was enacting something that was playing itself out in her mind (i.e., some sort of "internal argument").

The patient confirmed this and said her parents were quite unhappy and she had witnessed frequent quarrels. Such scenes seemed to have occurred before she herself could speak—in other words, quite early. It all led her to believe that she was a more trustworthy source than either her parents or her analyst. In the analyst's view, it put her in an 'anxious' spot because she would have rather been the child than the parent/analyst. The patient spitefully retorted that, if she had improved, it was no thanks to him, as he was a "terrible analyst." She went on to say that he had been angry and talked about putting an end to her analysis. The analyst thought that it was difficult for her to put up with the idea that she owed anything to her analysis and her analyst. He thought that part of her improvement resulted from his insistence on some sort of discipline. This became fodder for more argumentation on her part. He then interpreted that it was difficult for her to admit that she owed anything to her parents for being "tolerant." It was difficult for her to admit that she was indebted to some sort of discipline. How could she feel grateful for what she also despised (Bion, 2018, pp. 69–70)?

In contextualizing our assessment of Bion's difficult patient, it must be borne in mind that the analysis was conducted at the dawn of the time when borderline patients were being treated analytically. When American analysts such as Robert Knight (1953) first attempted to define a new kind of patient turning up in analysts' offices, there was considerable confusion and bewilderment about patients who presented with neurotic-sounding complaints but soon evinced transient psychotic episodes that resulted in a diagnostic muddle in the United States, with such terms as 'pseudo-neurotic schizophrenia' and 'borderland' patients being used before the term 'borderline psychosis' took root. It was only in 1966 that Otto Kernberg wrote the first of his many papers that attempted to define the syndrome and specify what altered treatment parameters might need to be in place in dealing with such patients.

Since Bion had already had considerable experience in analyzing psychotic patients in the 1950s, it would have seemed that treating borderlines would be less difficult. In fact, it was not the case. As we depicted in the initial presentation of this patient in Los Angeles, Bion found himself feeling overwhelmed by what, on the face of it, appeared to be a deteriorating situation. After 3 months of stable, on-going treatment, analysis became the scene of violent emotional disruptions, screaming, and menacing enactments. After the patient fell off the couch and reviled the analyst, he was left feeling profoundly worried and concerned about the patient's potential to harm herself once she set out on the streets of London. The shock, worry and concern led to further enactments on the analyst's part when he found himself feeling preoccupied with her personal safety while seeing his afternoon patients.

We start our analysis by emphasizing where Bion had put a foot right before reviewing how the analysis got off the track. His ideas about the abandonment of memory and desire stood him in good stead in the initial phases of treatment. It was clear that he could tolerate the 'full blast' of the patient's devaluations and sarcastic comments about how inadequate both the analyst and her family were in handling or understanding her "deplorable" state. He worked quickly with feeling overwhelmed and being unable to think, certainly a dramatic enactment of how the patient herself felt in her daily life. In digesting her violent enactment, he arrived at a definitory hypothesis—that she was intent on an omnipotent capture of his mind so that he might be as consumed by her as she herself no doubt felt by her own analysis.

In the midst of his working with her, as reported in the Buenos Aires Seminars, Bion (2018) was puzzled by her announcement of the need to go to the lavatory on account of her urinary tract infection. Here, the analyst proceeded as any analyst might—he wondered about the dynamic, unconscious meaning of her need to leave the room. This would have been standard technical fare for most analysts, and those trained in the Kleinian stream no doubt knew that Klein paid careful analytic attention to the child's occasional need to leave the playroom and use the lavatory. So, when the analyst posed the idea that perhaps there was a 'voice' involved in the patient's need to leave the room, she soon heard it as being told she was delusional and attempted to re-correct the perception—the only 'voices' she heard were his and hers. It was the analyst's persistence that escalated a tenuous situation—all before he switched his interpretative line and managed to reinstate a co-operative alliance when he wondered about her hearing her parents argue early in childhood. Switching interpretative tracks only momentarily saved the situation, and again the patient resumed her incessant attacks on the analyst as inadequate and off the mark.[14]

But perhaps one of the reasons that the analyst then found himself in a countertransference impasse—and this is only a conjecture—was that, sometime between having presented her in April 1967 and January 1968, when he relocated to live and work in Los Angeles, Bion (2018, p. 74) would have had to have at the back of his mind—as he said—that he would not be able to complete the analysis—and this for "non-analytical reasons." Since this was the case, it may have been one reason why he became so perseverative about the patient's need to leave the consulting room.

As it turned out, he would be leaving her—and the other analysands and supervisees working with him—when he decided to move to Los Angeles.

To the question of Bion's method of clinical inquiry: when he tried to make interpretations, an approximation of her current state of mind, he saw that, when his interventions did not alter the clinical situation, he was forced to make new ones and alter his understanding. Yet, in spite of this shift, it seemed that the patient perseverated in finding fault with his efforts, so that, whatever he said was 'wrong,' but, here, the patient herself anxiously vacillated, not knowing whether she wanted to help him to know what was going on or wanted to continue to deceive him. The analyst momentarily prevailed when he pointed out that something was being acted out, an 'internal argument' going on inside her. She momentarily confirmed this point, recalling her parents as unhappy early on and how they incessantly argued. She momentarily collaborated with him before moving back to her usual reproaching posture. Perhaps she needed to have it both ways, as if she was saying, "The law on non-contradiction does not apply to me." And all this is in the conscious realm. The patient could not tolerate the analyst being wrong and constantly reminded him of this. Yet she also could not tolerate his being right.

She caustically claimed that, if she had improved, it was no thanks to him. Perhaps, at this point, the patient was violently projecting her own inadequacy in coming to any understanding of the arguing internal couple, and, in addition, this projection was into reality as well. The analyst would not be able to complete the analysis because he was relocating to another city—hence his guilt about feeling he was also deserting her, perhaps another reason why he attempted to atone for his own felt sense of guilt and inadequacy by presenting her at two separate conferences.[15] The patient's chronic need to feel 'wronged' by those closest to her clearly grated on the analyst, and her reproaches got under his skin. So, in summary, it was *both* a negative therapeutic reaction *and* a countertransference impasse. The patient could and did continue her reproaches, project all sense of psychic agency elsewhere and say: "Look at what you have done to me." And, on this note, the analysis was discontinued.

Bion's Supervision of Horacio Etchegoyen's Analytic Case: Overview

During two meetings with members of the Argentine Psychoanalytic Association held in late July–early August 1968, Horacio Etchegoyen presented a case to Wilfred Bion, that of Mr. B, a single, 32-year-old Jewish male. Etchegoyen had just returned to Buenos Aires after his 1-year stay in London in 1966, where he himself was analyzed by Donald Meltzer. Mr. B's presenting problems were depression and drug involvement. The scant early history included leaving Europe in 1936 for Argentina during the Nazi period. His mother ran out of breast milk, and he was weaned at 2 months. He attended university but did not complete his degree; and he interrupted two previous analyses—one after 1 year, the second after 3 years. During his time with Etchegoyen, he lived with his elderly and well-off parents.

Mr. B initially appeared skeptical and wondered if his analyst was a novice. Was he the analyst's only patient? He frequently fell asleep during sessions. Bion interrupted early on and wondered if Mr. B's drug involvement might underlie a need to either misrepresent or distort his drug usage, so as to defend his habit. Perhaps he might put his drug-taking into the past to elude being asked about it in the present. Would the new analyst be any more suitable than the previous two and run out of milk early on?

Bion then suddenly wondered, almost out of the blue and amid these questions about the patient: was Mr. B saying, "I am cured, how about you?" Bion noted that he treated supervisions like a first session with a patient. One takes stock of what is going on, to decide if one can suitably understand and be of assistance.

Etchegoyen then introduced Mr. B's coprophilic dream material: in the first dream, he was served cat stew that smelled of feces in a restaurant. Mr. B felt disgusted and thought that somebody told him he should eat it and he would probably eat it if it was hare. The analyst wondered if this dream represented both a denial of analytic nutrition as well as a wish to feed himself. Bion expressed a number of reactions: is the patient now saying that he himself may be unsuitable for analysis (i.e., that he is the inadequate one)? Yet he could also have it both ways: yes, there is something wrong with him, but simultaneously maintain that the analyst and analysis are bad because they offer him such bad food. Bion expressed shock at the primitive level of the patient's material, sensing it was tied to early development.

In another session, Mr. B dreamed he was served a soda by a bar waiter that had a fly stuck in the cork part of the cap. He described his room at home as a mess and sometimes he would throw everything on the floor to tidy up. The analyst interpreted that Mr. B treated his own sessions similarly—he just throws everything about, expecting the analyst to be a maid that cleaned up after him. The patient merely expelled his dreams and provided few associations to them. Mr. B seemed to regard fecal matter as if it is a delicacy, yet complained to the waiter, who must be the analyst, that he feels forced to eat such rubbish.

Bion wondered about the patient's envy, a factor that would not let the analyst take any satisfaction in his work. He also wondered about what Mr. B was conscious of in terms of what led him to have such ideas. How did they originate? In Bion's words: "If the breast was so bad that it feeds with fecal matter, who placed that fecal matter there?" Perhaps Mr. B uses analysis to evade some deeper unconscious reality. The analysis itself appeared impeached because Mr. B felt that anyone who would tolerate this kind of filthy talk was also "dirty." Bion's surmise: "I think he is behaving as if he were associating freely and instead that he is defecating, in such a way that the analyst must pick up his excrements, he must make sense of what he the patient does." The mere evacuation of his anal dream life—with little expressed interest in trying to make meaning of it—represented an acting out, where the analyst was left to bear the interest in understanding what drove the patient's behavior. Mr. B distorted who was picking up after whom, so that he could feel that he was sorting out the mess and straightening things out and so could believe that he was healing himself.

Mr. B continued to present dreams, even ones from the previous analysis, such as one where a group of patients in front of a hospital ate human flesh out of a skull. Etchegoyen's reaction to Mr. B included a very rare example of a direct interaction: "You seem to identify eating somebody else's thoughts, discharging them as excrements and then eating them again as if they were your own and equate exquisite fecal matter with thinking." Mr. B's response: "Indeed, because now my mouth is watering."

To the extent that the analyst articulated Mr. B's state of mind, immediate contact was made that startled the patient. On this occasion, Mr. B felt he was having a fantasy, as if he was crying, having a sense of oppressive pressure in his chest and a lump in his throat. In short, he feared being abandoned by the analyst and plaintively said, "Don't leave me." Such moments were short-lived, brief interludes in his coprophilic evacuations. Bion was steadfast, however, in saying that Mr. B needed to be reminded that he was coming to analysis for something, not simply to malign the analyst. Yet, on the other side, Mr. B's envy might be such that, no matter how good the analysis was, he might very well color the analyst with his own envy-ridden brush. If the analyst was experienced as envious, it would be yet another reason to resort to self-feeding in his presence.

In Etchegoyen's next presentation to Bion a few days later, there was some material from Mr. B's analysis some 9 months after the initial presentation. Some progress had been made—the patient attended his sessions more regularly, yet worried about his capacity to co-operate. The content of the dream material shifted slightly—his anal preoccupations now manifested as an anxiety about keeping himself clean. It seemed that Mr. B required constant monitoring out of an inability to take care of himself. Mr. B still evacuated his dreams, but still showed little interest in understanding what drove his states of mind—he appeared as a small child soiling himself, someone who felt inadequate and ill prepared to wipe himself and stay clean. These anal fears and anxieties showed up strongly in the weekend material, replete with themes of feces and urine, prostitution and excessive consumption of drugs and alcohol.

Mr. B continued to rubbish interpretations—analysis was like a toilet he shat into. Yet, as Bion wryly noted, since defecation is a lifetime proposition, the patient could easily feel persecuted by its repetitive aspect, so that a correct and needed interpretation might also feel like being fed his own excrements by the analyst. On the other hand, the analyst's separate recognition of Mr. B's envious attacks also reflected a growing neediness and sense of his feeling humiliated by the analyst's separate mind. Envy also figured in Mr. B's intermittent problems in paying for treatment. After all, in previous treatment, he claimed to have no money and proceeded to interrupt his analysis. Problems with payment were thus linked to manic self-cure and the need to flee analysis.

Bion then summarized Mr. B's state of mind: (1.) that no matter how bad Mr. B is, the analyst must not abandon him, and (2.) it is as if the analyst must remain unconscious of his willingness to help him. Mr. B was like a baby who wanted to take things from the breast, but not acknowledge or look after it. But the question remained: how would the analyst speak to the defensive enclave embedded in the enactment? In Bion's way of putting it: "we must find a language that speaks louder than the action which speaks louder than words."

Mr. B also appeared inadequate and immature, donning the persona of a rather inept bumbler, as he made excuses for not being able to pay his monthly analytic bill in a timely fashion. Behind this façade lay contempt for the analyst, someone who Mr. B also thought didn't need his money. So momentary inadequacy resulted in still more denigration of the analyst. The irrational reasoning? Since the analyst was experienced as passing off rubbishy stuff, why should the patient have to pay for it? Yet the patient also continued an analysis he found to be an experience of some value.

When a corrupt dream figure appeared arm in arm with two prostitutes, Etchegoyen interpreted Mr. B's prostituting the analysis. The two prostitutes represent Mr. B's analysts—past and present—and, at a deeper analytic level, two analytic breasts that were degraded. Again, there was 'fecalization' of the breast and idealization of his bottom, and it is this that the patient fed from. Bion emphasized Mr. B's feelings of inadequacy—the end of analysis would terrorize him as "there wouldn't be anyone else to clean him." Bion then raised a fundamental point: how does the analyst ascertain whether he is accurately approximating the patient's own model of mind and not subtly imposing his own model of the patient's mind on his analysand? Mr. B felt hopeless and helpless in his contact with others. Taking the dream figures as various self-representations, Mr. B falsely congratulated himself for his self-control, or the control over his impulses—which was inadequate. It was the analyst who was made to appear unpleasant and dirty. Yet, despite these denigrating projections, a somewhat relieved Mr. B had come to feel more reliant on his analysis—and his dependency needs now appeared as a fear of a consuming voraciousness. All the patient knew was that he wanted more and more—even though he did not know what of. In Bion's words, it was the emphasis of quantity over quality—the patient just knows that he needs 'more' of something without thinking any further about it, whether it be more milk or more analytic sessions. In Bion's words, "The analyst can offer him good interpretations, but he can't resolve what he didn't get in the past."

Bion also raised the issue of a coprophilic couple—a father and mother "who have a relationship in which they mutually defecate and urinate on each other." It is as if Mr. B felt himself to be a shitty by-product of two fecal parents. The transference version of the two 'fecalized' parents is the analytic couple who maintain a dirty, filthy conversation where they pollute one another. Like mother and father, patient and analyst merely shit into each other; in the transference, a fecalized analyst and patient can only produce more waste. Again, in the last analysis, it was the analyst's responsibility to report back to the patient what he had been able to ascertain—namely, that another version of a fecalized partnership was a *folie à deux* aspect of patient and analyst merely rubbishing each other.

Bion's Supervision of Horacio Etchegoyen's Analytic Case: A Clinical Analysis

Bion the Clinician

Reading Bion's supervisions, I find him surprising, illuminating and continually helpful in my clinical work. I find it interesting that Bion, the highly innovative theoretician, is actually a traditionalist in his clinical stance. He believes that his job as a psychoanalyst is to provide understanding in words in the service of therapy. He presumes an established set of psychoanalytic understandings and procedures (explicitly Freud and Klein). Within this framework, his imagination is free to generate his surprising, illuminating and ultimately fruitful insights. They are based in the detail of a unique clinical situation, and yet I find them applicable to many of my patients, especially the recalcitrant ones. His insights enable me to speak to my patient where previously I had felt tongue-tied. Bion is focused on articulating the truth of that which is at hand at that moment. Within the at-hand—or manifest—lies the potential for therapy. When Bion speaks, his proximate aim is further understanding; his final aim is therapy. All this in his idiosyncratic brand of colloquial English. His criteria of selection and engagement, whether with patient or supervisee, derive from therapeutic usefulness. The most abstract of theoreticians, he is the most practical of clinicians.

I turn to the supervision of Horacio Etchegoyen's patient to illustrate some of the distinctive features of Bion's clinical stance.

Caution and Imagination

Bion's first intervention (2018, pp. 98 ff.) comes early, after the analyst's brief description of the patient's history and Etchegoyen's first consultation. Bion here demonstrates his capacity for great caution in claiming any understanding, on the one hand, and his capacity for imaginative leaps, on the other. Of all the reasons the patient gives for seeking a third analysis, Bion selects the patient's statement that he used to take drugs. This would make him feel uncomfortable, he says; he would even wonder if the patient is telling the truth or not ("I used to, but not now"). If he is a liar, then this is a serious case. While noting that Melanie Klein thought the prognosis when analyzing a liar was poor, he is not sure. He thinks, rather, it is really difficult to tell whether someone is lying or misjudging a situation, or whether it is a case of lying or splitting. In a couple of sentences, he opens up a spectrum rather than an either/or view of truth and lies. Bion moves on to select another fact: the patient's doubts about the analysis. He asks: "Who is he comparing the analyst with?" It would appear to be with his previous analysts. However, Bion goes on, "I would find this suspicious, and I would wonder if I am not really suitable, just like his previous analysts or even his mother who ran out of milk." Then comes the leap: "In this way, the patient seems to be saying 'I am cured, and how about you?'"

My own immediate reaction was: "Where on earth did Bion get that from?!" I will return to this. Bion then ends his intervention with a seamless transition to his practical aims. Before the first hour is up, Bion or any other analyst has to decide whether he will accept the patient. "This is a basic decision because you don't really know anything about the patient and you must decide if you can do something for him or not."

Never at Rest

Bion's next two interventions (2018, pp. 100, 102 ff.) relate to sessional material. The most striking feature of his clinical thinking is something best captured by the phrase "never at rest," a phrase I borrow from Richard Westfall's (1981) title of a biography of Newton. Bion never rests with one observation or thought; he immediately moves on to a question, then on to a tentative answer, which leads to a further idea—all this held in suspension—until he reaches a formulation which has grown out of the multiple linkages he's been making in the process. The formulation, typically in the transference, fits the unique clinical situation and informs what Bion might say to the patient. He also offers clinical generalizations. Earlier, we had truth and lies on a spectrum. Here, we get a lengthy exposition of why he considers it important, in certain situations, to take up conscious material.

At this point, Bion has heard detailed sessional material, including two dreams, where the manifest content is about the patient being given fecal matter to eat. While saying he thinks Etchegoyen's interpretations of the anal material are correct, Bion hears the material on the dynamic register: that of change and no change. He observes that something has changed in the analysis: the patient now admits that something is wrong with him, which means that the analyst is now in a position to do something for him (in contrast to the consultation where everyone else was unsuitable). This is progress, but in what direction? Yet, Bion notes, something else has not changed: "the analyst remains as bad as he was before, he offers terrible food, as the cat's faecal matter." All of this leads Bion to wonder whether this is the patient's way of reacting to his own jealousy and envy.

I now quote at length from his next intervention (2018, pp. 102–103):

> Here, again, we can appreciate some analytic progress ... it is very important for the analyst to realize this, because such an envious patient as this one won't let you get much satisfaction from your work ... we need to have a clear idea of the patient's progress and what direction that progress is taking. ... In this context I would offer the patient an interpretation with this aim, saying: "Well, you seem to agree with my interpretations, that they are more or less accurate, but what leads you to have these types of ideas?" (regarding faecal matter).

Then comes Bion's original generalization:

> it is not just psychopathology that concerns us, but also the external, real events ... very often the patient won't tell us exactly what is happening to him, what is conscious and known by him. Yet some ... patients, and this may be one of them, use analysis to evade reality and to take shelter in their own psychopathology. It is at that point that you will want not just to elucidate the unconscious

material, but also to analyse what is conscious, what is known by the patient. I would then say: "You must be really affected by the analysis, you must believe people who speak this way are really dirty people, people who speak about the kind of things that would be equivalent to what you would be eating, if, in truth, you ate cat's meat and faecal matter."

Note that Bion's explicit aim is to keep the patient in the immediate world of the analysis instead of letting him escape to a supposedly deeper world. Bion goes on to address the theme of the patient acting out in the analysis. Again, he agrees with Etchegoyen's interpretation that the patient appears to engage with his dreams, but actually does not—he makes a mess. And again, he goes beyond the acting-out to specify how the patient uses the analysis to evade the reality of being in the analysis.

I agree that the patient is using the analysis itself to do some acting out. I think he is behaving as if he were associating freely and instead of that he is defecating, in such a way that the analyst must pick up his excrements, he must make sense of what the patient does. However, there is a trap in this, as the patient will pretend that he is the one who fixes things and makes them orderly, picking them up from the floor when, in truth, what he does is drop them on the floor and make a mess. He pretends to be healing himself and that if something goes wrong the analyst is to blame.

Here we have got to a point where Bion's initial out-of-the-blue "I am cured, and how about you?" intuition reappears in a formulation of how the patient cures himself. The question is less where Bion got the intuition from and more how he uses the intuition. He holds it in suspension, together with other observations, until, at some point, the clinical material provides sufficient evidence to connect that intuition with others. Bion's formulation—namely, "He pretends to be healing himself, and if something goes wrong the analyst is to blame"—brings together a number of themes he has picked up from the beginning: truth and lies, change and no change, envy. His aim throughout has been to establish a real conversation with the patient rather than the appearance of one.

Use and Misuse of Theory

Typically, Bion does not refer to theories of Freud or Klein, and least of all to his own. In the *Buenos Aires Seminars*, as indeed in other supervisions, he repeatedly warns against the therapeutic misuses of theory.

When Bion is asked by Etchegoyen what he thinks of the patient's "thought disorder," Bion says: "In this case, again, I would insist—I would not try to think about the thought disorder or other psychoanalytic theories about the patient. I would think that the analyst cannot speak with the patient—and vice versa" (2018, pp. 119–120).

Bion is aware that the patient himself has given his inability to think as a reason for seeking the analysis. But, Bion says,

> in reality you would not know what this means ... you would wait for the meaning to appear at any moment. What the analyst should be capable of seeing is what is happening, which is the distortion in the relationship between the patient and himself.
>
> (p. 120)

I select one more quotation, because it illustrates Bion's conviction that it is dangerous to get into the habit of making interpretations because we have heard them from our own analyst or have read about them.

> This is obviously very different than making an interpretation because you have heard it during the session. I am sure that there is a big difference in the impact and penetrative quality of the interpretation if the patient feels that it is personal to him.
>
> (p. 115)

Denouement

Bion's clinical style is personal and reserved. It is personal in that, when he speaks to supervisee or patient, his voice is uniquely his own. Yet this has nothing to do with his personality—in the sense of his own desires or group affiliations. His sole aim is to understand the patient. The truth can be reached only through its manifestation in a particular moment in the analysis, provided there is genuine contact between patient and analyst. Recourse to theory is dangerous because it freezes time and it deadens the contact necessary for the emergence of the patient's personal truth. Evasion of contact is lethal for the same reason. Bion shows an acute awareness of the variety of specific ways in which the patient evades what he supposedly is coming to the analyst for. He is immensely acute in spotting psychic escape routes. If not spotted, such evasions result in a clinical situation I think most of us are familiar with: where many things appear to be changing, yet we feel fundamentally nothing is changing.

Conclusion—Bion's Method of Clinical Inquiry

How would we characterize how Bion worked clinically or supervised in 1967–1968? Is there anything distinctive about the way he worked in 1967–1968? We take up the evolution of Bion's method of clinical inquiry during this period.

First of all, he formalized what had long been one main point of orientation for his clinical work: all psychoanalytic observations were made in the present moment. Bion's (1967) existential approach did not tie current behavior, phantasies and emotions to an early infantile or childhood history. This was now Bion's defining analytic/technical signature, and, unlike some members of the London Klein group, he did not tie current transference conflicts to past infantile states or early states of unconscious phantasy.

Likewise, Bion expanded the notion of projective identification in a communicative as well as an evacuative direction, looking at the organizing impact that such 'words-as-actions' had on the analyst, both in terms of what he or she could know and interpret as well as how it impacted his or her own countertransference. Rather than discuss psychotic patients per se, he also now articulated the dynamics of the near-psychotic or difficult-to-treat patient in the borderline–narcissistic spectrum. Linked to a broader understanding of countertransference, Bion more fully embraced multiple communicative possibilities to expand the meaning from either side of the couch—for instance, in a more dexterous use of his own countertransference, where he drew upon the older Freud–Klein view of the analyst's disturbed emotional state as reflecting some residual 'personal interference' on the analyst's conflictual side, emphasizing more the unconscious-to-unconscious communications that, via projective identification, could also be informing.

Finally, during this period, particularly as the analyst's focus remained on the patient's internal, subjective, phantasmic experience, there was at times a certain strident attitude, regarding himself during this time as the sole epistemological agent in the consulting room, sometimes appearing to make intuitive clinical leaps, as he did when he supervised Etchegoyen in 1968. His analytic aim was to capture actively the unconscious in words, sometimes those actions that spoke louder than words. With severely compromised psychotic and near-psychotic patients, the analyst bore the curiosity to know the patient's enduring psychic reality, remaining the sane, meaning-seeking agent who observed the near-psychotic's attacks on his own mind that were, in turn, projected violently into the figure of the analyst.

Lastly, he expanded his method of clinical inquiry to now include how he went about the process of clinical inquiry in seminar situations. Here, he steadfastly refused to present his work in any sort of a way as a 'defining technique,' but insisted that his colleagues evolve their own method of clinical inquiry in response to how they understood how he worked both as an analyst and supervisor. So, for instance, he interrogated the 'question-and-answer' format, insisting that his colleagues take responsibility for their own learning, a principle that harkened back to his group work days. Likewise, he also made his own work the subject of self-inquiry with the audiences with whom he worked. With the case of the borderline patient in 1967–1968, he discussed his own failures of understanding, a form of inquiry that would continue intermittently for the rest of his life. Think here of his final paper, "Making the Best of a Bad Job," where he discussed one of his patients who committed suicide (Bion, 1979). It seemed that Bion deployed the seminar format as one where open-ended questions could be asked of either the clinical presenter, the clinical material or the facilitator himself. It was Bion's aim to extend the reaches of psychoanalytic inquiry into the realm of the unknown, towards which he maintained an attitude of open-ended curiosity.

Notes

1 While there had been some interest among American psychoanalysts in the treatment of psychotic patients, there also seem to exist a division between east-coast ego psychological approaches (e.g., Jacobson, 1967), as well as Sullivanian-derived models (Searles, 1965), and west-coast emphases derived from the work of Ernst Federn and his notions of 'ego deficiency' in schizophrenic patients (Wexler, 1965). There was no mention of any of these approaches in the audience queries put to Bion in the *Los Angeles Seminars*.
2 Having heard Bion's work at previous IPA Congresses, Grinberg had already formed a small study group in advance of Bion's coming to Buenos Aires, so that some of the analysts who came to hear Bion's work in 1968 were already familiar with his as well as other Kleinian ideas (Grinberg, 2000, in Bion Talamo, Borgogno and Merciai, p. xx).
3 Bion outraged some of the analysts in Topeka attending his second paper, "On a Quotation from Freud," when, in the midst of speaking extemporaneously (rather than reading from a prepared text), he said: "I want to say something which sounds like saying something for the sake of saying it; and perhaps it is, I don't know: 'Bloody cunt. Bloody vagina'" (Bion, 1977, p. 308). While he went on to discuss the differences between spontaneous and clinical anatomical language, Roy Menninger, who had been in attendance, was so flabbergasted by Bion's manner of speaking at this particular point that he abruptly got up and left the lecture (Bennett Roth, personal communication).
4 At one point, at the New York seminars in 1977, when he had already received and responded to a number of questions attempting to draw him out on the theme of memory and desire, Bion became annoyed when pressed further on the same issue: "When I feel a pressure—for example, 'I'd better get prepared in case you ask me some question'—I say—'To hell with it; I am not going to look this stuff in Freud or anywhere else, or even in my past statement—I'll put up with it.' But of course I am asking you to put up with it too—an impromptu affair of this sort" (Bion, 2014, Vol. 10, p. 282).
5 Bion was invited in 1968 to be the guest of honor at a cabaret show hosted by the Argentine Society's training committee. In the midst of it all, Bion recounts how he was treated: "The dancing and singing were, to my eye and ear, pretty usual folk lore though with great verve and in a pervading spirit of good humour and kindliness. I was placed in a kind of throne—the Royal Box—which I tried to occupy with proper dignity" (Bion. 2014, Vol. 2, p. 174).
6 Bion addressed group themes throughout the Italian seminars (e.g., Seminars 8 and 9), and one poignant example came with a questioner who felt encouraged to express a "wild thought": "But when I decided to express my thought, I felt anxious about the dependence and loneliness that could arise if someone were to listen to me and then go away" (Bion, 2014, Vol. 9, p. 174). Bion interacted directly with the questioner, who seemed to express the sentiments of the group. Is the listener just going to be 'better off' staying quiet and recover his 'capacity for internal listening'? He also took up the 'alone and dependent' position, saying that it is fundamental to life itself—even before language. Yet it is also fundamental "to be able to communicate with the most important person in this context, namely ... yourself." Bion's efforts took root with his Italian listeners and, within a few years of his 1977 visit, there would be a long line of Bionian-inspired publications, beginning with an entire issue in 1981 of the *Revista di Psicoanalisi*, where Italian analysts published their commentaries on Bion's ideas.
7 In the fourth seminar in Los Angeles, Bion (2013, pp. 81–91) gave an extensive report of his analytic work with a young female analysand of about 30 years of age. I have made the case that Bion (2018, pp. 67–81) continued the presentation of this quite problematic patient in the fifth seminar in Buenos Aires on account of the quite striking similarities—for instance, the details provided about the patient's family background

and two previously failed analyses (Aguayo, pp. xxv, in Bion, 2018). Some of these themes developed there have been taken up by Eshel (2022).

8 Etchegoyen's extensive presentation of a muddled narcissistic patient with coprophilic features was taken up by Bion (2018, pp. 85–111) for supervisory comment in both the sixth and seventh seminars in Buenos Aires. The same patient was the subject of a later publication by Etchegoyen (1982), in which, in spite of the fact that he commented on the same dream material presented in 1968, he did not mention his supervision with Bion. In an interview at the IPA Congress in Buenos Aires with Samuel Zysman, one of Etchegoyen's closest collaborators, he revealed that Etchegoyen had never mentioned to him the supervision with Bion (Zysman, 2017). Etchegoyen's (1991) supervision with Bion was also not mentioned in his *magnum opus* on psychoanalytic technique. However, months before he passed away on 2 July 2016, when interviewed by Lia Pistiner de Cortinas, Etchegoyen was asked what he remembered of Bion in 1968. He said: "I don't really remember the patient, but having been supervised by Bion was a very interesting and extraordinary experience" (Bion, 2018, p. xxx).

9 In Bion's supervisory comments about another adult psychotic male, who had made a severe attempt on his own life, the analysts in Los Angeles were keen to hear what Bion might say. The patient had engaged in self-endangering and self-mutilatory behavior, having cut himself seriously and having discovered bleeding profusely in his bath. In agreeing to treat such patients, Bion put forth a position quite familiar to his London Kleinian colleagues: "I think that there's something about the whole subject which means that whether we like it or not, we shall be *bound* to have to treat patients of this kind. And whether there's any question of being able to do anything for them or not, nevertheless we'll have to deal with them" (Bion, 2013, p. 59).

His (2013, p. 60) point was clear: he insisted that analysts extend the range of the types of patients they treated. While Bion's ideas about treating psychotics would have hardly surprised his London Kleinian colleagues, his use of new conceptual language would have appeared idiosyncratic to them—for example, statements such the patient's violent projection of his "'beta-element,' these elements of the personality which are just not perceptible to us in the ordinary way, even if we have a good deal of intuition and understanding, a good deal of experience in dealing with human beings, but which are nevertheless brought into the sphere of our own activities by virtue of the fact that we are psychoanalysts" (2013, p. 61).

Bion's London colleagues, however, would have been quite familiar with his use of part-object, symbolic anatomical interpretative language, something that Bion demonstrated in his interpretative remarks about the suicidal patient: "I would have said that, 'You feel that you have something very bad inside you. And although you describe this as something which is outside of you and slashes your wrists and arms and so forth, actually I think it is felt to be an object which is inside you, which has no regard for your personality or even your anatomy, but breaks out by cutting you from inside outwards. ... You are afraid here, of being surrounded by an extremely cutting, painful, dangerous excretion; urine, in which it cuts into you, and destroys you, because it is such very, very bad stuff; it's nothing good, it is something very *bad*'" (Bion, 2013, p. 62).

London Kleinians, such as Segal (1964) or Meltzer (1967), would have been quite familiar with this staple of the Kleinian interpretative method, as it dates back to Klein's early work on unconscious phantasy and how it manifests in various forms of bodily expression, such as when the child's various sadistic attacks—oral, anal and urethral—are directed against the depriving breast (1932, p. 129).

10 Bion had already given an impromptu talk on memory and desire at the British Psychoanalytical Society on 16 June 1965. However, this less well-known version remained in the Archives of the British Society until it was rediscovered in an audio-taped form by Joanne Halford, the Society's archivist in 2014. The full text of this paper can be found

in Bion (2014, Vol. 6, pp. 3–17). While this talk created no noticeable stir in London in 1965—as British analysts were quite familiar by this point with working analytically in the 'here and now'—it was received quite differently in Los Angeles, where the traditional practice of presenting background historical material of patients in analysis still obtained. There were no such reconstructed 'background' histories in any of Bion's Los Angeles presentations, and, no doubt, this form of existential presentation, one that started from recent session work with the patient, may have struck a discordant note with some of Bion's American listeners. As published in the Los Angeles-based journal *Psychoanalytic Forum* in 1967, "Notes on Memory and Desire" astonished some readers, bewildered others and became the object of intense scrutiny and criticism from some of its five commentators (Bion, 1967, pp. 274–288, 2013, pp. 139–149). There were no clinical examples in either the 1965 talk in London or the 1967 "Notes."

11 Bion's mode of presentation drew his listeners in with more of a rhetorical rather than a clinical emphasis. What would his analytic listeners think if they were in his place? This kind of borderline/psychotic presentation is exactly what he had outlined in *Learning from Experience* (1962): this is a psychotic expression of "word-as-actions" in which a "beta-screen" of screams, defensive maneuvers and reproaches are meant to induce or evoke a strong negative countertransference response in the analyst. The beta-screen is so forcefully expressed that it disrupts the analyst's alpha-function in the contact barrier, leading to its potential reversal. This form of unconscious-to-unconscious communication organized the analyst in a role-responsive direction, which in this instance led to the momentary experience of an inability to think or formulate a response (Bion, 1962, pp, 24–25).

12 Besides the patient's two previously failed treatments, Bion made mention of having had contact with the patient's family prior to the beginning of her analysis. He made mention of her emotional violence and suicidality from the beginning of treatment. She also insisted on his analyzing her and, in his words, "reiterated her intention to commit suicide if I did not accept her as a patient" (Bion, 2018, p. 68).

13 From the time of Robert Knight's (1953) description of what came to be known as 'borderline patients,' this American interest crossed the Atlantic and garnered some attention from London Kleinians, such as Herbert Rosenfeld. Bion's (1959) interest in borderline psychotic patients began with his observation of their propensity for "attacks on anything that links one subject to another" (2014, Vol. 6, p. 138). These were patients who didn't seem to suffer their experiences, but rather imposed their disturbances—at times rather violently—on the analyst. Bion (1965) also described a borderline psychotic as someone who could have a breakdown during the course of treatment. Friends and family start noticing how strange and bizarre their behavior can be, creating a kind of situation that would make any analyst think about whether he or she had done anything to contribute to a worsening and deteriorated situation (Bion, 2014, Vol. 5, p. 132).

14 The patient's need to render the analyst's understanding 'inadequate' would have long been familiar to Bion. His colleague, Roger Money-Kyrle (1956) had written about "normal countertransference" in which the patient induced disturbances of thought in the analyst; it only became problematic when such responses went undetected and unmetabolized by the analyst, hence opening the door for the analyst's momentary disturbance to be in turn inflicted upon the patient. Money-Kyrle also defined the normal reparative parental 'functions' carried by the analyst and, insofar as he or she performed his or her normal metabolic function, the analytic work went well. But, when the patient succeeded in infecting the analyst's mind, this projective identification could induce disturbed emotions in the analyst, which, if unchecked, could in turn re-disturb the patient. Money-Kyrle (1956, pp. 362–363) gave a clinical illustration of countertransference disturbance, when he felt that he had introjected a patient's illness in the form of feeling robbed of his wits by him. His patient arrived at his session not being able to work in his office, feared being in an accident on the way to his session and despised himself for

being useless. Whatever understanding the analyst offered fell on deaf ears—and the analyst reflected privately that he had been reduced to the state of "useless vagueness" and that the patient had "put him on the mat," "asking questions and rejecting the answers the way his legal father did." The patient, on the other hand, identified with the critical interrogating father and attacked his "impotent self" projected into the analyst. But, ultimately, for any clarity to emerge, the analyst had to differentiate between his own sense of inadequacy and the "patient's contempt for his impotent self." Money-Kyrle (ibid.) here directly buttressed his point by referring to Bion's (1955) work of making these types of discriminations an "important part of the capacity to use one's countertransference in the interests of analysis."

15 This case seems to have made an indelible impression on Bion because he appeared to speak about her again—years later—in the Italian seminars (number 4, 13 July 1977; 2014, Vol. 9, p. 138): "A greedy patient can behave in such a way that when his hour is over, you are so bothered about what he will get up to next that you take up the next patient's time in thinking about the previous patient."

References

Aguayo, J. (2011). 'The Role of the Patient's Remembered History and Unconscious Past in the Evolution of Betty Joseph's "Here and Now" Clinical Technique (1959–1989),' *International Journal of Psychoanalysis*, 92: 1117–1136.

Bion, W.R. (1951). 'Letter to Francesca Bion.' In The Complete Works of W.R. Bion, Vol. 2. London: Routledge, p. 174.

Bion, W.R. (1955). 'Language and the Schizophrenic.' In M. Klein, P. Heimann and R. Money-Kyrle (Eds.), *New Directions in Psycho-Analysis* (London: Tavistock), pp. 220–239.

Bion, W.R. (1959). 'Attacks on Linking.' *International Journal of Psychoanalysis*, 40: 308–315.

Bion, W.R. (1962). *Learning from Experience* (London: Heinemann; reprinted in paperback, London: Maresfield Reprints, 1984).

Bion, W.R. (1965). *Transformations* (London: Heinemann).

Bion, W.R. (1967). 'Notes on Memory and Desire.' *The Psychoanalytic Forum*, 2: 272–273, 279–290.

Bion, W.R. (1975). 'Brasilia Clinical Seminars.' In W.R. Bion and F. Bion (Eds.). (1987). *Clinical Seminars and Four Papers* (Abingdon: Fleetwood Press).

Bion, W.R. (1977). 'On a Quotation from Freud.' In *Borderline Personality Disorders: The Concept, the Syndrome, the Patient* (New York: International Universities Press), pp. 306–311.

Bion, W.R. (1979). 'Making the Best of a Bad Job.' *Bulletin of the British Psycho-Analytical Society*, 20. Reprinted in *Clinical Seminars and Four Papers* (1987).

Bion, W.R. (1980). *Bion in New York and Sao Paulo* (Perthshire: Clunie Press).

Bion, W.R. (1990). *Brazilian Lectures* (London: Karnac).

Bion, W.R. (1994). Brasilia Clinical Seminars. In W.R. Bion and F. Bion (Eds.). (1987). *Clinical Seminars and Four Papers* (Abingdon: Fleetwood Press).

Bion, W.R. (2013). *Wilfred Bion's Los Angeles Seminars and Supervision*. Edited by. J. Aguayo and B. Malin (London: Karnac).

Bion, W.R. (2014). The Complete Works of W.R. Bion, 16 Volumes. Edited by C. Mawson and F. Bion (London: Karnac).

Bion, W.R. (2018). *Bion in Buenos Aires*. Edited by J. Aguayo, L. Pistiner de Cortinas and A. Regeczkey (London: Karnac).

Bion, W.R. and Bion, F. (Eds.), (1987). *Clinical Seminars and Four Papers* (Abingdon: Fleetwood Press).

Eshel, O. (2022). 'Bion's Long Road towards Intuiting the Patient's Suffering: "Theoretical" vs. "Clinical" Bion.' Presentation at the New Center for Psychoanalysis, 22 February 2022.

Etchegoyen, R.H. (1982). 'The Relevance of Here and Now Transference Interpretation for the Reconstruction of Early Psychic Development.' *International Journal of Psychoanalysis*, 63: 65–75.

Etchegoyen, R.H. (1991). *Fundamentals of Psychoanalytic Technique* (New York: Brunner/Mazel).

Etchegoyen, H. and Zysman, S. (2005). 'Melanie Klein in Argentina: Beginnings and Development,' *International Journal of Psychoanalysis*, 86: 869–894.

Freud, S. (1912). 'Recommendations for Physicians on the Psychoanalytic Method of Treatment.' In *The Standard Edition of the Complete Psychological Works of Sigmund Freud*, Vol. 12, pp. 109–120.

Grinberg, L. (2000). 'Foreword.' In *W.R. Bion—Between Past and Future*. Edited by P. Bion-Talamo, F. Borgogno, and S. Merciai (London: Karnac).

Grinberg, L., Sor, D., and Tabak de Bianchedi, E. (1975). *Introduction to the Work of Bion* (Perthshire: Clunie, Roland Harris Educational Trust).

Hartocollis, P. (Ed.). (1977). *Borderline Personality Disorders. The Concept, the Syndrome, the Patient* (New York: International Universities Press).

Hinshelwood, R.D. (1994). 'Foreword.' In G. Bléandonu (1994). *Wilfred Bion, His Life and Works, 1897–1979* (London: Free Association Books), pp. ix–xii.

Jacobson, E. (1967). *Psychotic Conflict and Reality (The Freud Anniversary Lectures)* (New York: International Universities Press).

Joseph, B. (1971). 'A Clinical Contribution to the Analysis of a Perversion,' *International Journal of Psychoanalysis*, 52: 441–449.

Joseph, B. (1975). 'The Patient Who Is Difficult to Reach.' In *Psychic Equilibrium and Psychic Change*. Edited by M. Feldman and E.B. Spillius (1989). (London: Routledge), pp. 75–87.

Kernberg, O. (1975). *Borderline Conditions and Pathological Narcissism* (New Jersey: Aronson).

Klein, M. (1932). *The Psychoanalysis of Children*. In (1975). The Writings of Melanie Klein, Vol. 2. Edited by R. Money-Kyrle et al. (London: Hogarth).

Knight, R.P. (1953). 'Borderline States.' In R.M. Loewenstein (Ed.), Drives, Affects, Behavior (New York: International Universities Press), pp. 203–215

Meltzer, D. (1967). *The Psychoanalytic Process* (London: Heineman). Reproduced in 2008 by Karnac, The Harris-Meltzer Trust Series.

Money-Kyrle, R. (1956). 'Normal Countertransference and Some of its Deviations.' *International Journal of Psychoanalysis*, 37: 360–366.

Pistiner de Cortinas, L. (2018). 'Introduction.' In W.R. Bion, *Bion in Buenos Aires*. Edited by. J. Aguayo, L. Pistiner de Cortinas and A. Regeczkey (London: Karnac).

Searles, H.F. (1965). *Collected Papers on Schizophrenia and Related Subjects* (New York: International Universities Press).

Segal, H. (1964). *An Introduction to the Work of Melanie Klein* (Basic Books: New York).

Westfall, R. (1981). *Never at Rest: A Biography of Isaac Newton* (Cambridge: Cambridge University Press).

Wexler, M. (1965). 'Working through in the Therapy of Schizophrenia.' *International Journal of Psychoanalysis*, 46: 279–286.

Zysman, S. (2017). Interview Conducted by Joseph Aguayo and Sira Dermen, Buenos Aires, 1 August 2017.

6
The Brazilian Clinical Seminars

Nicola Abel-Hirsch

In the 1970s, Bion (now in his 70s) conducted clinical seminars in Brazil. Fifty-two of these were published in The Complete Works of W.R. Bion series (2014) and are the focus of this chapter. Further seminars have since been transcribed and can be found in *Bion in Brazil*, Vol. 1 (Junqueira de Mattos, de Mattos Brito, & Levine, 2017) and *Bion in Brazil*, Vol. 2 (Levine, de Mattos Brito, & Junqueira de Mattos, 2024).

What can we learn of Bion's method of clinical inquiry from his supervisions? Analysts, because their work is so intensive, only have a limited number of patients during their working lifetimes, and, consequently, we only hear about a small number of patients in their presentations and writing. In contrast, Bion's clinical seminars give access to a breadth of experience relating to his clinical method: we hear his thinking about the many different patients presented in the seminars and can listen for patterns in his clinical method that emerge across the cases. Although my selection of examples is subjective, I have chosen to illustrate what I've come to understand as his method of clinical inquiry throughout the Brazilian seminars.

It is important to note that these supervisions are not the same as Bion's work with his own patients. The speed at which everything happens is one way the supervisions differ! There is little of the slow and difficult processes of analysis. Indeed, often in analysis, not much can be seen for long periods of time. Instead, the seminars offer some sense of what Bion thought mattered in clinical work, how he communicated with the presenters/seminar group, and how *he* might have talked to the patients concerned.

Layout of the Chapter

- Beginnings: the first thing Bion says is most often a question
- The heart of the supervision: Bion's use of abstraction in the formulation of the patient's core way of relating
- A note on the 'shadow' of past and future in the present of the session
- On 'knowing' and 'being' in Bion's method.

DOI: 10.4324/9781003401926-7

Beginnings: The First Thing Bion Says Is Most Often a Question

In most of the seminars, the presenter begins with a paragraph or so about the patient. The content varies from aspects of the patient's history to recent events or concerns or an account of a session's beginning. Bion comes in to speak quite quickly and, most often, asks a question: he does this in 19 out of the 24 Brasília seminars and in 19 out of 28 Sao Paulo seminars. A few of his questions are requests for information. However, most often, Bion is not looking for an answer but inviting the presenter (and seminar group) closer in to the material.

Example 1: Questioning the Apparently Obvious

Bion's initial questions are often unexpected and frequently about something the patient and presenting analyst are taking for granted. Here is an example from Seminar 4 in Brasilia in 1973:

Presenter: ... she [the patient] heard there was a very famous psychoanalyst in Brasília. ... She said she was carrying on an inner dialogue with the following argument: "If I ask her [if the patient were to ask the presenting analyst], I know she won't give me the answer; if I don't ask her, I shan't know where the meetings are going to take place." So she decided to speak out and to explain the situation to me. I pointed out that the conversation with herself was a way of avoiding speaking directly to me.
Bion: Why did she say she knew she wouldn't get an answer?

Because analysts do not answer questions, the reader may think! Bion, however, questions the apparently obvious. As the supervision goes on, he suggests that the relationship evident in this opening material can be seen to be recurring in other relationships the patient has. Involved in this process is his abstraction of the key elements in the relationship – 'famous analyst + she won't get an answer.' Here are some of his comments:

> Bion: It seems to me that she feels guilty and frightened because she is having an experience which doesn't accord with the psychoanalytic rules – as she knows them. I think that the 'famous analyst' is a person she doesn't feel able to talk to, and that famous analysts are not people who talk to her either. How does she know that the 'famous analyst' wouldn't have anything to do with her?...So there is anxiety about this 'famous analyst' who is sometimes her analyst, sometimes herself, sometimes her baby, and sometimes something which will emerge.
> (Bion, 1987/2014, pp. 25–28)

The "famous analyst" is not assumed just to refer to the actual famous analyst. Bion never links the reference to himself, although he *is* the famous visiting analyst.

"The famous analyst" is identified as "the person she doesn't feel able to talk to" and "who won't talk to her." This is variously "sometimes her analyst, sometimes herself, sometimes her baby, and sometimes something which will emerge." As well as talking about the patient, it is possible that Bion is also implicitly addressing the presenter (who may have felt she couldn't dare talk properly to him), as well as the other members of the seminar and their relation to ideas that might 'emerge' in them throughout the discussion.

Reading all the seminars, I began to wonder whether Bion might be actively on the lookout for the 'obvious' (e.g., analysts don't answer questions). Is it possible that presumed assumptions might be particularly good hiding places for unconscious content? It is as if Bion is looking in a rock pool and knows from experience that, beneath certain rocks, one will find certain sea creatures. Do presumed assumptions function like apparently insignificant day residues that appear in dreams – the day residues unconsciously chosen because of a connection to unconscious phantasy.

Example 2: Why Did You Say That to Her?

In this example, Bion's first intervention is to ask a question. This time, he questions the analyst's assumption that he must say something to the patient. (This contrasts to the previous example, where the assumption was the patient's: that 'analysts don't answer questions'). In this example, Bion questions the assumption that the analyst ought to speak. At first sight, the presenting analyst's comment to the patient seems a sympathetic acknowledgement that the patient is anxious. The example is from Brasília Seminar 15 (1975):

Presenter: The patient, who had been absent for a few sessions before this one, came into the consulting room and sat in the chair. She remained silent and appeared to be suffering some sort of anxiety. I told her that I sensed her anxiety and that she was consequently experiencing some difficulty.
Bion: Why did you say that to her? ... it is a matter of some consequence because otherwise one gets into a habit of thinking that the important thing is to say something to the patient. ...
Presenter: She [the patient] smiled and said, "Yes, it has been difficult to come. It isn't agreeable here, and it's boring."
Bion: She doesn't have to come, so what is the problem? If that is all that is troubling her, she only has to stay away and do something else. ...
Presenter: It seemed to me that she could not tolerate feeling anxiety in front of me, that she was perhaps ashamed. ...
Bion: It seems to me that you are trying to find an excuse for her, but I don't see why you should, and I don't see why you shouldn't expect her to say why she has come.

(Bion, 1987/2014, Seminar 15, pp. 75–76)

In Bion's view, the analyst is finding an 'excuse' for the patient. The analyst is assuming that the patient is behaving as she does because she is in difficulty (anxious, ashamed). We don't know why she has been absent, what she may be anxious about, and whether she is, in fact, ashamed. The analyst may wish to reduce the uncomfortable experience the patient seems to be having. Uncomfortable for whom is, of course, a question. The analyst may be trying to put something right that hasn't been properly experienced or understood. This seems a relatively straightforward point, although there may be a debate to be had about when one is foreclosing an experience or, alternatively, is helpfully 'keeping the conversation going for the time being.' But, what of Bion's comment "I don't see why you shouldn't expect her to say why she has come"? Bion wants as little as possible to be taken for granted, and this may be implicit in 'expecting the patient to say why she has come.' It's important to bear in mind that neither the question nor any answer would necessarily take an explicit cognitive form. That said, the question (and the analytic position inherent in the question) places more responsibility with the patient than we may be familiar with. On reflection, we can trace Bion's emphasis on keeping responsibility with the person concerned right back through his analytic work, and further back to his work in the Northfield hospital in World War II.

In this particular case, the presenting analyst may also have not entertained the thought that the patient could hold a critical – possibly accurate – view of the analyst. In a whole number of supervisions, Bion puts into words what the patient may be thinking and not necessarily saying or may not even be conscious of themself.

Bion's insistence that analysts avoid reassuring or excusing the patient can be seen in his behaviour towards the presenting analysts: he neither reassures nor excuses them. By not fitting in with the implicit agreement between presenting analyst and patient, Bion's questions give a potential message that 'stuff,' previously unobserved, may be about to have a place. This way of proceeding is linked with Bion's own clinical practice and something he discusses during his disagreement with Greenson in Los Angeles in 1967 (Aguayo & Malin, 2013). Greenson is critical of Bion for the lack of reassurance and support he seems to show patients and suggests Bion uses his patients for his own observational interests (the insults fly both ways). Bion responds by commenting that, by not fitting in with what the patient elicits, the patient may sense that Bion is available for aspects of them that haven't had a place before. In the clinical seminars, Bion's opening questions may well give the message that he is not going to fit in with the familiar, anticipated functioning that is established between the presenting analyst and his or her patient.

The Heart of the Supervision: Bion's Use of Abstraction in the Formulation of the Patient's Core Way of Relating

As we have already observed in the context of his first questions, Bion focuses on the relationships between 'objects': between the patient and others; the patient and analyst; the patient and their internal objects; and, in the following example, between the patient and his envy (his envy being treated, perhaps somewhat humorously, as an object in its own right). Bion abstracts from the various relations to determine what the recurring qualities of the relations are. The objects may vary, but something in the relationship between them stays constant.

Example 3: "Somebody Seems to Have Been Controlling Somebody"

The patient tells the analyst that he (the patient) had felt envious of his wealthy brother, but knew envy was destructive "and this time he had managed to control it."

Bion: What did he expect to happen if he didn't control it?
Presenter: I asked him what he meant by controlling his envy. ... After a while he said he felt very distressed and, "You are trying to confuse me because I wasn't able to control my aggressiveness."
Bion: Well, somebody seems to have been controlling somebody. ...
Bion: He controlled envy, and his envy is extremely annoyed about it.

Bion further comments – from the point of view of the patient – "The analyst is controlling my envy, trying to control my mind" (Bion, 1987/2014, Seminar 9, pp. 49–50).

The relationship "somebody seems to have been controlling somebody" has been traced between the patient and his brother, the patient and the analyst, and, in the patient's internal world, between himself and his envy.

A well-known relationship identified by Bion is that between the container and the contained. My impression, although he doesn't explicitly refer to the concept in the clinical seminars, is that container–contained is implied in Bion's thinking about relationships within them. While his work on container–contained tends to be identified with his earlier thinking (late 50s/early 60s), it is, in fact, most fully elaborated in his later 1970 book, *Attention and Interpretation*, which was published just 5 years before the clinical seminars in Brasília. In *Attention and Interpretation*, Bion comments that each of us tends to have a characteristic relationship between container and contained:

> According to his background a patient will describe various objects as containers, such as his mind, the unconscious, the nation; others as contained, such as his money, his ideas. The objects are many but the relationships are not.
> (Bion, 1970/2014, p. 324)

With this in mind, "somebody seems to have been controlling somebody" may be inherent in the patient's characteristic relation between container and contained – the container controlled by the contained and vice versa. The analyst might assume the patient to be feeling benignly contained, while the patient views the analyst's 'containment' as controlling him.

Example 4: 'A Suspicious Relationship'

In a second example, we hear of the patient's stomach-aches, his relation with his wife, and his recent visit to his bank during which he has a long conversation with a female bank employee. Here is what Bion comes to say:

Bion: It might perhaps be wiser to say, "You don't seem to feel that you could trust anybody – or at any rate, any woman. Although you seem to have relationships with these creatures we call women – a wife, a bank employee – I think you are very suspicious of them."

(Bion, 1987/2014, Seminar 17, p. 92)

Bion goes on to talk about 'the dangerous woman' also being inside the patient. He comments that, if he were the analyst, he would take up the relation to a 'dangerous woman' in the transference. He thinks the patient would reject the interpretation, but that this doesn't necessarily mean he wouldn't have understood it.

Again, Bion focuses on the relationship between objects: the patient's relationship to his wife and the bank teller, his relationship to his internal objects (as indicated by his stomach-ache), and his relationship to his analyst. The pattern that emerges when Bion abstracts from these relationships is of a relationship between the patient and a dangerous woman, a relationship characterised by suspicion, regardless of whether the woman is outside or inside him (the stomach-ache). If he, Bion, were the analyst, he says he would consider saying that he is felt to be a dangerous woman "whether I am outside you or inside you."

Example 5: 'A Hostile Object Covered Up with Publicity'

Presenter: The motives that brought him to analysis were twofold: he was going to work as a publicity agent – he said he usually destroyed everything he most loved, and this agency was something he had always dreamt of doing all his life; and he had a bad relationship with women. ...

Bion: I think that he feels he has a very hostile object inside him which he covers up with all this publicity and family affairs in order that he cannot look inside himself and see what this very bad thing is which he calls "hypertension" ...

Bion: ... he attacks this bad thing inside him: he throws amphetamines at it, he throws food down his gullet so as to hit it, to kill it; he tries to starve it out of existence. Whatever he does, this bad thing which is felt to be a bad part of himself might just as well be somebody else because he has no control over it. He is only a sort of publicity agent: it is his business to look nice, to act as a disguise or cover for this bad thing inside him which is greedy, violent and hostile.

(Bion, 1987/2014, Seminar 22, pp. 113–116)

We can hear Bion's intense sense of the patient's experience under threat from an internal bad object. In the supervisions, there is little time for the 'continued observation of facts'; Bion comes quickly to his formulations. It raises the question of whether – in the clinical seminars – we see him working with clinical theory and experience more familiar to him, instead of the states of mind in which he is more exposed to what is not known.

A Note on the 'Shadow' of Past and Future in the Present of the Session

The following quote is taken from Brasília Seminar 10, the supervision of work with a child who has been 'pretending' to telephone her father. Bion checks first that the father is thought to be a good father. He then continues:

Bion: The telephone makes it possible to have a contact with something she has forgotten or never really worked through properly. There is a 'getting into contact' with a love affair she hasn't had yet – with the father of the family. She may be aware of something behind the actual father and mother. It is the future casting its shadow before, as well as the past casting its shadow on the present.

(Bion, 1987/2014, Seminar 10, p. 57)

In the quote, Bion refers to the "future casting its shadow before, as well as the past casting its shadow on the present." In the following comment from the Brazilian lectures (which he gave around the same time), Bion talks about a "peculiar experience," which is not a memory or a prophecy (of the future), and describes how he might speak to the patient about this:

Or to put it in other terms, "I think I remember something like what you are saying. I think that one day I shall understand what you are talking about." It glances back; it intuits "the shape of things to come." It is that peculiar experience which is not an interpretation, not a memory, not even a prophecy. A 'present' experience is past, is present and is future; it is timeless – unless someone can invent space-time, psychoanalytic time and space.

(Bion, 1973/1974/2014, p. 86)

Bion also talks about "germs" of the future that can be picked up in the present if we are able to be sufficiently discriminating:

When you hear a baby scream or shout, you will have to be a specialist to say that that particular scream has no future to it, and that particular scream is turning into something. If we can develop our powers and capacity for discrimination we may be able to see, and to be correct in thinking that we can see differences.

(Bion, 1973/1974/2014, p. 139)

And he refers to the "Future casting its shadow before" in his novel *Memoir of the Future* (again of the same period):

> It was probably the Future casting its shadow before; sometimes it is disguised as the Past casting its memory forward.
>
> (Bion, 1977/2014, p. 40)

Wanting to be in the future (wanting the end of the session to come, the summer holiday to come) is different to discerning the shadow of the future in the present and the germs of the future in the present. By "psychoanalytic time and space" he means the capacity to be in the present and sense the past and the future in the present.

On 'Knowing' and 'Being' in Bion's Method

I have described how Bion's method of clinical inquiry focuses on the formulation and interpretation of the patient's characteristic/problematic core relationship (a controlling relationship, a suspicious relationship, a relationship that covers things up). At first sight, this clinical approach would seem to be closely related to 'knowing.' At the same time, from the mid to late 60s onwards, Bion clearly stated that psychoanalysis needs to work at the level of 'being' ('O') instead of 'knowing' ('K').

The use of the letters 'K' and 'O' allow us to mark a subject that can then be inquired into. The American psychoanalyst Michael Eigen puts what is meant by 'O' like this:

> What is crucial is how one relates to whatever one may be relating to. ... If, for example, one's emotional reality or truth is despair, what is most important is not that one may be in despair, but one's attitudes toward one's despair. Through one's basic attentiveness one's despair can declare itself and tell its story. One enters profound dialogue with it. If one stays with this process, an evolution even in the quality of despair may begin to be perceived, since despair itself is never uniform.
>
> (Eigen 1981, p. 429)

It is not only the patient's difficulty with 'being' that concerns Bion, but also the analyst's 'being' properly in the session with the patient. It is worth mentioning that Bion remained strict throughout about the analytic setting.

Bion's differentiation of 'O' and 'K,' so clearly drawn in his writings, is very interesting to think about in relation to the Brazilian clinical seminars. He doesn't talk about 'O' explicitly. However, it is evident that he is committed to bringing the presenting analyst and members of the seminar closer to the patient. This requires the avoidance of assumptions being made by the analyst (as far as possible).

What effect might there be on the patient of the analyst making fewer assumptions and potentially being in closer contact with him or her? Might the patient feel more claustrophobic? In *Attention and Interpretation*, Bion suggests that the patient actually feels less possessed by an analyst who is eschewing memory and desire. What of the effect on the presenter and seminar group? I wonder if some of the presenters might be frightened by the possibility of a deeper analytic contact with their patients, as well as a deeper contact with Bion.

Bob Hinshelwood asked me whether I thought Bion had given up interpretation in favour of provoking some kind of alpha-function in the other. It's an interesting question and linked with the image of digging up the soil of assumptions, which came to me when reading the seminars. As is clear in the clinical seminars, Bion hasn't given up making interpretations, but one could certainly say that the function of the interpretation is to provoke alpha-function.

Conclusion

I have asked what we can learn of Bion's method of clinical inquiry from his supervisions.

I drew attention to how, in the majority of the seminars, Bion starts by asking a question. A few questions are requests for information, but, most often, Bion is not looking for an answer. Instead, he is inviting the presenter (and seminar group) closer in to the material. I gave three examples from the seminars:

- "Bion: Why did she say she knew she wouldn't get an answer?" His formulation was of there being a famous analyst (her analyst, her baby, a new idea) who she doesn't feel able to talk to and who won't speak to her.

In the second example, his question was:

- "Why did you say that to her?" And his discussion was of the analyst's assumption, first, that he should speak and, second, that the patient would want to be a favourite.

Second, I considered the heart of the supervision: Bion's use of abstraction in the formulation of the patient's core way of relating.

I gave three examples:

- "Somebody seems to have been controlling somebody"
- 'A suspicious relationship'
- 'a hostile object covered up with publicity.'

So we have a controlling relationship between container and contained, a suspicious relationship between container and contained, and a hostile relationship between container and contained

Then, in the third part of the paper, I looked at how Bion's work on the difference between 'K' and 'O' might be present in the supervisions. What is most striking in the supervisions is his questioning of the assumptions made by patients and analysts. The effect of this is to bring patient and analyst closer into being in the session.

The image that came to me while reading the seminars was of impacted soil being dug into by Bion's questions. It doesn't sound like the seminar members expressed very much explicit surprise in relation to Bion's questioning, which is itself striking. It is possible that what was happening was happening on a deeper level than that of cognitive surprise.

References

Aguayo, J., & Malin, B. (Eds.). (2013). *Wilfred Bion: Los Angeles Seminars and Supervision*. London: Routledge.

Bion, W.R. (2014). The Complete Works of W. R. Bion. C. Mawson & F. Bion (Eds.). London: Routledge.

Bion, W.R. (1970/2014). Volume 6, *Attention and Interpretation: A Scientific Approach to Insight in Psycho-Analysis and Groups*. London: Routledge.

Bion, W.R. (1973/1974/2014). Volume 7, *Brazilian Lectures 1973; São Paulo 1974; Rio de Janeiro 1974; São Paulo*. London: Routledge.

Bion, W.R. (1977/2014). Volume 9, *Memoir of the Future*. London: Routledge.

Bion, W.R. (1987/2014). Volume 8, *Clinical Seminars Brasília 1975; São Paulo 1978; New York 1977; São Paulo 1978*. London: Routledge.

Eigen, M. (1981). The area of faith in Winnicott, Lacan and Bion. *International Journal of Psychoanalysis*, 62: 413–433.

Junqueira de Mattos, J.A., de Mattos Brito, G., & Levine, H.B. (Eds.). (2017). *Bion in Brazil: Supervisions and Commentaries*. London: Routledge.

Levine, H.B., de Mattos Brito, G., & Junqueira de Mattos, J.A. (Eds.). (2024). *The Clinical Thinking of W. R. Bion in Brazil Supervisions and Commentaries*. London: Routledge.

7

Conclusions on Bion's Method of Clinical Inquiry

Similarities and Differences

Joseph Aguayo, R.D. Hinshelwood, Sira Dermen and Nicola Abel-Hirsch

We initially gathered as a group of Anglo-American psychoanalysts and researchers to address one main question: if we went back to Bion's actual clinical and supervisorial examples from his published work, could we ascertain if he had a particular way of working? With the exception of the famous "Notes on Memory and Desire" (1967), Bion was quite disinclined to write about analytic technique, perhaps something that might have established him in a position he did not want: a dependency group leader. As he ironically commented in *Learning from Experience*, to put oneself forth on the basis of analyzing trainees "smacks of an esoteric cult" (Bion, 1962, p. i). Earlier on, in 1955, he also frankly admitted he wouldn't know where to start in terms of defining his technique.

When our group began working in earnest to sift through Bion's clinical examples, Sira Dermen early on captured our sense of what Bion was up to in and outside the consulting room when she labeled his approach an "implicit method of clinical inquiry" (IMCI). We define it here: IMCI pertains to a loosely saturated concept based on a clinically inductive method of reasoning—the analyst orients to his session material with an organizing set of preconceptions and gathers the data of clinical experience. He/she then can take that data and transform it into analytic concepts, which in turn shed light on particular classes of patients. When a sufficient number of concepts have been gathered, they in turn can be used to form models—and, with sufficient experience, new theories, which in turn can be linked to new observational data for further consideration. In his clinical work, Bion evinced a certain cast of mind that is manifest throughout his work, one that our group has endeavored to formulate. We asked: what were the enduring features, if any, of his IMCI? Did his method vary over time and circumstance? Did his clinical work also vary as a function of important mentors and influences at play in its evolution?

We decided to start at the beginning, realizing that, on the one hand, Bion's method informed how he intervened with either his patients or his supervisees, all of which, at times, led to clinical concepts that might broadly apply to a certain class of patients (e.g., 'attacks on linking' might be represented in the psychotic's fragmented and elliptical statements). On the other hand, Bion's clinical concepts in turn also formed the basis of a new metapsychology that revised the work of

DOI: 10.4324/9781003401926-8

Freud and Klein (e.g., an attack on linking in the model of container–contained was theoretically reformulated as the patient's beta-screen attack on the analyst's alpha-function).

In presenting our conclusions regarding Bion's *implicit* method of clinical inquiry, we thus regard it as a Janus-faced model, a loosely saturated set of concepts that extend to the technical interventions an analyst might make with his patients on the one side and, on the other, how these clinical concepts inform the building of theoretical revisions. One key paper that best represents the Janus-faced nature of IMCI is Bion's "On Arrogance" (1958b). In that paper, he reads fresh meaning into the figure of Oedipus as representing the analyst's epistemological task: to inquire and establish the psychic truth of the patient's living emotional experience, a position that can and does lead to unforeseen ends in terms of the varying responses from patients. The analyst's commitment here is to inquiry itself, what Bion (1978) later called a form of "disciplined curiosity." Along the way, Bion (1963) thought enough of the analyst's main role as inquirer to make it part of his Grid (Column 5). Parthenope Bion tells us that, in his original conception of the Grid, he termed what became the inquiry column the "Oedipus column."

Putting these ideas in a different way, Bion took up the central importance of the clinical/inductive method as it informed his clinical work. In effect, this meant how any analyst's theoretical preconceptions oriented how he/she focused on and gathered clinical data from analytic sessions in order to arrive at clinical generalizations. It was also the other way round, where preconceptions established the field of observation, and the field of observation, in turn, sometimes yielded new sorts of clinical data that the analyst was hard pressed to understand. *Relevant here would be Bion's preconceptions that oriented him at the outset of his group period.* Hinshelwood recounts how Bion delineated the group as a field of study—how the group defined its social space, its work task and intra-group tensions and its relationship to leadership. The observing psychiatrist had the task of displaying the problem to the social group and assigning responsibility. It is, of course, very difficult to imagine that Bion's war experiences as a young tank commander in World War I didn't have a profoundly shaping influence on how he conceived of the nature of groups, especially men in combat situations. At a theoretical level, through his collaboration with his ex-analyst John Rickman, Bion also drew upon Lewin's field theory (1951), looking at social forces in action.

In World War II, at Northfield Hospital, Bion regarded individual group members as taking up varying roles that resulted in intra-group tensions (e.g., 'workers' vs. 'shirkers') which the entire group was held communally responsible for resolving. Since each member made 'anonymous contributions' to the overall mentality of the group, it was also up to the leader to interpret and understand what kind of leader they expected him to be. In the peacetime groups run by Bion as leader, he deployed his capacities to directly observe what roles the group members were attempting to recruit him into, drawing upon his introspective capacities and training analysis. If functioning properly, the analyst would recognize the role he was being recruited into and, instead, produce verbal understanding in the hopes of helping the group resolve their conflicts with one another. Put differently, the analyst allowed for the momentary recruitment into particular roles, reflecting on these processes—and thus become a leader of an inquiring group. By way of interpretations, he reported his findings back to the group. Thus, through his use of intuition, emphasis on group members' responsibility, non-sensuous perception and communication in plain and intelligible language, the group leader served an inquiring function.

Turning now to Bion's career as a psychoanalyst, there were definite preconceptual carryovers in his IMCI from the group period as he embarked on the analysis of psychosis. Most apparent were two principles he learned from John Rickman, ones that just as easily applied to groups as they did to the analytic couple: (1.) the subjective examination of the roles of both partners in the transference–countertransference interaction, and (2.) the reflection on those roles required of the analyst and the patient. Both cases, a psychoanalytic session as described by Rickman and the group as observed by Bion, pointed to two principles of technique: the psychoanalyst (1.) does no more than momentarily accept the role required, and (2.) interprets the roles and requirements, thus becoming the leader of an inquiring group or the instigator to inquiry in the analytic session.

Characteristic of his post-war work with groups as well as a result of his analysis with Melanie Klein and supervision with Paula Heimann, Bion's IMCI also reflected his attempts *to observe and understand in a vigilant manner what was occurring in the present moment. All emotional issues in analysis were dealt with at the point of urgent anxiety in real time.* He deployed three crucial structuring concepts in his technique in the 1950s: (1.) Rickman's accentuation of unconscious role-recruitment deployed by the patient; (2.) Klein's notions of projective identification and unconscious phantasy occurring mainly in the present moment; and (3.) Heimann's (1950) advocacy that the analyst introspect on direct emotional experience, so that he or she might tunnel out of disturbing countertransference impasses with patients. The countertransference was both the analyst's great obstacle and ally, interfering as well as informing.

Bion fully embraced Klein's (1946) programmatic agenda to analyze psychosis, one that recast Freud's version of the psychotic as primarily narcissistic, auto-erotic, non-libidinally attached to a patient dominated by omnipotent defenses against a fundamental need for a breast. Like Herbert Rosenfeld and Hanna Segal, Bion was hardly aware that he *was* helping to birth a 'novelty of method,' an implicit clinical technique in the 1950s. Yet, for all his participation in the Klein's group agenda, Bion also went about it in an idiosyncratic way. While the others might exclusively focus on understanding and analyzing the patient's internal, phantasmic and subjective states of mind, Bion augmented his IMCI by not focusing on linking the patient's early history to current transference manifestations. After all, his point of entry to the Klein group was through his group work, not as a child analyst who would emphasize the patient's development over time. Thus, Bion here veered away from Klein's (1952) definition of transference as a "total situation," which adhered to Freud's notion of transference as a repetition from the past (Spillius, 2007, p. 5).

So, for instance, Bion's (1950) case of "The Imaginary Twin" (published in 1967) referred to the 'Twin's' traumatic early familial losses but did not explicitly attempt to tie them to active, present-tense transference work. He instead accentuated present-tense unconscious phantasy, active and organizing in the here and now. He focused on the unconscious roles into which the slippery/elusive Twin recruited him, emphasizing his own enduring subjective reactions as he slowly tunneled out of a recruited countertransference position. On this point—just like in his group work—he relied upon his direct emotional experience and countertransference to his patient *before* considering their transference to him.

Such experiences accentuated the fallaciousness of what Bion had assumed was a correct understanding of the Twin's internal state of mind. The patient and analyst *were* in fact operating with two different models of the mind. The analyst's model of what was operative in the patient's mind had run in a parallel track to the Twin's model of his own mind. The central point here was how the analyst had been unwittingly recruited into the position of 'imaginary twin,' a recreation of the phantasized lair to which the Twin was adhered.

Bion arrived at these conclusions through his present-tense emphasis on a more total communicational gestalt, one that understood the present moment differently, broadening and embracing potentially available meanings with patients who were split off from themselves, all while introspecting on his own direct subjective reactions in the form of disturbed emotional experience in the patient's presence—or outside the session.

Yet, for all these carryovers from his group to his initial period as a psychoanalyst, Bion also effected a caesura in his IMCI by the mid-1950s when he began to focus on new observational data streams, namely the physical movements and sensory impressions conveyed to him by his psychotic patients. Extremely puzzled by what he witnessed—fragmented, elliptical speech that carried little semantic meaning—he simply inquired about the accompanying physical and sensory experiences. Neither he nor the patient made any initial sense of its possible meaning—they existed as so much sensory noise in the consulting room—but, here, Bion kept the question open, another key feature of his IMCI. There was something happening that was not understood, something in the realm of the non-representational. So, he formulated a hypothesis of an 'ideo-motor activity,' a private conjecture that assumed that the physical gestures carried some implicit meaning, but one not yet known (Bion, 1954). It was akin to his notion of 'proto-mental systems' from his group period, ideas associated with inactive basic assumptions. Think of it: if a psychotic communicated in a fragmented as well as elliptical way, the analyst would need some auxiliary method to make a communicative link with the meaning-making part of the patient's mind. Just as Klein had originally deployed the child's play with toys, along with its rudimentary verbal associations, so that a more complete communicational gestalt might evolve, so Bion now played in the motoric gestures of his patients, all in the service of broadening the communicative potential with his patients.

Bion now expanded the present moment to include fragmented speech and motoric gestures of a non-representational kind, thus broadening the net of potentially available meanings with patients who experienced themselves as 'partial personalities.' Linked to a broader understanding of countertransference, Bion more fully embraced multiple communicative possibilities to expand the meaning from either side of the couch—for instance, the wider notion of countertransference, which was first and foremost unconscious and could only be accessed through a careful tuning into his own disturbed emotional experience in the patient's presence or away from him, outside the session. Bion had the added flexibility of still being able to draw upon the older Freud/Klein view of the analyst's disturbed emotional state as reflecting some residual 'personal interference' on the analyst's conflictual side vis-à-vis unconscious-to-unconscious communications that, via projective identification, could also be informing.

Finally, during this period, particularly as the analyst's focus remained on the patient's internal, subjective, phantasmic experience as well as his own subjective experience, there was, at times, a certain strident attitude, almost as if the analyst regarded himself during this time as the sole epistemological agent in the consulting room. With severely compromised psychotic and near-psychotic patients, the analyst bore the curiosity for knowing the patient's enduring psychic reality, remaining the sane, meaning-seeking agent who observed the psychotic's attacks on his or her own mind that were in turn projected violently into the figure of the analyst.

In the later 1950s, Bion consolidated his clinical findings, broadly deploying them as the basis of innovative conceptual formulations that now began to expand his reach as both a practicing psychoanalyst and budding theoretician who began a revision of existing Freudian and Kleinian theories. Dermen also differentiated Bion's IMCI from technique per se, maintaining the importance of explicating its basic features of how the analyst went about inquiring about the psychoanalytic process itself. Allowing for the "analytic situation to evolve, and then interpret the evolution" enabled him to discover his most innovative ideas about early mental development, ideas he began to articulate in abstract/theoretical terms. From his everyday practices, his analytic posture now became one of avoiding foreclosure, doing so through an accentuation on what he did not understand. His fundamental presumption was: "I am missing something," and he did not treat *any* insight, however hard gained and temporarily illuminating, as a definitive resting place. What mattered was what happened next—what the analytic situation was evolving towards, living the uncomfortable premise that every gain in analysis will come at a cost—to patient and analyst alike. Insight is a way station on the stormy journey of therapy.

Bion's (1958a, 1958b, 1959) papers, "On Arrogance," "On Hallucination" and "Attacks on Linking," all shared a commonality of now deploying clinical findings as a basis for innovative clinical concepts that, in turn, became the basis of further inquiry and new clinical generalizations, such as the hypothesis that projective identification is a "primitive mode of communication that provides a foundation on which, ultimately, verbal communication depends" (Bion, 1958a, p. 146). As explicated in "On Arrogance," we can see how Bion worked inductively, showing a rare capacity to take his clinical experience as the basis of far-reaching formulations. In his innovative rereading of the Oedipus myth, the inquiring analyst-as-Oedipus assumes the position of laying bare the patient's psychic truth. This position as an epistemological agent with an enduring commitment to psychoanalytic inquiry also renders him, from the patient's perspective, an accessory to the crime he or she feels to be perpetrated against him or her. Bion here augmented what he had learned about psychotic mechanisms—such as the mutilating attack not only on reality but on the very organs of awareness which apprehend reality—to ask: what is there in reality that makes it so hateful to the patient that he or she must destroy the ego which brings him or her into contact with it? Again, the emphasis was on what eluded understanding, what was missing. Put differently, Bion's IMCI now combined intuition with rigorous reasoning about what he did not understand. In these endeavors, he maintained an awareness to hear a part of the patient who was collaborating in the analysis, however rudimentarily—and this was now reflected in interpretations that marked the minute shifts in the patient's movements towards collaboration with the analyst.

In so doing, Bion's IMCI was now characterized by an emerging distinctiveness of understanding a dialectical relationship between the analyst's commitment to verbal communication as the primary way in which he delivered the fruits of inquiry to the patient and the patient's own separate model of communicating through other means, such as motoric gestures with no apparent representational meaning. Bion here emphasized the perspectival differences between analyst and patient as a form of reciprocating communicative projective identification. This mind set of focusing on what made for difference in the analyst's conception of the patient's mind vis-à-vis the patient's implicit conception of his or her own mind was now made apparent in discoveries such as the patient's experience of the analyst as an obstructive object. In effect, these were the patient's reactions to the analyst-as-analyst, a move that now shifted and expanded the original meaning of projective identification as an organizing unconscious phantasy to a newer meaning of communicating an organizing gestalt based on new combinations of ideo-motoric gestures and elliptical, fragmented communications. If the analyst's stance represented the primacy of verbal communication as a method of making the patient's problems explicit, it could be directly experienced as attacking the patient's methods of communication. This gave Bion's IMCI additional dexterity, as there could be different aspects at play; it encompassed: traditional countertransference, where the analyst might be contributing to acting like an obstructive object; Kleinian ideas about envy, in which the patient's resentment of the analyst's sanity could render the former obstructive to furthering the aims of inquiry in the analysis; and, of course, situations in which both partners contributed to obstructive the overall aims of inquiry, as we saw in the impasse underlying the *folie à deux* in "The Imaginary Twin" case.

With this newfound dexterity that broadened, say, normal projective identification as the first mode of communication and differentiated it from that in the service of evacuation, Bion now touched upon the importance of how the analyst also subjectively and internally processed these types of communications by way of allowing for these necessary bits of the patient to be modified by their 'sojourn' in the analyst's (and mother's) psyche. These statements would soon become a cornerstone in Bion's container–contained model of mental development.

The move from clinical findings to new theoretical concepts was also on display on "On Hallucinations," where his amalgamating sensory/motor and non-representational forms of experience, evident in the psychotic's experience of daytime hallucinations in and out of analysis, now led to the discovery of the nature of psychotic dreaming. As Dermen has set out, Bion here expanded and began to revise Freud's dream theory, heretofore restricted to more commonplace phenomena of the reporting of nighttime dreams by his neurotic patients. He extended this experience to include the importance of attending to and interpreting the patient's bodily movements, which in effect rendered the daytime hallucinatory experience as a form of what Bion now termed "psychotic dreaming," which also formed one fundamental divide between psychotic and non-psychotic aspects of the personality. Whereas splitting and projective identification dominated the psychotic aspects, they existed in complementarity to the neurotic aspect governed by repression and other mechanisms of defense. What now emerged was a newfound capacity to appreciate the operation of primitive forms of defense, such as the psychotic deployment of the sense organs as a way to expel as well as receive outer communications.

These not-yet-psychic and motoric activities helped Bion to appreciate the continuum from psychotic to neurotic forms of dreaming. He wrote: "I felt that the 'dreams' shared so many characteristics of the hallucination that it was possible that actual experiences of hallucination in the consulting room might serve to throw light on the psychotic dream" (Bion, 1958b, p. 346). He advanced the hypothesis that, when the psychotic patient spoke of having a dream, it was his or her perceptual apparatus expelling something, and that "a dream is an evacuation from his mind strictly analogous to an evacuation from his bowels." "In short, to the psychotic a dream is an evacuation of material that has been taken in during waking hours."

In the last of these three groundbreaking papers, "Attacks on Linking" focused on the psychotic aspect of the patient making destructive attacks on anything which he or she feels to have the function of linking one object to another. Bion synthesized findings from previous papers—for instance, further elaborating his new theory of psychotic dreaming, now linked to hallucinations. There was a new appreciation of the patient who reported having no dreams, so that this apparent dreamless state was now likened to an "invisible-visual hallucination." Put differently, these types of dream experiences consisted of material so minutely fragmented that they were devoid of any visual component. The clinically applicable thesis? That *dreams could only be reported when they contain visual objects*. Bion concluded: "I felt that the 'dreams' shared so many characteristics of the hallucination that it was possible that actual experiences of hallucination in the consulting room might serve to throw light on the psychotic dream."

Another fundamental contribution was a newfound appreciation of the experience of *containment*, which originated with the clinical finding of the complex situation observed when a patient feels he or she is being allowed, in the analysis, an opportunity of which he or she had been cheated in the past. "The poignancy of this deprivation is rendered the more acute and so are the feelings of resentment and deprivation." "Gratitude for the opportunity coexists with hostility to the analyst as the person who will not understand and refuses the patient the use of the only method of communication by which he feels he can make himself understood." The denial of projective identification is real in external reality, *and* the denial will inevitably be lived as real in the transference. Hence, another reason for Bion *not discussing reconstruction and early history with the patient.*

Dermen encapsulated the major technical advancements of Bion's IMCI for the late 1950s:

1. He has the capacity to avoid foreclosure. His fundamental presumption is "I am missing something." Equally, "something has changed, but I have failed to notice it."
2. He combines intuition with rigorous reasoning about what he does not understand. "I am missing something: there must be another element at play."
3. He has the capacity to hear a part of the patient who is collaborating in the analysis, which makes his interpretations even-handed and establishes an atmosphere of mutual inquiry.
4. He has the capacity to spot and be curious about that which might appear to be insignificant. We have seen how he homes in on "it" in "On Arrogance." The context indicates that progress is being made as the patient is offering useful thoughts, so one could easily have missed that the meaning of "it" is unclear. But Bion sees "it" as the problem that "awaits solution." We see the same capacity to focus on the apparently insignificant in other papers. For example, in "On Hallucination," when crucial understanding of the nature of psychotic dreaming is emerging, Bion focuses on the fact that the patient has called his dream "peculiar." He inquired further about why the patient thought his dream 'peculiar.'

When we transit to Bion's epistemological work in the 1960s, there is a striking contrast reflected in his IMCI that now became a source of his enduring interest. The findings of the group and psychosis periods now became a way of clinically situating his epistemological innovations in a more comprehensive theoretical fashion. Put differently, his clinical findings were used as a way to evolve experientially near models. For instance, in *Learning from Experience* (1962), and from the vertex of Bion's own clinical practices in the 1960s, he restlessly shifted his sightlines (as Abel-Hirsch puts it), looking one way then another, so that he could interrogate his clinical data from as many possible theoretical vertices as possible.

He simultaneously extended his analysis of psychotic states of mind to encompass a newly identified class of patients, the so-called "borderline patients," those who could feel but not suffer their experiences. Akin to the psychotic patients he had analyzed, the borderline patients' intolerance of frustration and inability to be thoughtful resulted in evacuative projections, so that the analyst was made to 'bear' or 'suffer' the mental pain and anguish that the patients themselves were unwilling or unable to suffer. The borderline patient, as a fresh source of new observational data, gave added meaning to previous distinctions, such as psychotic/non-psychotic, and thus extended the Kleinian analysis of psychotic states to less disturbed kinds of patients, such as those with borderline and narcissistic disorders. Bion (1962) gave a clinical example of a patient who could do no more than receive a decent interpretative feed from the analyst before feeling dissatisfied. Analytic sustenance did no more than momentarily sustain the patient emotionally. The taking-in of analytic milk, warmth or the good breast essentially remained indistinguishable from the evacuation of a 'bad breast.' Such a patient is left railing about needing 'more analysis, more analysis' as a hungry infant might feel in wanting 'more milk, more milk.' Taking this material, Abel-Hirsch draws our attention to the missing element of the patient's capacity for thinking that would make insight possible.

Bion himself differentiated between the "actual milk" and the "psychical quality of the milk" and went on to explore the splitting between the two in a disturbed relationship. Tacking back to the infant at the breast—there can be some aggressive 'obstruction' (from either the infant's or the mother's side) to the point that it interferes with the impulse to obtain sustenance. While love can decrease the obstruction, it can also increase it, especially when envy is involved, as "love is inseparable from envy." Hate cannot arise if love is not present, and thus the split between material and psychical satisfaction develops (Bion, 1962). While Bion conceptualizes his clinical results a bit differently, it is not substantially different from the conclusions he reached in "On Arrogance," where the patient's envious attacks can themselves render him or her into an obstructive object—or, alternatively, the analyst who insists on verbal communication can appear as obstructive to the patient's preferred means of communication by way of projective evacuation.

In *Elements of Psycho-Analysis*, Bion (1963) continued the process of shifting his conceptual sightlines with the Grid, now emphasizing the kind of mental and emotional work the analyst must do *outside* the consulting room. In positing the Grid, the analyst could see to what ends the patient's (and his own) communications were put to outside the session, the way a musician might practice scales between concerts. Bion clinically illustrates his own use of the Grid: "Suppose the patient had said, 'I know that you hate me'" (Bion, 1963, p. 73), a statement that can then lead the analyst to deploy various Grid categories as a way to play imaginatively with various meanings (e.g., words used as concrete actions, perhaps defensively disguising an attack; or it could be a dream, or part of a phantasy or an enactment—or even an oracular pronouncement, such as Tiresias might have made at the beginning of the Oedipus myth). Abel-Hirsch concludes: "Bion wants to give himself the widest of possibilities to choose from. He also wants a means of checking his work, a form of self-supervision." Bion was formalizing a way in which he could discuss his work with himself, with the Grid providing some neutrality.

Abel-Hirsch here takes into account the difficulties posed by patients who vacillate between using words-as-actions and drawing upon them as ordinary semantic meaning. Bion was drawing our attention to what has become known nowadays as enactment taking place between the analyst and the patient, a process that can be seen as early as Bion's (1950) case of "The Imaginary Twin" (1967), where the patient involved himself unwittingly in acts of reversible perspective. This theme continued as a distinctive signature of Bion's evolving conceptual work—the capacity for perspectivism, or understanding how the same clinical material looked different from the vantage point of the analyst vis-à-vis the patient. So, where other Kleinians—for example, Segal (1964)—focused on both paranoid-schizoid and depressive positions as defining the patient's pathology, Bion (1967, p. 22) augmented these positions as *also* defining the analyst's internal states (e.g., P/S as chaos, insecurity and persecution leading to the analyst's security and integrative understanding in D). Bion's illustrations here reflected his need to try out different perspectives on the clinical material on the one hand and the need to abstract from particular experiences of both patient and analyst in their session work on the other.

Taking a clinical example from *Transformations* (1965), Bion's description of "a method of critical approach to psychoanalytic practice" (p. 131) now encompasses an epistemological question that the analyst can pose to him- or herself: how does the analyst know what he or she knows, especially as his or her work generally veers in the direction of unknown psychic territory? As Bion now includes clinical data from 'borderline psychotic' patients, he attempts to encompass some of the differentiating characteristics. So, where the psychotic analysands treated by Bion in the 1950s were already certified and/or psychiatrically hospitalized, the phenomenon of the borderline analysand presented new problems: what if the 'breakdown' occurred not before, but *during* the course of the analysis when there is a "sudden deterioration," the patient is morose and appears to be hearing voices and seeing things? Relatives and the family doctor are alarmed, as more and more people become involved in what appears to be a catastrophic reversal akin to a psychic disaster. Has the patient deteriorated while under the analyst's care—has the physician's cardinal principle of "First do no harm" been violated? To address this issue, Bion wonders if these sorts of catastrophic events can be masked by symptoms appearing under other names (e.g., somatic symptoms) (Bion, 1965, V, pp. 133–134). Here again, the question of sightlines (or vertices in Bion's terminology) arose: do we consider what happens from the vertex of the patient's own experience, or the analyst's listening vertex—or its familial/group transformation when worried relatives effect what could be termed a 'lateral communication,' all of which is worrying to the analyst? Bion (1965, V, p. 132) writes: "There appears to be reason for the analyst to be alarmed, or, if not he is not, to lay himself open to grave miscalculation and consequent blame." In this instance, Bion combined afresh what he had learned from his group, psychosis and epistemological periods.

In *Attention and Interpretation*, Bion (1970) rehearsed different sightlines on the same material. When the Grid is used, for example, its versatility comes to mind insofar as the analyst is free to put any particular response in a separate other category. Through the 1960s, Bion was restlessly working to improve his observational capacity. Dermen has drawn attention to his question of 'what am I missing?' To this, Abel-Hirsch adds: "How can I look from different points of view?" (what he comes to call vertices). It is not only sense-based observation or observations based on sensuously derived models involved in this endeavor (in fact, he becomes increasingly critical of the use of such models); he becomes increasingly freer to draw on his own experience of difficulty thinking (derived from his World War I trauma). He seems free to use his imaginative conjecture in opening up very early, even fetal, functioning to the possibility of our noticing it in sessions.

In one respect, by the time he published what turned out to be a landmark paper in 1967, "Notes on Memory and Desire," it represented a formal statement of what he had done for the past 20 years. His analytic work with groups, then psychotic and now borderline patients all occurred in the register of the present moment at the point of the most urgent anxieties. He seemed to be never at rest clinically, experimenting with different ways of looking at the same material. In one sense, there is a continuity between the Grid and the discipline of memory and desire—the Grid, a more concrete instrumentality, evolving through the 1960s into the discipline of memory and desire, and Bion moving from what analysts should do (the Grid) to how they need to be (discipline of memory and desire). It is in this sense that the 1967 paper formalizes something he had already been doing clinically.

Did Bion's conceptual thinking through the 1960s go ahead of his method of clinical inquiry? Abel-Hirsch has drawn attention to the fact that *Transformations* (1965) contains a radical discussion of the discipline of memory and desire, but not overt clinical illustrations of its use. What we do see clinical illustrations of are the maintenance of the analytic position through the observation of invariants (possibly in contrast to a more theory-based analytic identity) and his attention to the different perspectives on clinical material that are possible. Likewise with other theoretical concepts, such as O. There are no clinical illustrations left by Bion himself of what 'O' looks like in clinical practice. What is clear in the illustrations from the beginning of the 1960s (and before) is his attention to what does and doesn't have a clinical effect.

As it stands in the next period of Bion's clinical seminars, in various IPA regions (1967–1978), we have ample opportunity to look at how the main aspects of his IMCI were reflected and broadened in both his analytic and supervisorial work. To orient the reader here, we take note of the fact that many of the patients discussed by Bion in this period were on the borderline/narcissistic spectrum. It is a consistent feature of the way he analyzed and interacted with colleagues around clinical material that he was generally reluctant to answer direct questions about technique, resisting being put in an explicit leadership position vis-à-vis the group. He ventured 'second opinions' and encouraged others to develop their own practice style, contrasting basic assumptions that "kill curiosity" with genuine inquiry that was "a disciplined and informed curiosity" (1978, Seminar 2). He embodied his own distillation of Kleinian clinical technique, doing so in a style distinctly his own.

To a clinical example of a distraught borderline female ('A') presented both in Los Angeles and Buenos Aires in 1967–1968: Bion (2013, 2018, p. xxv) here demonstrated how he analyzed both near-psychotic patients, reprising his paper on memory and desire on the occasion of his US visit. In "Notes on Memory and Desire," Bion (1967) at last *explicitly* rendered his idiosyncratically Kleinian technique, accentuating the present moment in the analytic encounter. Clearing the obstructions of memory and desire made a path for crisp observations about his patient, which in turn could lead to a creative evolution. Psychoanalytic observation concerns itself with neither the past nor the future, but only with *what is happening now*. The analyst's true trajectory is towards the unknown, which he referred to as "tomorrow's session," one we know nothing about. It was important to forget what one knows in the immediacy of the current session, so that some new (and heretofore unknown) pattern might evolve.

Bion differentiated a relaxed receptivity from the actual analysis of countertransference—its analysis was an ideal process, in which one has the time, awareness and resources to handle it. The workaday analyst often doesn't have time for such measured reflection and must, for good or ill, enter the next session as he or she is, so better to aspire to patience and security because the workaday reality will often be persecution and depression.

In the fifth Buenos Aires seminar in 1968, Bion now retrospectively understood the analysis of 'A' differently, having shifted his sightlines. He confessed errors he had made, such as talking with members of her family and trusting their reports. Threatened from the outset by a patient who expressed suicidal wishes if he did not treat her, an analysis was begun under extorting emotional circumstances.

Initially, the analysis started off smoothly, but then became disrupted by a seemingly everyday incident. 'A' stated a physical need to interrupt her session to go to the lavatory. When her lavatory behavior persisted, interpretations were met nonresponsively. A suggestion that perhaps she was hearing 'a voice' when she left the room led to denials on her part, and, after a short while, she felt misrelated to. The atmosphere escalated and polarized, with 'A' feeling she was being told she was delusional and 'hearing voices' (Bion, 2018, pp. 69–70). A further antagonism occurred when the analyst concluded that her behavior was making analysis impossible. Now beleaguered, he thought he was being cast as a 'bad analyst' who didn't know what he was doing. He reprised the 'angry voices in the room' interpretation, ones where 'A''s parents were engaged in a heated argument that she enacted (Bion, 2018, p. 72). Then, 'A' calmed down for the moment, agreeing, but soon this momentary collaboration vanished, as she reproached him for not making this intervention earlier! An insurmountable impasse formed: 'A' persisted with violent rage, and, finally, the analyst felt that he had had enough—with his 'minimum work conditions' being violated, he unilaterally interrupted her analysis (Bion, 2018, pp. 69–70).

To the question of Bion's implicit method of clinical inquiry, the here and now analysis also reflected a disinclination to focus on early trauma or history, yet he momentarily and uncharacteristically reached for it with 'A.' Free to ask questions about the reasons 'A' came for analysis, he initially demonstrated how he had been role-recruited as a 'bad' and inadequate analyst, but his sitting with these violently induced countertransference reactions—with which he momentarily identified—led to an organizing formulation that 'A' was effecting an omnipotent 'capture' of his mind. It put the analysis back on a proper footing.

When Bion presented 'A' in Buenos Aires, her attacks emotionally pierced the analyst in such a way as to lead to some perseveration about her unconscious motives, aggravating a polarized situation. Perhaps 'A' needed to have it both ways—as if she were saying, 'The law on non-contradiction does not apply to me.' And all this is in the conscious realm. The patient could not tolerate the analyst being wrong—and constantly reminded him that neither could she tolerate his being right.

Bion's implicit method of clinical inquiry here appears consistent with how he analyzed patients in the 1950s: the introspective attitude on his observations, the processing of his direct subjective experiences with patients; a sensitivity to role-recruitment as well as keeping an eye on potential countertransference impasses. Yet, at the same time, and this would become a common experience among analysts treating borderlines for the first time in the 1960s, it seemed that the treatment of this particular near-psychotic patient could prove more trying than the analysis of the psychotic patients from the 1950s.

Alongside Bion's own clinical work, we have examples of his 1968 supervision of Horacio Etchegoyen's case of 'B,' a single Jewish male, who quietly and passively devalued the analyst, wondering if the analyst was inexperienced, or, alternatively, frequently falling asleep during sessions. Questions abounded for Bion: would the new analyst be any more suitable than the previous two or would he run out of milk early on? Had 'B' effected his own self-cure with drugs? Where others might have foreclosed on the meaning of 'B's perverse behavior, Bion kept such questions open, saying it is difficult to tell whether someone is lying or misjudging a situation, and opening up a spectrum of potential views rather than an either/or view of truth and lies.

Bion then came up with a sudden, precipitating intuition regarding the omnipotence of self-cure, a true leap beyond what had been presented. This out-of-the-blue reaction, as if 'B' was saying, "I am cured, how about you?", opened up many interpretative possibilities: omnipotent self-sufficiency, counter-dependency, the hostile devaluation of the analyst or an overreliance on a perverse concoction of self-feeding. Leaving this question open, Bion's manner is characterized by his restlessness, rarely foreclosing on one meaning, but generally moving on to other questions, other tentative answers, which lead to a further idea—all this held in suspension—until he reaches a formulation based on multiple linkages. The formulation attempts to address a unique clinical situation and informs what Bion might say to the patient.

In taking up 'B's coprophilic pathology, Bion (2018, pp. 102–103) came up with an original generalization about consciously held misperceptions about everyday life. It is essential to elucidate the unconscious material, but also material consciously misperceived by the patient. How could 'B' not think that analysts were "really dirty people, people who speak about the kind of things that would be equivalent to what you would be eating, if, in truth, you ate cat's meat and fecal matter?"

The analyst also had to bear knowing about B's profound anxiety about emotional self-regulation, all in the face of B's little-developed introspective capacity. 'B' appeared as a small child soiling himself and the analyst, rubbishing interpretations, so that he could equate understanding with being fed his own excrement. On the other hand, the recognition of 'B''s envious attacks also reflected a growing neediness and sense of his feeling humiliated by the analyst's separate mind and capacity for understanding.

Bion then raised the perspectivist question: how does the analyst ascertain whether he or she is accurately approximating the patient's own model of mind and not subtly imposing his or her own model of the patient's mind on his or her analysand? 'B''s denigrating projections could make it appear that it is the analyst who was unpleasant and dirty, yet, at the same time, he increasingly relied on his analysis to the point of fearing a consuming voraciousness. He wanted more and more—even though he did not know what of. In Bion's words, it was the emphasis of quantity over quality—the patient just knows that he needs 'more' of something without thinking any further about it, whether it be more milk or more analytic sessions.

We can take up the evolution of Bion's implicit method of clinical inquiry to this point. Next to his reluctance to prematurely foreclose on meaning, he deploys projective identification in a communicative as well as an evacuative direction, looking at the organizing impact that such 'words-as-actions' had on the analyst, both in terms of what he could know and interpret as well as how it impacted his own countertransference. He now articulated the dynamics of the near-psychotic or difficult-to-treat patient on the borderline/narcissistic spectrum. Linked to a broader understanding of countertransference, Bion more fully embraced multiple communicative possibilities to expand the meaning from either side of the couch—for instance, in a more dexterous use of his own countertransference, where he drew upon the older Freud/Klein view of 'personal interference' on the analyst's conflictual side, emphasizing more the unconscious-to-unconscious communications that, via projective identification, could also be informing.

Finally, the consultant's focus on 'B''s internal world sometimes appeared a bit strident, as if he regarded himself as the sole epistemological agent in the consulting room, sometimes even making intuitive clinical leaps. He strove to capture actively the unconscious in words, those actions that spoke louder than words. With severely compromised psychotic and near-psychotic patients, the analyst bore the curiosity for knowing the patient's enduring psychic reality, remaining the sane, meaning-seeking agent who observed the near-psychotic's attacks on his or her own mind that were in turn projected violently into the figure of the analyst.

Lastly, he expanded his method to include the process of inquiry in seminar situations. Here, he now made his own work the subject of self-inquiry and reflection.

With 'A,' he discussed his own failures of understanding, a new form of inquiry that would continue intermittently right down to his final paper, "Making the Best of a Bad Job," where he publicly discussed one of his patients who committed suicide (Bion, 1987). The seminar format could be one where open-ended questions could be asked of either the clinical presenter, the clinical material or the facilitator himself. It was Bion's aim to extend the reaches of psychoanalytic inquiry into the realm of the unknown, towards which he maintained an attitude of open-ended curiosity.

Turning now to Bion's clinical seminars in the 1970s, what more can we learn of his method of clinical inquiry from his supervisions? There are, of course, differences between reporting analytic cases—a small number in any analyst's lifetime, where movements develop slowly over long periods of time—and supervisions, where the emphasis is on an immediate intervention, usually conducted in a fairly circumscribed period of time. With the many supervisory examples provided by Bion during his visits to Brazil in the 1970s, in Abel-Hirsch's words:

> we can listen for patterns in his clinical method that emerge across the cases. ... We can get some sense, however, about what Bion thinks matters in clinical work, how he communicates with the presenters/seminar group and how he himself might talk to the patients concerned.

After hearing the presenter's opening, Bion generally asks an open-ended question, inviting participants to get closer to the material—and *not* be held at more of a distance by their own preconceptions. One aim is to get at something that is being taken for granted. Sometimes, the patient has unwittingly boxed themselves in by way of a closed-ended construction: with one patient who hears there is a famous analyst in Brasília, her conundrum is the expectation that any direct question she puts to the analyst will only be analyzed, and she won't have an answer. Bion questions the obvious here—analysts don't answer questions—and looks beyond this to see how this opening material recurs in other relationships the patient has. Involved in this process is his abstraction of the key elements in the relationship—"famous analyst + she won't get an answer" (Bion 2014, Vol. 8, Seminar 4, Brasília, 1973, pp. 25–28). Abel-Hirsch concluded:

> Reading all the seminars I began to wonder whether Bion might be actively on the lookout for the 'obvious' (i.e. analysts don't answer questions). Is it possible that taken for granted assumptions might be particularly good hiding places for unconscious content?

Are taken for granted assumptions like insignificant day residues in dreams? In addition, Bion sometimes looks at the presenting analyst's own taken-for-granted misperceptions that impact the analysis (Bion 2014, Vol. 8, Seminar 15, Brasília, 1973).

To expand a bit on Bion's use of questions, he also focuses on the relationships between 'objects': between the patient and others, the patient and analyst, the patient and their internal objects, and, in the following example, between the patient and his envy (as a sort of object). He abstracts from the various particular relations to determine what the recurring qualities of the relations are. The objects may vary, but something in the relationship between them stays constant. For an envy-ridden patient, for example, there would seem to be a constant search for links that would demonstrate to the patient that his preconceptions are justified (Bion, 2014, Vol. 8, Seminar 9, Brasília, pp. 49–50). It is from such linkages that patterns emerge—the emotional key being a sense of suspiciousness about a 'bad' internal or external object (Bion, 2014, Vol. 8, Seminar 22, pp. 113–116). We hear Bion's awareness of how internally threatened the patient feels. This has a familiar Kleinian ring to it as an experience under threat from a bad internal object.

Dimensions of Difference

In a group-authored book, it would be odd if there were total unanimity, and this book is no exception in throwing up debatable differences about Bion's clinical approach. As, for instance, John Wisdom concluded in his critique of *Learning from Experience*:

> In non-academic circles criticism is often confused with antagonism. Antagonism, however, means finding mistakes *without* understanding, while criticism means finding mistakes *with* understanding, so it is an exacting exercise. There are few works that are worthy of criticism.
>
> (Wisdom, 1987, p. 605, ftnote)

Differences are for inquiring into 'with understanding,' in a spirit of Bionian curiosity.

Perhaps it is first of all important to mention the fulcrum that generated Joe Aguayo's interest in getting together our study group—that was Sira Dermen's idea of a 'method of clinical inquiry,' distinct from a clinical technique. Is it necessary to have a clear-cut idea of this conception at the outset for the reader to follow in the development of Bion's work, or, in contrast, is the book a process of clothing that term with qualities which, by the end, will have become apparent to the reader (and authors)?

On the whole, the latter view prevailed and seems to have resulted in crediting Bion with an approach to his clinical work (and his seminar activity) with a cast of mind that is enduringly inquiring and persistently hesitant to allow foreclosure. One difference debated was to question the degree to which Bion inquired more of his clinical material than other psychoanalytic researchers. Was it in fact possible to outdo Freud in never foreclosing on a set of conclusions and theories? The reader can mull their own opinion.

In relation to that and trying to capture the difference between a method of clinical inquiry and a technical approach, it was necessary to bring into use another term—cast of mind. That is, Bion's approach was not merely a set of technical rules or steps, though he did at times set out rules, such as 'no memory or desire'; there is also his mental attitude of how to inquire into those technical steps.

One proposed definition of a method of clinical inquiry emphasized the focus as not the curiosity of a scientific kind about an inanimate object. Instead, Bion's was a more subjective engagement with another subject who could waver around being a partner in disclosing their own unconscious. However, some of the group found that subjective engagement as more or less taken for granted as the cast of mind of analysts in general.

Another formulation was that Bion's implicit method of clinical inquiry was a propensity for inductive leaps, taking the reader (and perhaps his patients) from the experience in the clinical work to creative and overarching generalizations. At the same time, we in the group recognized that, in part, we were doing our best to avoid following such theoretical leaps since that was the focus of so much written material on Bion, which we were attempting to balance by sticking to the clinical work. The place of theory was a subject of debate for the group. We partly moved away from Bion and his very wide reading—outside the psychoanalytic literature as well as inside. But it was partly inevitable that we had to acknowledge we could see Bion drawing into his clinical work extraneous theory, such as Lewin's social field theory, such as Poincaré's selected fact (1911/1914), such as Jung's container–contained and, above all, such as Klein's projective identification. The difficulty was to decide how influential those background ideas were, how much he was using them to formulate interpretations and, in addition, how much he was using his clinical work and the responses he got in order to question and test those ideas.

Bion's group work in the war and in the later 1940s was viewed by some as of little relevance and partially set aside since it is pre-psychoanalytic. Bion qualified at the end of that decade and was believed to have been encouraged by Klein to drop his group interests. Others in the group thought they could discern clear continuities from way back—in fact, from his psychotherapy training at the Tavistock Clinic, with its Jungian influence, right through to his last psychoanalytic book in 1970 and into the final years in Los Angeles.

One emphasis in the group period was Bion's reliance on intuitive introspection on what a patient was *doing* to the analyst's mind, just as much as interpretation of semantic and symbolic meanings of the material. This some thought significant in his 1970 contrast of sensuous signaling—that is, apperception via information from the senses—and non-sensuous appreciation of others' minds, which he called intuition. This was his advocacy of something more like empathic attunement and identification. One can appreciate someone else's anxiety, even though anxiety itself cannot be seen or touched, heard or smelled. How important is this non-representational kind of engagement between minds? Bion clearly linked this with the communicating form of projective identification. That use of the concept led some to '*label*' Bion a continuing Kleinian to the end, although others felt that label would be rather against Bion's own preference.

Much debate centered on whether Bion was completely out on his own, or whether he was a man of his times. It is true that Bion was not very thorough in giving references to his sources, and that makes him more difficult to place. It is anticipated that, for the reader of this book, a central question will be how loyal Bion remained to Melanie Klein—a good deal, or not at all. This book does not give a definitive answer. Indeed, it has not been able to assess how far an analyst's new ideas take him from the orthodox school he once belonged to; this was the fundamental dispute in the British Society's Controversial Discussions in 1943–1944—had Klein herself moved too far from Freud to be considered a Freudian? That is a dispute not settled today. It compares with the dispute over Bion's ideas and whether he should be severed properly from Klein.

Evidence that Bion was a Kleinian could be assumed to be the case only during the 1950s when he was part of the group that was researching the use of Klein's theories of schizoid mechanisms when working with acute psychotic states of mind. Once Bion left that project and eventually moved, geographically, out of Britain, he could be seen to be moving out of the so-called 'rigid' Klein group. In contrast, others say Bion's use of intuition as a means of working with countertransference and its re-emerging in the mid-1960s, together with other Kleinians' development of 'normal' countertransference, kept him a member of the group, evidenced by his proposal to rejoin them in 1979, just before he died.

Bion's emphasis on the non-representational mode of interaction with another mind was slow to evolve, and he created new terms (I believe they are new), such as 'proto-mental' or 'ideo-motor' as he tried to define the non-verbal mode of communication indicated by Freud's idea of unconscious-to-unconscious communication, the impact of countertransference and his commitment to intuition as radically different from language and the ordinary communication of the senses. Bion's work on this kind of impact was certainly persistent, and he did emphasize it more perhaps than anyone. However, others could say that, although Bion took things further, it was in a context of a long-standing thread of psychoanalytic research.

Much weight was put on Bion's interest in curiosity as a significant indicator of his special gift for inquiring more deeply than others. This focused around the title of the paper "On Arrogance," which described a constant conjunction of curiosity, stupidity and arrogance as personality features covering over a "primitive disaster" as Bion called it. In contrast, others thought this was not the main point of the paper, and indeed Bion does not seem to make reference ever again to this constant conjunction. Instead, the main point of the paper was the recognition that the Oedipus complex had a dimension of curiosity that was as important, or more so, than the dimension of rivalry and murder. The latter point of view, however, seemed, it was suggested, to ignore the fact of Freud's own implicit recognition of the Oedipal story's relevance for a psychoanalytic curiosity about the unknown (the epistemophilic component of the libido as Freud called it at the time), and indeed ignored how Klein exposed much more explicitly, in her early papers in Budapest with Ferenczi (including her membership paper for the Hungarian Psychoanalytic Society), the resistance to, and struggle over, curiosity in latency-age children.

Some attributed Bion's idea, now almost his signature—the container–contained—to the paper "On Arrogance," rather than the explicit model developed in his "Attacks on Linking." It is true that the two papers were presented within 2 months of each other in 1957. Almost certainly, they were both intended, in that year, to give support to Klein who, after the publication of her contentious work on envy in 1957, saw a number of her previously close supporters take to their heels—including Paula Heimann and Donald Winnicott. Alternatively, Bion's persisting loyalty at this stage could also be seen as quite the opposite and his own step to dependence by advocating the importance of the external (m)other that Klein was supposed, by many, to deny.

Returning to Bion's membership paper in 1950 on "The Imaginary Twin" (1967), this can be claimed as a tribute to the here-and-now focus. The focus in the write-up of the case for examination was Bion's understanding of the interplay of figures in the present. In particular, it was the analyst who was maneuvered for 2 years into an accommodating figure who supported a phantasy defense in which the analysis was conducted so that little contact was made with the realities of the pain the patient was trying to bring. It was this present reality that Bion could eventually expose as a demonstration of his worthiness for membership of the Society. The analyst changed from the obliging assistant supporting the patient's defenses to become a persecuting figure who reduced the patient to an abject state of pain. In short, the therapeutic benefit was seen in the mutual understanding of the parts played out by patient and analyst in the immediate session and, illustrating Klein's aphorism "transference, the total situation" (in 1952).

This inquiry into the here-and-now predicament of patient and analyst could be seen as an innovation of Bion's and, therefore, an exemplar of his implicit method of clinical inquiry. However, in contrast, it could be argued that this focus *now* was not an exclusive advance of Bion's but stemmed at least from Strachey's 1934 paper on the mutative interpretations and the 1943 argument in the Controversial Discussions by Susan Isaacs (1943/1948) that transference came from active unconscious phantasy now, and not from fixation points in the past (see also Glover's 1945 criticism of Klein as no longer an analyst because she dropped the idea of regression and fixation points).

There is a possibility too that Bion's focus on roles played out now in the analytic session was not particularly Bionian but a core of the technical approach in much of the British approach to 'object-relations.' As mentioned, Strachey took this approach in 1934, and it echoed again perhaps in Klein and her work with children, published in her 1932 book but illustrated in her publications since 1923. The role of toys in her play analysis and the role of the figures in an adult session could be seen as entirely comparable in terms of the hidden unconscious material.

The place of Bion's fascinating but challenging lapse into epistemology/metapsychology between 1958 and 1967 is contentious—and, indeed, it was the contention that started this book. What is the place of clinical work in Bion's opus? The general approach among analysts, as we have stated, is to follow his exciting diversions into theory. He gives little clinical material after 1959. So, can we follow his implicit method of clinical inquiry when his presentation of clinical material is so sparse? We seem to be gazing at a distant nebula. In fact, apart from the detailed process presented in the group period, the case presented in his 1958 paper "On Hallucination," and a patient presented in two seminars in 1967–1968 in Los Angeles and in Buenos Aires, these represent the detailed material that illustrates his clinical work and ideas. So, some would contend that his available work allows only inferences, rather than showing the evolution of original trends from persistently observed clinical occurrences.

A similar question was debated by our group over the supervision material presented by others in the many international seminars after 1967. Can those supervisory comments (in fact, very many of them merely challenging questions) adequately demonstrate his clinical work? It could be argued that his inquiring approach to the work of presenters in his seminars gives a window into his inquiring approach to his patients. On the other hand, there are sprinkled pieces of clinical material and thinking used as illustrations, which could be examined for a specific approach, or method of inquiry. In fact, a lot of our discussions focused on the demonstration of his restless unwillingness to allow himself or others foreclosure on clinical opinions. In fact, a collection of reminiscences of analysands and supervisees of Bion's does confirm this restless inquiry. Those quotes back up the opinion on his willingness to remain in a state of uncertainty and unsatisfied curiosity. It was also a state of mind in which he promoted a kind of partnership in the inquiry with his analysands and supervisees, as he had with the various groups he had worked with in the 1940s. He cajoled them into taking as much responsibility as the analyst in the exploration of their own unconscious mind. It remained debatable how much Bion sought a partnership with his patients and how much he sought an authority to know what generalizations were illustrative for him and his reader, and what were questionable.

These dimensions of debate in our group, perhaps like many of the others, seem to chime with a possible dimension of Bion's own character. He had a powerful presence which implicitly placed him, in the eyes of others, as an authority to learn from, whose teaching they should accept. At the same time, he appeared in so much of his work—with both groups and individuals—to seek an equal partnership and to give play to an anti-authoritarianism. These separate attitudes, the Edwardian military man and the rebel against the Establishment, come through in much of his writings, including his autobiographical texts. It might be worth now giving pause for thought about whether such a to-and-fro within Bion might be implicitly recreated as a dynamic underlying the unresolved debates in our group. In other words, does our long discourse together over many years represent, in part, something taken from Bion's own character? This being a so-called parallel process, paralleling in the group a conflict in the topic of our discussion, could we expect to resolve such conflicts on behalf of Bion?

References

Bion, W.R. (1967). 'The Imaginary Twin,' in W. Bion, *Second Thoughts: Selected Papers on Psycho-Analysis*. New York: Basic Books.

Bion, W.R. (1954). 'Notes on a Theory of Schizophrenia.' *International Journal of Psychoanalysis*, 35: 113–118; also in: *Second Thoughts*, New York: Basic Books, pp. 23–35.
Bion, W.R. (1958a). 'On Arrogance.' *International Journal of Psychoanalysis*, 39: 144–146.
Bion, W.R. (1958b). 'On Hallucination.' *International Journal of Psychoanalysis*, 39: 341–349.
Bion, W.R. (1959). 'Attacks on Linking.' *International Journal of Psychoanalysis*, 40: 308–315.
Bion, W.R. (1962). *Learning from Experience*, London: Heinemann (reprinted in paperback, London: Maresfield Reprints, H. Karnac Books, 1984).
Bion, W.R. (1963). *Elements of Psycho-Analysis*. London: William Heinemann Medical Books.
Bion, W.R. (1965). *Transformations*. London: William Heinemann Medical Books.
Bion, W.R. (1967). 'Notes on Memory and Desire.' *The Psychoanalytic Forum*, 2: 272–273, 279–290.
Bion, W.R. (1970). *Attention and Interpretation*. London: William Heinemann Medical Books.
Bion, W.R. (1978). *Four Discussions with W.R. Bion*. Perthshire: Clunie Press.
Bion, W.R. (1987). 'Making the Best of a Bad Job,' in *Clinical Seminars and Other Works*, W.R. Bion and F. Bion (Eds.) (Abingdon: Fleetwood Press).
Bion, W.R. (2013). *Wilfred Bion's Los Angeles Seminars and Supervision*. Edited by J. Aguayo and B. Malin. London: Karnac.
Bion, W.R. (2014). The Complete Works of W.R. Bion. 16 Volumes. Edited by C. Mawson and F. Bion. London: Karnac.
Bion, W.R. (2018). *Bion in Buenos Aires*. Edited by J. Aguayo, L. Pistiner de Cortinas and A. Regeczkey. London: Karnac.
Glover, E. (1945). 'Examination of the Klein System of Child Psychology.' *Psychoanalytic Study of the Child*, 1: 75–118.
Heimann, P. (1950). 'On Countertransference.' *International Journal of Psychoanalysis*, 31: 81–84.
Isaacs, S. (1943, revised 1948). 'The Nature and Function of Phantasy.' *International Journal of Psychoanalysis*, 29: 73–97. Republished (1952) in M Klein, P. Heimann, S. Isaacs and J. Riviere, *Developments in Psychoanalysis* (pp. 67–121). London: Hogarth.
Klein, M. (1932). *The Psycho-Analysis of Children*. London: Hogarth. Republished (1975) as *The Writings of Melanie Klein, Volume 2*. London: Hogarth.
Klein, M. (1946). 'Notes on Some Schizoid Mechanisms.' *International Journal of Psychoanalysis*, 27: 99–110.
Klein, M. (1952). 'The Origins of Transference.' *International Journal of Psychoanalysis*, 33: 433–438.
Lewin, K. (1951). *Field Theory in Social Science*. New York: Harper.
Poincaré, H. (1911/1914). *Science and Method*. New York: Dover.
Segal, H. (1964). *An Introduction to the Work of Melanie Klein*. Basic Books: New York.
Spillius, E. (2007). *Encounters with Melanie Klein: Selected Papers of Elizabeth Spillius* (London: Routledge).
Strachey, J. (1934). 'The Nature of the Therapeutic Action of Psychoanalysis.' *International Journal of Psychoanalysis*, 15: 127–159. Republished (1969), *International Journal of Psychoanalysis*, 50: 275–292.
Wisdom, J.O. (1981). Metapsychology after forty years. In Grotstein, J.S. (ed) *Do I Dare Disturb the Universe?* p. 602–624. Beverley Hills: Caesura Press.
Wisdom, J.O. (1987). Bion's Place in the Troika. *International Review of Psychoanalysis*, 14: 541.

Index

Abel-Hirsch, N. 3, 5, 6, 138, 139, 140, 141, 145
Abraham, Karl 48
abstraction (used in Brazilian clinical seminars) 124–127
Aguayo, J.: Betty Joseph's analytic technique 34; Bion on memory and desire 2; Bion's analysis of psychotic states of mind 43, 49
'alone and dependent' position 115
alpha elements 76, 77
alpha function 76, 77
Argentine Psychoanalytic Association 101–102
arrogance: "On Arrogance" 58–61, 132, 135–136, 148–149; curiosity and stupidity 58, 59, 60, 148
assumptions (basic model) 27, 132, 145
"Attacks on Linking" 68–75, 137, 149
Attention and Interpretation 8, 28, 86–89, 125, 141
authority, suspicion of 11

"bad" sessions 63–65, 142–143
Banet, Anthony 11, 28
basic assumption model 27, 132, 145
Beckett, Samuel 52
beta elements 6, 82
Bion's implicit method of clinical inquiry (IMCI): combines intuition with reasoning 136; conclusions regarding 50–51; definition 131; generalization from a few cases 57; in "Imaginary Twin" case 41–42; as Janus-faced model 132; learning about 35; overview 3–6; technical advancements of 138
Bion, W.R.: Anthony Banet Interview on Groups 98; "On Arrogance" 58–61, 132, 135–136, 148–149; "On Group Dynamics" 47; "Attacks on Linking" 68–75, 137, 149; "bad" sessions 63–65, 142–143; borderline female analysands 99–106, 142; Brazilian Seminars 2, 122–124, 124–127, 127–128; Buenos Aires Seminars 1, 95–98, 101–104, 106–113; "Development of Schizophrenic Thought" 42; "Differentiation of the Psychotic from the Non-Psychotic Personalities" 42–45, 49; 'Four Discussions' 96; "On Hallucination" 61–68, 137, 150; patients and supervisees (accounts) 89–92; illustration from Bion's own practice 78–80; on implicit method of clinical inquiry 113–114; independence of mind 48; Italian Seminars 97–98, 115, 118; "Language and the Schizophrenic" 46, 49; Los Angeles Seminars 1, 95, 115–117; on memory and desire 1; Menninger's Borderline Conference 96; New York IPTAR Seminars 97, 115; Northfield Hospital experiment 132–133; "Notes on Memory and Desire" 1, 141, 142; "Notes on Schizophrenia" 47; rhetorical style 96–98, 122–124; sees wood as well as the trees 88; supervision of Etchegoyen 106–113, 116, 143; traditionalism of 110; *Wilfred Bion: His Life and Works 1897–1979* 6–7
Bléandonu, Gerard: Bion's life and work 6–7; J.A. Hadfield as 'Mr-Feel-It-in-the-Past' 52; marginalizes significance of *Clinical Seminars* 2
borderline patients 68–69, 99–106, 117, 139

Brazilian clinical seminars: questioning by Bion in 122–124; 'shadow' of past and future in the present 127–128; use of abstraction in 124–127
breakdown during the analysis 83–84, 117, 140
breast (good/bad) 79–80
Brenman Pick, Irma (supervisee) 91
Brown, L., countertransference in the work of Reik and Heimann 51–52
Buenos Aires Seminars and Supervisions: borderline patient 101–104; Horacio Etchegoyen's analytic case 106–113; overview 95–98; as starting point 1

cast of mind 146–147
caution in claiming understanding 3, 58, 59, 110
Civitarese, Giuseppe, dreams and cinema 7
clinical work (1960s): *Attention and Interpretation* 8, 28, 86–89, 125; *Elements* 7–8, 81–83, 139; eschewing memory, desire, and understanding 88–89; illustration from Bion's own practice 78–80; *I Scream/Ice-cream* illustrative model 87–88; *Learning from Experience* 77–81, 138; overview 76–77, 92–93; *Pander and the Whore* illustrative model 87; patients and supervisees 89–92; *Transformations* 8, 83–86, 140, 141
communicational gestalt 51
"complex situation" 73
"constant conjunctions" 8
container–contained relationship 61, 77, 78, 125
containment 72, 125, 138
coprophilic pathology 107–108, 109, 143–144
countertransference 46–47, 48
curiosity 58, 59, 60, 74, 148
curiosity, arrogance and stupidity 58, 59, 60, 148

delusions, functions of 67
depressive position 67
Dermen, S., Bion's implicit method of clinical inquiry 3, 110–112
"Development of Schizophrenic Thought" 42
"Differentiation of the Psychotic from the Non-Psychotic Personalities" 42–45, 49
disharmony/unity 24

dissociation 63
double stance 5
dreams: coprophilic 107–108; psychotic 65–67, 70–71, 137
dream theory 7

ego functions 49–50
Elements of Psychoanalysis 7–8, 81–83, 139
enactment 140
epistemology/metapsychology 7–9, 80, 132, 136, 138, 140, 149–150
Etchegoyen, H.: re-analysis with Donald Meltzer 102; supervision with Bion 106–113, 116, 143
evasion of contact 4
excusing the patient (by analyst) 123–124
existing analytic theories and the Psychosis Papers 46–50, 86, 147

fecalized analyst/patient 108–109, 112, 144
Ferro, A., Bion's use of metaphor in the analytic field 7
field theory 4, 7
fight/flight group 26
First World War 11
fragmentary, elliptical speech 42–43, 51, 134–135
'free-floating attention' 99
Freud, S.: Schreber case 54; 'Two Principles of Mental Functioning' 47, 48
functions, theory of 78–79
future ('shadow' of in the present) 127–128

Glover, E.: critique of Klein system 52; iatrogenic disorders 47
Greenson, Ralph 124
Grid, the 80, 81–82, 139–140
Grinberg, L. 95, 102; study group on Bion's ideas in Bueno Aires 115
Grosskurth, P., on Bion's independence of mind 48
group mentality 25–27, 29
group work: anti-group 18; basic assumption model 27, 132; coming together as group 26; connection between members 24; crisis point 22; dependency 26, 131; expectations in 21–22; fight/flight group 26; later manifestations of 28–30; leadership 20, 132–133; method of approach 15–17; 'non-sensuous' perception 23; officer selection 12, 15; pairing

26, 28; process in 22, 27–28; reality (unwilling to accept) 22; responsibility of group members 18–19, 20, 124; role emergence in 12, 13, 14, 15–17, 18–19, 20–22, 132–133; *see also* Northfield Rehabilitation Experiment; Tavistock Clinic group work

Hadfield, J.A. 36, 52
hallucinations ("On Hallucination" paper) 61–68, 137–138, 150
Heimann, P. 46–47, 51–52; countertransference 34, 53; intuition and countertransference 133
here and now focus 35, 41, 43, 50–51, 63, 89–90, 113–114, 133–134, 142, 149
Hill, J. (supervisee) 90–91
Hinshelwood, R.D., on Bion's group work 4

"ideograph" 45
ideo-motoric activity 43, 62, 66, 134–135
"Imaginary Twin" case: early history of patient 36; emotional atmosphere of 37–39; emotional contact 40; implicit method of clinical inquiry in 41–42; overview 34–35; personification of splits 40–41; pseudo-analyst in 37, 39–40, 134; pseudo-patient in 37–40, 134; unconscious phantasy in 36, 38
inductive leaps 147
infant-mother situation 78–80
Insight in Psychoanalysis and Groups 28
instrumentality, psychoanalytic 80–81
introspection 4, 19, 29, 41, 147
intuition 26, 29, 136, 147, 148
invisible-visual hallucinations 70, 137
IPA Congresses: Boston (2015) 3; Buenos Aires (2017) 3; Geneva (1955) 42; London (2019) 3; Vancouver (2021) 3; Zurich (1949) 34, 53, 102
I Scream/Ice-cream illustrative model 87–88
Italian seminars (1977) 97–98

Joseph, Betty 34

K (knowing): and L(loving), and H (hating) linking 80–81; and O (being) 128–129
Klein, M.: Bion's analysis by 5–6, 48; Bion's emphasis as recognizably Kleinian 36, 148, 149; Bion's training analyst and analytic technique 33; on countertransference 54; paranoid-schizoid position 27, 50; projective identification 43, 46–47; project to analyze psychosis 133; *see also* London Klein group

"Language and the Schizophrenic" 46, 49
Learning from Experience 77–81, 138
lies 110
linking: "Attacks on Linking" paper 68–75, 137, 149; K (knowing), L(loving), and H (hating) 80–81; search for links 146
London Institute of Psychoanalysis 33
London Klein group 2, 35
Los Angeles Seminars and Supervision: borderline patient 99–101, 115; overview 95–98, 115–117; as starting point 1

Meltzer, D. the psychoanalytic process 116
Memoir of the Future, A - The Dawn of Oblivion 5–6
memory, and desire 1, 141, 142
Menninger, R. 115
Menninger's Borderline Disorders Conference (1976) 96–97
misuse of theory 112–113
Money-Kyrle, R., normal countertransference 47, 117–118
mother-infant situation 78–80
motor activity 43, 62, 66, 134–135

Necessary Dream, The: New Theories and Techniques of Interpretation in Psychoanalysis 7
neurotic islands 50
'non-sensuous' perception 23
Northfield Rehabilitation Experiment: general method of approach 15–17; rehabilitation ward 12, 16; Vignette 1 12–13; Vignette 2 13–14; Vignette 3 15
"Notes on Memory and Desire" 1, 141, 142
"Notes on Schizophrenia" 47

'O' 92–93, 128
obstructive object 60, 68
Oedipus myth 58, 132, 136, 148
officer selection 12, 15
Ogden, T., Bion's style of writing 1
omnipotence phantasy 100–101
omnipotence of self-cure 110, 112, 143
"On Arrogance" 58–61, 132, 135–136, 148–149

"On Countertransference" (Heimann) 34
"On Group Dynamics" 47
"On Hallucination" 61–68, 137, 150
'openness' 86

Pander and the Whore illustrative model 87
paranoid-schizoid position 8, 27, 33, 50
part-object experience 46
past and future ('shadow' of in the present) 127–128
patients and supervisees (accounts) 89–92
'personal interference' 51
'personification' 41
pleasure principle 67
presentation style (Bion's) 96–98, 122–124
present moment focus 35, 41, 43, 50–51, 63, 89–90, 113–114, 133–134, 142, 149
primary narcissism 75
process 22, 27, 57–58
projective identification: Bion's examination of 47, 48–49; denial of 60–61, 73, 74; excessive 73; importance of normal 72; overview 43–44, 45–46
pseudo-analyst (in "Imaginary Twin" case) 37, 39–40, 134
pseudo-patient (in "Imaginary Twin" case) 37–40, 134
psychoanalytic instrumentality 80–81
Psychosis Papers: "On Arrogance" 58–61, 132, 135–136, 148–149; "Attacks on Linking" 68–75, 137, 149; "Development of Schizophrenic Thought" 42; "Differentiation of the Psychotic from the Non-Psychotic Personalities" 42–45, 49; "On Hallucination" 61–68, 137, 150; "Language and the Schizophrenic" 46, 49; "Notes on Schizophrenia" 47; prelude to 33–34; questioning of existing analytic theories and 46–50, 86, 147; *see also* "Imaginary Twin" case
psychotic bombardment 100–101, 117
psychotic dreams 65–67, 70–71, 137
psychotic islands 50

question-and-answer format 96–97

Reading Bion 7
reality principle 48–50, 67
recalcitrant patients 3, 61
recourse to theory 4, 113
responsibility: leader 19, 132–133; members 18–19, 20, 124

reversible perspective 77, 82–83, 140
rhetorical style (Bion's) 96–98, 122–124
Rickman, J.: as Bion's mentor 4–5, 11, 17; on unconscious role-responsiveness 34, 53–54, 133
role emergence in group work 12, 13, 14, 15–17, 18–19, 20–22, 132–133
Rosenfeld, H.: advocate of Klein's technique 34, 50; psychotic states of mind 43

Schreber case 54
secondary literature 6–8
Segal, H.: advocate of Klein's technique 34, 50, 96; part-object symbolic interpretation 116
self-cure (omnipotence of) 110, 112, 143
self-observations 5
seminar publications (overview) 1–2
sense organs 62, 64
sexual anxiety 59
'shadow' of past and future in the present 127–128
speech (fragmentary, elliptical) 42–43, 51, 134–135
Spillius, E.: on Klein's analytic technique 35; supervisee 91–92
splitting 40–41, 45; different forms of 63; individual's disowned parts 25, 28, 46, 50
stammering 69
stasis 82–83
stupidity, curiosity and arrogance 58, 59, 60, 148
suicidal patients 116
superego 74–75
supervision: Hill, J. 90–91; Brenman Pick, Irma 91; Spillius, Elizabeth Bott 91–92; *see also Buenos Aires Seminars and Supervisions*; *Los Angeles Seminars and Supervision*

Tavistock Clinic group work: Bion's correspondence about 17–18; Experiences in Groups I 19–22; Experiences in Groups II 23–25; Experiences in Groups III 25–27
theories (existing) and the Psychosis Papers 46–50, 86, 147
theory of functions 78–79
traditionalism of Bion 110
transference–countertransference interaction 29, 133
Transformations 8, 83–86, 140, 141
Trist, Eric 22

Trotter, Wilfred 28
Tustin, Francis (patient) 89–92
"Twin" paper *see* "Imaginary Twin" case
"Two Principles" paper (Freud) 48, 49

unconscious phantasy 33–34, 36, 38

Vermote, R., Bion's conceptually-laden theoretical work 7–8
vertices 84, 86, 92, 138, 141

Wilfred Bion: His Life and Works 1897–1979 6–7
Winnicott, D.W.: on Bion's case in 'Differentiation of Psychotic from Non-Psychotic' 53–54; on Bion's case of the 'Imaginary Twin' 52–53

Zysman, S. (collaborator of Etchegoyen), interviewed by J. Aguayo and S. Dermen, (2017) 116, 120

For Product Safety Concerns and Information please contact our EU representative GPSR@taylorandfrancis.com Taylor & Francis Verlag GmbH, Kaufingerstraße 24, 80331 München, Germany

Printed and bound by CPI Group (UK) Ltd, Croydon, CR0 4YY

30/05/2025

01888659-0001